About the Author

Annette Henderson has been writing full-time since 2005. Prior to that, her working life took her to the United Kingdom, Africa, Indonesia and remote Australia. With her husband, Win, she travelled overland from Calcutta to London in a Kombivan, in which they later journeyed from London across the Sahara Desert to Equatorial Africa. Her life changed forever in 1975 when they both took jobs in a mineral camp in remote mountainous forest in Gabon, West Africa. On returning to Australia, she embarked on a career as an anthropologist.

Annette is a committed conservationist, a zoo parent of the lowland gorillas at Taronga Zoo and the adoptive parent of a juvenile orangutan in Borneo. Her articles on Australian birds and reptiles have appeared in *Wildlife Australia Magazine*. Annette and her husband share seven acres of bushland near Brisbane with koalas, wallabies, powerful owls, over 100 species of native birds and their ridgeback cross, Bentleigh. She is a classically trained singer, enjoys regular workouts at a gym, and runs half marathons.

wild spirit

How a year in the African rainforest changed an Australian woman's life

Annette Henderson

WILLIAM HEINEMANN: AUSTRALIA

A William Heinemann book
Published by Random House Australia Pty Ltd
Level 3, 100 Pacific Highway, North Sydney NSW 2060
www.randomhouse.com.au

First published by William Heinemann in 2009

Addresses for companies within the Random House Group can be found at www.randomhouse.com.au/offices.

National Library of Australia
Cataloguing-in-Publication Entry

Henderson, Annette Elizabeth, 1945–.
Wild spirit.

ISBN 978 1 74166 671 7 (pbk).
Henderson, Annette – Travel.
Anthropologists – Gabon – Biography.
Culture shock – Gabon.
Endangered species – Effect of human beings on – Gabon.
Gorilla – Conservation – Gabon.
Gabon – Description and travel.

301.092

Cover photograph © Annette Henderson
Cover design by Christabella Designs
Internal design by Midland Typesetters, Australia
Typeset in Mrs Eaves 14/16 pt by Midland Typesetters, Australia
Printed and bound by Griffin Press, South Australia

The quote on page 253 is taken from *One Dry Season: In the Footsteps of Mary Kingsley*, by Caroline Alexander, and is reproduced with the permission of Caroline Alexander and Bloomsbury Publishing.

The names of some of the people in this book have been changed to protect their privacy.

Random House Australia uses papers that are natural, renewable and recyclable products and made from wood grown in sustainable forests. The logging and manufacturing processes are expected to conform to the environmental regulations of the country of origin.

10 9 8 7 6 5 4 3 2 1

For Win, who dragged me kicking and screaming into a life of adventure and introduced me to the natural world

Author's note

The United Nations has declared 2009 the 'Year of the Gorilla'. My hope is that this book will contribute to the long-term survival of one of our closest relatives, now critically endangered in the wild. A percentage of the proceeds from its sale will be donated to the conservation of western lowland gorillas.

Contents

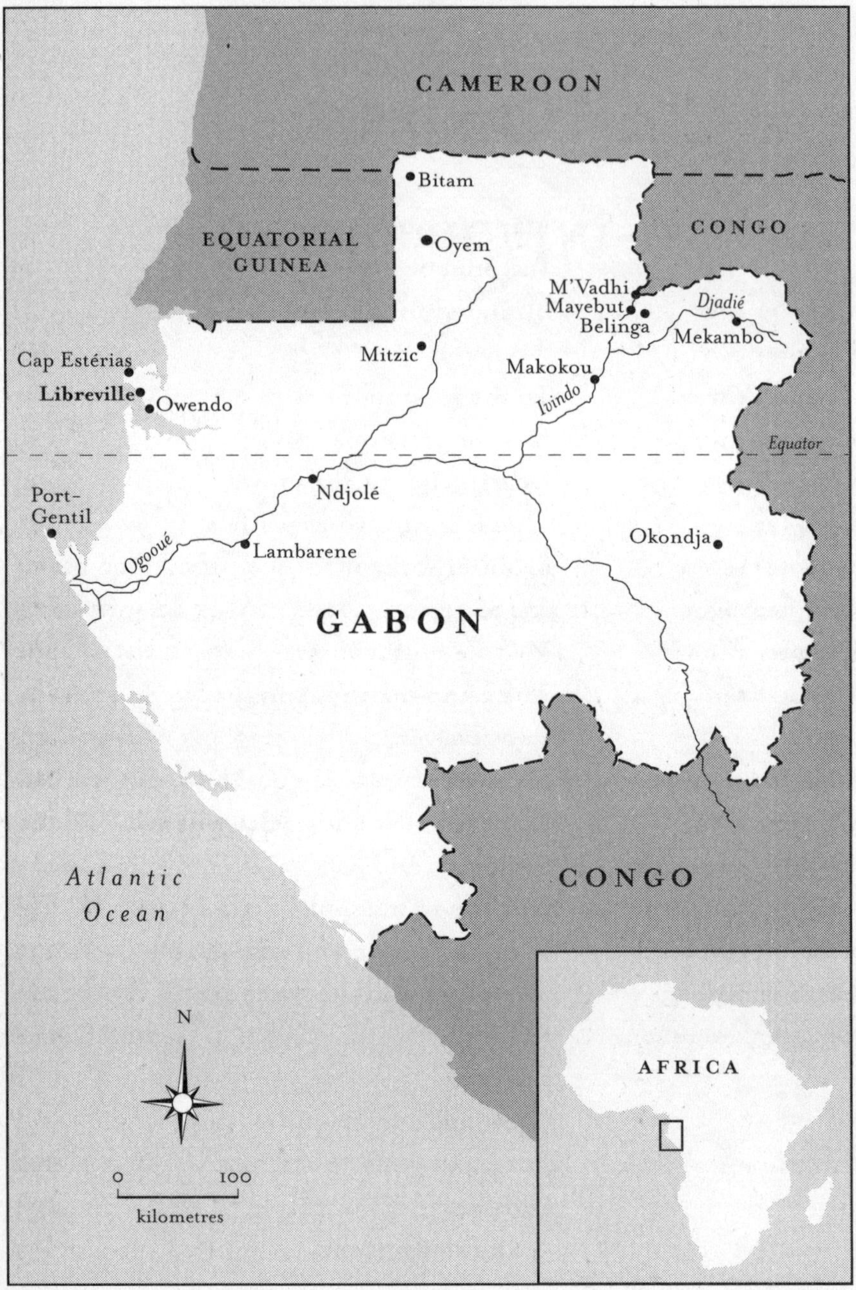

CAMEROON
EQUATORIAL GUINEA
CONGO
Bitam
Oyem
Mitzic
M'Vadhi
Mayebut
Belinga
Djadié
Mekambo
Makokou
Ivindo
Cap Estérias
Libreville
Owendo
Equator
Port-Gentil
Ndjolé
Ogooué
Lambarene
Okondja
GABON
Atlantic Ocean
CONGO
N
0
100
kilometres
AFRICA

Introduction

Belinga Camp, Gabon, West Africa, July 1975

At 2 am a noise outside the Kombivan woke me. I sat up in bed, held my breath and listened. I didn't have to wait long before it came again – a low-pitched rasping cough, not human. I climbed out of the van into the canvas annexe and crept towards the clear plastic window. It sounded a third time – a hoarse guttural exhalation that sent a chill through me. My eyes darted to check that the flap of the annexe was tightly zipped.

Win had woken. 'Did you hear that?' I whispered. He had, but even with his knowledge of wildlife, he couldn't identify it. He handed me the torch. 'Just shine the beam through the window. You might pick up something. Whatever it is, it's pretty close.'

The night was moonless. A symphony of small clicks and buzzes issued from the forest. I switched the torch on and panned the thin beam around through the window. At first I saw nothing. Then the sound came again, closer. I pointed toward it with the torch and then I saw it. In the middle of the dirt road that led up to the generator shed, a gaunt big cat stood motionless, its eyes glowing amber in the beam.

'Quick, look at this!' I hissed under my breath. Win was out of bed in a second to stand beside me at the window, his eyes alight with excitement.

'You realise what that is? It's a leopard! It's come in following our scent trail.'

We stood breathless at the window as the leopard padded down the road towards us, sniffing the air and smelling the ground. My pulse raced, half in excitement, half in fear. Leopards are solitary nocturnal hunters, wary of people and seldom seen in the deep forest. Our passion for wildlife was a major part of what had lured us to Africa, but a rare encounter like this was beyond imagining. This was not a game park, and we were no longer tourists. We were here to work and the leopard had entered our living space.

This was the first time I'd seen a large wild animal in its native surroundings: I watched, spellbound. Was this what our life here would be like all the time?

Several metres from the annexe, it stopped and looked around. Close up, we could see that its coat was in poor condition and its body so thin that the flesh seemed to hang off its bones.

'That looks like an old animal to me,' Win said. 'It's probably having trouble getting enough food and has come into camp hoping for an easy meal. We'd better get back in the van and close the sliding door. If that leopard is really hungry, this annexe won't keep it out.'

The leopard stood for perhaps a minute, sweeping the darkness with its eyes, then turned and ambled back up the road again until it was out of range of the torch.

We climbed back into bed and I lay beside Win, my mind racing. Since we'd met five years earlier, our life had been a continuous adventure. My girlhood in Brisbane seemed like a distant dream, and my twelve years of officework felt like part of someone else's life. Now we were here, in Equatorial Africa, two hours from the border with the Republic of the Congo in a world of forested mountains and mighty brown rivers. There were no railways, airfields or main roads here – just the river and long dugout canoes to connect us with civilisation.

Moving to the camp seven days before had been the most profound change yet of my twenty-nine years. In the months ahead, our lives would be played out against the majesty of the great forest and shared with the wild animals whose home it was.

Lying in the Kombi, deep in the equatorial forest in the hours before dawn, I realised my fear of the leopard had turned into awe. Perhaps the leopard was a harbinger of the change Africa would work in me.

In the morning, I was woken by the voices of the men from the village assembling for the day's work in the forest. I pulled on a pair of old jeans and a jumper and unzipped the flap of the annexe. Mist lay over the great forest, trailing off the high canopy in wispy fronds. I looked at the ground outside. At my feet, the powdery red dirt bore large four-toed paw prints, clearly visible in the soft light. The leopard's tracks led around the annexe and down the hill towards the village. It must have returned for a closer look.

The workmen greeted me: '*Bonjour, madame! Vous voyez? L'empreinte de pas de léopard!*' They had seen the tracks too, and pointed to the imprints at my feet. '*Attention, madame – il est très méchant!*' They were warning me, as the newcomer, to be careful. I smiled my thanks at the men, rugged up in their long-sleeved pullovers and woollen hats, then walked across to the guesthouse for breakfast.

Africa first beckoned to me during the depths of a London winter – February 1974, to be precise. Win and I had been married just fourteen months and were renting a bedsit in a red-brick Victorian house in the leafy suburb of Willesden Green. We'd deliberately avoided Earls Court and the other hangouts of expatriate Australians, as we didn't want to be labelled as beer-swilling, loud-mouthed, football/cricket-mad philistines.

Our one concession to the stereotype of globetrotting Australians was that we owned a Volkswagen Kombivan. But we hadn't bought it at the 'used car yard' outside Australia House in the Strand: we had shipped it, and another just like it, brand new from Germany to Calcutta early in 1973, and travelled the overland route to London through the Khyber Pass, Afghanistan, Iran and points west. That trip had been our honeymoon, but we had shared the first six months of our marriage with thirteen other people from Brisbane.

Our life together was never going to be conventional on any count – I had married an adventure-trip leader nineteen years my senior. It had been his job to plan and lead the trip and ensure that everyone reached England safely.

Shortly after we arrived in London in July we sold one of the Kombis but kept the other. Win began work in his trade as a master builder, and I found a well-paid secretarial job in the West End, not far from Savile Row.

We had no ties, no responsibilities, no jobs back in Australia to return to. Anything seemed possible.

My family in Brisbane had had several years to become accustomed to the idea that my life partner had been married before, had less formal education than I had, and had four adult children all roughly my age. Still, I think Mum and Dad thought I had taken leave of my senses when I announced we were planning to marry. My brother, Phil, a medical student, had taken to Win straightaway – they sparked off each other like two stand-up comics. Sadly, Mum and Dad were not able to see that I had found the soul mate I had always dreamed of: the perfect intellectual companion, best friend and tender lover.

I was in love with everything about him – the craggy face with the bald head and Renaissance beard; the strong, well-built body (a legacy of years as a builder, a canoeist and a surf lifesaver at Bondi Beach); the buoyant sense of fun; the love of life; and the passion for nature. The night we met, at the Adventurers' Club in Brisbane, Win was bronzed from a month on the Barrier Reef leading two camping trips back-to-back over Christmas and New Year. The first thing I noticed about him was the smile; the second was the shapely legs in tailored shorts. I could talk with him as though we had always known each other. And he was a sensational dancer, one of only two men I had ever met who could dance like I could. He was forty-three and I was twenty-four, but I was hooked. That night we talked and danced and talked some more. By three in the morning, over coffee in my flat, I realised I had found someone who would be a friend for life.

Still, I trod warily. I had had two offers of marriage in the preceding five years, and had hurt two good men when I had refused them. I had no intention of hurting this good man, who had weathered many rough patches in his life. I was going to do things the right way.

From the start, Win and I drew each other into our respective lives. I became a member of the Adventurers' Club and began my education in camping, wilderness knowledge and the skills of canoeing and snow skiing – a major shift in direction, as I'd had a sedentary life up to that time. I also began to share his passion for jazz music and nature. Meanwhile, I introduced him to all my singing friends and the world of classical music. We went to concerts, ballets and plays. We maintained separate apartments, but as the months went by, I realised our partnership was a seamless fit – more than the sum of us both.

My life had had several turning points before we met. My job as a secretary had left me unfulfilled and frustrated, so I'd gone to night school and matriculated to university. Dad had two degrees in engineering and Phil had graduated in economics and was now studying medicine – tertiary education in our family had been only for the men. At twenty-two, I broke the mould and enrolled part-time in French language and literature at the University of Queensland, still working as an executive secretary during the day.

About the same time my spiritual yearnings surfaced, and I became an Anglican. I had kept up my lifelong interest in singing, and had been invited to join an excellent four-part choir singing the best of church music from the Renaissance to the twentieth century.

Nevertheless, as a teenager in Brisbane in the late 1950s and early 1960s, a kind of torpor had lain over my world, as though the subtropical heat and humidity had rendered everyone too lethargic to think expansive thoughts, to look outward, to attempt brave things. We lived in Wilston, a comfortable middle-class suburb where nothing exciting ever seemed to happen. Most of the time I'd felt as though I was in limbo, waiting for life to touch me, anxious that it never would.

In all of this, though, I had never envisaged myself as an adventurer. I was cautious, never leaving my comfort zone. I had never travelled outside Australia and had no plans to. But that was before . . .

I had slotted in to officework in London without a ripple. For me, being in London was like being at the centre of the world. Everything happened there. I read the good newspapers, *The Guardian* and *The Observer*, savoured the colour supplements that came with the weekend editions, and opened my mind to everything. It drew me into a cosmopolitan consciousness, a world away from the suburban outlook I had grown up with, and I came to understand why Samuel Johnson had written that he who was tired of London was tired of life. Our two incomes allowed us to splurge on seats at the opera, ballet and theatre, and at weekends we travelled in the countryside, devouring the history, architecture and landscape. We attended lectures at the Royal Geographical Society, where people like Iain Douglas-Hamilton spoke about elephant conservation in Africa.

Just one thing bothered me. The longer Win and I lived

in London, the more I became aware of a growing discomfort with my job as a secretary. Most of the people we mixed with were professionals and I began to feel like a lesser being. As polite and hospitable as people were towards us, I couldn't shake my feeling of not meeting them on level ground. It niggled at me.

One day at work I pushed my typewriter aside, drew out a blank sheet of paper and wrote down all the things I dreamed of doing. It was a long and visionary list, including wildlife photography, museum curating, travel writing, archaeology – bits and pieces of ideas I had gleaned from reading.

At much the same time, Africa entered my consciousness, not as merely a place on a map where other people went, impossibly remote and eternally mysterious, but as a place where people we knew had been, and had returned from enraptured. The mainstream newspapers constantly carried news of Africa, too – it was little more than a decade since Britain had lost its empire, and events in the former colonies still had immediacy. Each week we would pick up the free newspaper aimed at expatriate Australians, and find it full of ads for overland trips from London to Cape Town by ex-army four-wheel drive truck.

One night, over drinks in our bedsit, I found myself saying what I had been thinking for some time: 'Why don't we go to Africa?'

'What, on one of those commercial trips?'

'No, silly, in the Kombi! Just the two of us.'

'What, and cross the Sahara?'

'Yes. People are doing that in Kombis.' There was a long silence. I had planted the seed. Now all I had to do was wait for it to germinate.

***

The preparations took us a year. We studied maps, read books and saw films, devouring every piece of information we could find, and saved all we could. It would be a six-month trip from London to Cape Town, where we would board a boat to return to Australia. We would travel up the Congo on a car ferry and make our way slowly through the game parks of Kenya and Tanzania. Win had modifications made to the Kombi to protect it against structural damage and fit it for desert conditions. I did a first-aid course, applied for all the visas and brushed up on my French. It soaked up all of my restlessness.

We left London on 25 March 1975, with six months' supply of dried food, a boat ticket from Cape Town to Perth, and an array of jerry cans and spare tyres on the roof-rack. Win would do the driving, as I lacked a manual driver's licence. He would also prepare meals – cooking was one of his passions – and look after the vehicle. I would be the chronicler, keeping a journal and taking photographs, and would navigate, translate and interpret, as most of North Africa was French-speaking. We would share the hard physical tasks of lifting gear and digging out.

Two months later, we had survived the Saharan crossing – just – but war had broken out in Angola, and its ripple effect had brought us to a standstill in Libreville. This is the story of what happened next, halfway through Africa, and how we were thrown into the path of that leopard.

chapter one

STRANDED IN LIBREVILLE

Libreville, Gabon, 2 June 1975

The curve of beach lay deserted in the morning light, unlike the day before, when dozens of French families had picnicked on the sand with their dogs. The grey-green Atlantic lapped gently at the shore. Seated in folding camp chairs, we stared at the horizon; the soft, white sand was warm under our bare feet, and a cool breeze from the ocean rustled the coconut palm fronds overhead. The Kombivan stood nearby, coated in jungle mud and crammed with jerry cans, freeze-dried foods and survival gear. Sign-writing on both its sides proclaimed our origins – Brisbane, Australia – just in case someone, somewhere on our marathon journey assumed we came from a country that had fallen out of favour.

We were on the old 'slave coast', over 7000 kilometres and two months by car from London, halfway across the African continent. We should have been jubilant: we had crossed the Sahara, battling 44-degree heat and a vehicle breakdown, and survived arrest at submachine-gunpoint in Algeria, where the army was convinced we were spies.

Now we were almost on the equator, in Gabon, part of francophone West Africa. We should have felt at least some satisfaction in making it thus far. Instead, we were miserable, as miserable as we had ever been.

A three-day torture drive through the jungle had left us demoralised and exhausted. National Highway 1, proudly signposted at the Gabon–Cameroon border, had turned out to be a quagmire of red clay that sucked at the tyres like a living thing. With deserted quarries the only resting places, we had passed sleepless nights in them, powerless to escape the onslaught of the biting insects. By day, we had dug the Kombi out of bogs, or cut saplings with a machete to make a surface firm enough to drive on. The humid air had lain over us like a blanket, saturating our filthy jeans with sweat and making every movement an effort. As if that weren't enough, our arms and legs, florid from countless insect bites, itched and stung incessantly, and we hadn't been able to shower for weeks.

Worse, war had broken out in Angola far to the south, and Zaire (now the Democratic Republic of the Congo) had closed its borders. At a stroke, this had consigned to the scrapheap our planned trip up the Congo to East Africa. But our problems didn't end there. Our already strained budget had been dealt a deathblow twelve hours earlier, when a thief had crept into our camp and stolen our last wad of ready cash.

Our options for getting out of Gabon were now limited. We could retrace our route north back to Nigeria or board a coastal freighter to Namibia in south-west Africa, and thus bypass Angola. Or we could sell the Kombi and all our gear and fly out.

***

We had arrived in Libreville the day before, a Sunday. The outskirts of town were a jumble of decaying iron-roofed shanties sprawled over hillsides, where purple bougainvillea and giant *Ficus decora* threatened to engulf every structure. Clumps of palms beside the road shaded rickety wooden stalls where local traders sold French bread, fruit, peanuts, maize and chillies, and small groups of Gabonese strolled barefoot along the verges, dressed in bright, patterned cotton cloth. The city centre, by contrast, could have been anywhere in the West. Chic boutiques, French supermarkets, gift shops and luxury appliance retailers indicated an affluent urban elite. Libreville lay on a wide bay, skirted by a sickle of pure white sand. An esplanade led past graceful colonial-style buildings with pillared porticoes, surrounded by brilliant stands of purple and red bougainvillea. Luxurious embassy residences, shops and nightclubs adjoined an up-market residential sector with high-rise hotels and French restaurants.

The morning after the robbery, I felt like a victim, as if a malevolent African fate had deliberately targeted us. I looked across at Win and saw exhaustion and despair etched on his face. Normally he was the resilient one – a fit forty-eight-year-old, tanned and muscular from a life of outdoor activity – and also the optimistic one, whereas I had enough pessimism for both of us. But this situation had got to him badly. I had never seen him so down. We'd always known there would be many factors along the way beyond our control, but we hadn't expected to have to abandon the trip halfway through.

Still, I didn't hate Africa for thwarting us: in fact, I loved it, even though it had pushed us close to desperation at times. Perhaps it was that very unpredictability that excited me – that, and the untamed rawness. My greatest disappointment was that we would miss the game parks of Eastern and Southern Africa; they were what had drawn us to Africa from the beginning. With our savings so depleted, too, it seemed unlikely that we would return in the future.

But it was useless wallowing – we had to do something about our immediate situation. I reached for a notebook and pen and made a list of the things in our favour. When all else fails, I always resort to writing things down. It gives me a sense of security, as if I can anchor a capricious fate by making marks on a page. Now, I discovered there were more positives than I had expected. We loved each other. We weren't physically ill – in fact, after all our exertions digging the van out of sand bogs in the Sahara, I was probably fitter than I had ever been. The Kombi was in working order. We had boat tickets from Cape Town to Perth for ourselves and the Kombi, which we could cash in if necessary. We had instructed our London bank several weeks earlier to send £100 to its correspondent bank in Libreville. And I spoke good French – a legacy of my year studying French at university. As a bonus, the air was cool as we sat staring at the ocean, even though Libreville lay just four degrees north of the equator. It could be worse, I told myself.

'Are you going to have any breakfast?' I asked Win.

He shook his head. 'I couldn't face it. But another mug of tea would help.'

I put the kettle on and continued to mull over the situation. We had just one US$20 traveller's cheque left, and we needed to buy fresh food. Libreville was reputedly the most expensive city in Africa. Our tourist visas would expire in ten days.

I reviewed what I knew of Gabon. Its people hadn't

experienced the horrors that their neighbours in the Congo had endured under colonialism. The French had been essentially benevolent, although they'd left little infrastructure behind: eighty-five per cent of the country was still equatorial rainforest. Tracts of swamp covered much of the lowlands, and a huge river system – the Ogooué-Ivindo – drained the country from east to west. Politically, one feature distinguished it from much of Africa: since independence in 1960, its history had been essentially peaceful. The pro-western head of state, El Hadj Omar Bongo, had been in power eight years. (He is still in power at the time of writing.) Per capita it was one of the wealthiest countries in Africa, riding a mineral and oil boom, although little of this prosperity filtered down to the village level.

What I knew of pre-colonial Gabon had come entirely from the writings of a famous nineteenth-century British explorer, Mary Kingsley, who had travelled alone to West Africa, hungry to learn about the customs and beliefs of the people and to collect specimens of plants and fish to take home. In her voluminous skirts, high-necked Victorian blouses, leather boots and hat, she had ventured far up the mighty Ogooué River in a pirogue – a dugout canoe – accompanied by Gabonese interpreters and guides, relying on the hospitality of traders and missionaries where there were any and local villagers where there weren't. In the Kombi was the abridged edition of her famous book *Travels in West Africa*, a gift from my boss back in London. Now I was here, on the old slave coast, where she had been a century before.

Win and I drank two mugs of hot tea each, then drove into town to report the burglary to the police – an official report could be useful if we wanted to claim on insurance. We had slept poorly after the robbery; my eyes felt gritty, salt from our swim in the ocean the day before caked my skin, and my grimy jeans stuck to my legs. As we drove, my mind fizzed with anxieties. According to our guidebook, Libreville had no camping facilities, and we had no money for a hotel. We could see no way of exiting the country quickly. We were stranded. All we could hope was that our money had arrived from London.

That morning, the main route into town was a riot of colour. Festive banners announced that the 1975 OPEC conference would take place in Libreville that week. President Bongo was to become the new chair of OPEC. The flags of all the oil-producing nations lined the route, dancing in the steady onshore breeze. The central business district looked spotless. Somehow it seemed the ultimate irony: Libreville was celebrating, while we were in extremis. I gritted my teeth and peered hard at the names on buildings, looking for the police station.

The grey, multistorey concrete building looked forbidding. I had never reported a robbery in a foreign language before. As we climbed the stairs, I hoped the Gabonese police would be friendlier than the Algerian variety, whom we had come to know better than we would have liked six weeks before. I got my wish: Sergeant Christian Girard was young, French, and immaculate in khaki and black, with abundant gold braid and rows of polished brass buttons, and he smiled and motioned us to two wooden chairs in his office. 'How can I help?'

I smiled back, introduced myself and Win, and began in my best French: 'We've been robbed, and would like to report the incident.' I fought fatigue as I related the events of the night before. When I mentioned where the theft had occurred, Sergeant Girard grimaced knowingly: we had innocently chosen to camp at a beach notorious for robberies, the haunt of unemployed immigrant labourers from Benin and Senegal.

'Is there *really* nowhere we can camp near town?' I asked.

'Not legally. The safest place would be a hotel.' The muscles in my abdomen tightened into a cramp – hotels were out of the question on our budget. While a clerk typed the report of the robbery, I explained our circumstances – that we needed to find a way out of Gabon, possibly to sell the van. Soon I realised that he felt genuinely sorry for us.

'I'll make some inquiries for you,' he said. We sat and listened as he placed a series of phone calls – to the port, to car dealers, to friends and colleagues – and wrote out the details of shipping agents, second-hand car yards and departure schedules. For the hundredth time on this trip, I blessed my love of the French language. As we waited, I explained to Win, who spoke no French, what was happening.

An hour later, Sergeant Girard handed me two copies of the report, and the list of useful contacts he had compiled. As we left, he called after us, 'Come back and see me. Let me know how you get on.' I thanked him and said we would. A spring crept into my step as we reached the street: we now had an ally we could call on if we needed to. It was a chink of light.

'We'd better get a move on,' Win said. As we strode to the Kombi and climbed in, his whole body was tense, his face drawn. His mind was already focused like a laser on the next task: 'Everything closes at noon for three hours. We've got half an hour to find the bank where our money from London was sent, or at least to cash the traveller's cheque. We can't do anything without money.'

Win's stoicism never deserted him. I'd seen a lot of it during our desert crossing. He kept going under duress, regardless of how he felt. I knew he was still exhausted, hungry and bitterly disappointed, but he kept it to himself. I took his cue and turned my attention to finding the Banque Nationale de Paris.

As we drove slowly through the business district, my eyes lighted on the name over a door – Banque de Paris et des Pays-Bas – surely there couldn't be two banks with such similar names. We parked outside. The red and white Kombi, with our expedition gear on the roof, its 'Brisbane, Australia' sign sprayed with mud, stood out among the urban traffic: unlike many African cities, Libreville was off the well-travelled overland routes.

Suddenly a voice behind us was saying, 'You're from Brisbane?' The speaker was a well-dressed European man, French, but speaking perfect English. 'My name is Pierre Rochet. I'm an architect. I've worked in Brisbane with Ian Ferrier, the architect. Do you know him?'

Win gasped. 'Do I know him? I've worked with him – I'm a builder!' They started swapping stories, and I looked at my watch. Precious time was elapsing. Pierre thrust one of his business cards into Win's hand: 'Come home and have dinner with us. Give me a ring. Don't forget, will you?'

We barely had time to react when a second voice said, ''Ello. My name is André St Just. You are Australian?' We nodded, incredulous. 'My wife is Australian. She would love to meet you!' My head spun. Just hours ago, we had known no-one.

'Please, come to our house!' André insisted. 'Come tonight – for dinner.'

'We'd love to,' I said, 'but please forgive us – we must rush now.' We agreed to meet him outside the bank at seven-thirty that evening, shook hands and strode towards the bank. It was six minutes to midday. We half ran through the gate and up the concrete path towards the door, but before we reached it, another voice called out, 'So you're from Brisbane?'

We whirled around. Why was everyone in town with a Brisbane connection converging on this spot now? The speaker was a tall man, tanned, around forty, wearing an open-necked business shirt, tropical slacks and horn-rimmed spectacles. He could have passed for Cary Grant; his clipped speech even carried the hint of an American accent. He stepped forward and extended his hand. 'I'm Doug Hunt. We lived in Brisbane for three years. Is there something I can do to help?' By now we were beyond surprise. Anything could happen.

Win's face creased into a wry smile. 'We're desperate to get into this bank to see whether some money has arrived for us. We were robbed last night and we've got no cash.'

'No problem,' Doug said, 'I know the manager personally. Follow me.'

By the time we discovered this was the wrong bank, it had closed for the three-hour lunchbreak and we still had no money. We waited on tenterhooks as Doug exercised his persuasive powers on the French bank manager to get him to cash our one remaining traveller's cheque. Eventually, I grasped a small pile of Central African francs, thanked the bank manager in French, and we walked with Doug back out into the street.

'We're very grateful,' I said. 'It's been a rough twenty-four hours.'

'No trouble. You might have difficulty finding the Banque Nationale de Paris though: it's hidden away at the other end of town. How about I take you there now, then you'll be right for when it reopens?'

The bank was on the first floor of a nondescript building. He was right, we'd never have spotted it.

We'd worked out that Doug was a Kiwi – the vowels gave it away. The chances of meeting a fellow Antipodean in this francophone slice of Equatorial Africa must have been millions to one.

'What brings you to Gabon, Doug?' I had him pegged as a professional of some kind.

'I'm a geologist. I'm running a mineral project up in the mountains.'

I glanced at Win. I knew what he was thinking, because I was thinking the same: a geologist in the mountains of Equatorial Africa? How romantic was that! Doug seemed reluctant to leave: 'Look, when you've collected your money, why don't you call around to my office for coffee late this afternoon, and we'll talk about Brisbane. We loved our life there. I'd be interested to know what it's like now. Here's my card – the office address is on it.'

'We'd love to.' Win smiled and shook his hand. 'And thanks again for your help.'

'Okay. See you then.'

The card showed Doug was the director of a company called SOMIFER. We stood on the footpath, our heads spinning. In only three hours, we had a network of contacts in the city – people of goodwill, people we could call on for help, people who spoke English. We even had money for food and a dinner date. We looked at each other and burst out laughing. The whole thing was bizarre. I half-danced back to the van with relief, light-headed from hunger and lack of sleep.

We drove down to the esplanade and parked on a grass verge under the coconut palms. Thick cloud hung low over the bay, a murky grey with no breaks. We stretched out on the bed in the van and closed our eyes, hoping for sleep while we waited for the town to wake from its three-hour lunchbreak.

I must have dozed off, because the next thing I knew it was two o'clock. To while away the last hour, I pulled out our *Travellers' Guide to Africa* and opened it at the chapter on Gabon. The country relied heavily on imported food and consumer goods. There was no commercial agriculture, and much of the population depended on subsistence agriculture, hunting and fishing. The only major manufacturing industry was a massive plywood mill at Port-Gentil on the coast. Gabon's economy was critically linked to world demand for its minerals, offshore oil and timber. The *Guide* also highlighted the government's flagship project – a plan to build a railway from the port of Owendo near Libreville to a vast iron-ore deposit at Belinga in the remote north-east. When completed, the railway would bring out the mined ore for export. Construction on the railway had not begun, and no ore had been mined.

At three o'clock we were back at the Banque Nationale de Paris, where I explained to a melancholy French clerk about our funds transfer. I wasn't hopeful. After a thorough search of the records, he returned with the news that the money had not yet arrived – perhaps we would care to call back next week? Out in the street we took stock again. We had nowhere to camp legally, and probably just enough cash for one day's food. Our new contacts in town would be critical for our survival.

Hunger and fatigue set in again, so we drove to the far end of town, where we found a European-style hypermarket, Mbolo, crammed with luxury French food and alcohol.

'We'll try for some salami,' Win said. He chose a piece twenty centimetres long, looked at the price and instantly dropped it, hissing an expletive under his breath. It cost four times what it would in Paris. Stunned, we chose a piece half that size and a small baguette from the bread display. By the time we had paid, it was almost four o'clock and there was no time to eat. We were due at Doug's office for coffee.

On the walls of Doug's office, geological maps jostled for space with black-and-white aerial photographs of a minuscule clearing in thick forest, where a scatter of tin-roofed buildings perched on a hillside. Above the desk, the latest official portrait of the president of Gabon, El Hadj Omar Bongo, looked out imperiously.

We sat in black vinyl armchairs and sipped the strong coffee brought by Doug's bilingual French secretary. Intrigued, Doug eyed us both in our soiled jeans. 'So what have you been doing in Africa? Where've you been?'

Win and I exchanged glances, took deep breaths, and began. After we'd finished the story, Doug sighed deeply. 'That's a hell of a tale. My wife would love to hear that!'

Doug had worked as a geologist around the world and had been in Gabon for just six months. On arrival, he had spoken no French and had no African experience. His brief as director of SOMIFER was to: reopen an old mineral exploration camp in mountainous forest 600 kilometres from the coast, in a region with no roads, airfields or railways; coordinate surveying, mapping and test drilling of the area; establish supply lines for provisioning the camp; and provide housing for up to twenty expatriates and over a hundred Gabonese workers and their large families.

'What is this project?' I asked.

'It's an iron-ore exploration project at a place called Belinga,' Doug said.

'Belinga?' We both sat bolt upright. 'We read about that only today. Isn't it supposed to be the biggest iron-ore deposit in Africa?'

'It is! Come over to the desk and I'll show you.' He spread out prospectuses, photographs and maps, and on an aerial photo, pointed to a clearing in dense forest. 'That's the camp. We're cutting a road through to it at the moment, but it'll be a while before we reach it because of the wet season.' This was the flagship project for which the Trans-Gabonese Railway would be built.

'We've been slowly opening up the camp over the last five months. At the moment, we have a Sicilian geologist and a handful of Gabonese labourers up there. They're manually clearing the old tracks through the forest ahead of our team of British surveyors, who're due here in a fortnight.'

'How do you get up there?' Win asked.

'It takes two days. We fly to the nearest town, Makokou, then go upriver in a motorised pirogue – a dugout – which takes between five and twelve hours, depending on the height of the water. Then we go by Land Rover seventeen kilometres up into the mountains. The route is steep and full of hairpin bends, so it takes about forty-five minutes.'

Win's eyes had lit up. 'How do you communicate with people in the camp when you're down here?'

'We have an army-style field radio here in the office, another one at our base in Makokou, and one in the camp. Twice a day we have scheduled radio links to coordinate movement of supplies and people and sort out any problems.'

I sat on the edge of the armchair. The project sounded like the plot of an adventure film. It had all the right elements – remoteness, danger, challenge and the mystery of Equatorial Africa. I forgot how tired and hungry I was. I just wanted to hear more. For Doug, the project was clearly more than a job – it was a way of life that combined his love of wild places with a satisfying career.

'We're about to embark on an accelerated building program at the camp,' he said. 'We need six timber houses built quickly.' Doug was unaware he was sitting opposite a builder. A flicker passed across Win's face; he had always believed that when opportunity knocked, one should race to open the door. A hint of a smile played around his mouth. 'Not looking for a good builder, are you?'

'Matter of fact, I am. I'm about to telex someone I know in Brisbane to see if he's interested. But it's hard to get people to come here.'

'Well look,' Win said, still playing with the idea and not really serious, 'I'm a builder. If you pay me US$30,000 a year tax-free, I'll build your camp for you.'

I think he expected a flippant reply to the effect that it wasn't so simple. Instead, Doug leaned forward, focused: 'Okay, you're on. There's no problem with the salary, as long as you only work for six months. But it won't be much fun for your wife. You'd have to live in a tent.'

Win's eyes widened and his jaw dropped. Doug turned to me. 'How would you feel about being the only white woman there?'

How would I feel? The 'only white woman' part wouldn't faze me at all, but going back into that forest, to those minuscule biting insects, for six whole months – I couldn't face it. Mosquito nets and insect repellents were useless against their onslaughts. I glared at Win as he began to discuss the possibility seriously, without even asking my opinion. His imagination was on fire; I was speechless. Thoughts ricocheted in my head: 'What is he doing? I won't go back into that jungle – we've just escaped from it!' I kicked his foot hard under the table.

It was now dark outside, but Doug was wound up, deadly serious about recruiting this builder who had dropped into his lap. 'Look, why don't you come home to my place and we'll have a drink and talk about it?' We still had not eaten, and it had been a long and tumultuous day. The last thing we felt like was socialising over alcohol, but Doug wasn't about to give up: 'If you give me a few minutes, I'll be finished here and we can drive there in convoy.' It was settled before I had a chance to demur. Only much later we remembered our arrangement to meet the Frenchman with the Australian wife at seven-thirty that night for dinner – by the time we had, it was too late.

We left Doug's office in silence and walked to the Kombi, parked just outside. Flushed in the face, I climbed into the passenger seat, and let fly. 'What do you think you're doing? Don't I have any say in this?'

'You do realise I was only joking at first, don't you? I had no idea he'd take me up on it. But can't you see? It would be a way out of the mess we're in. Besides, I think it could be really interesting. Let's just hear what he has to say.'

'But what about the biting insects? It was bad enough for three days. How do you imagine we'd cope with six months of that misery?' I could handle staying in Africa, but I couldn't begin to contemplate a situation where we couldn't escape the torture of those insects. But Win was already there in his mind – I knew that look in his eyes well. I call it the Boys' Own Adventure syndrome. He couldn't resist a challenge, and this one would be a whopper.

'Why don't we just wait and see?' he asked calmly. He seldom rose to my anger – a fact that sometimes exasperated me – and I knew this was his way of saying I was overreacting. Reluctantly, I had to admit to myself the idea had merit – being on a payroll would solve all our problems. But I was in no mood to say so.

chapter two

A WAY OUT

We followed Doug's car in silence to the luxury residential quarter on the seafront. He pulled in to a paved entryway surrounded by flowering tropical shrubs and vines. My jaw was set – I wasn't about to be bulldozed into anything, especially six months of sustained insect attacks. Then we climbed out into the fragrant early-evening air, and in an instant I was back in Brisbane, in the garden of my grandmother's home, gulping in the perfume of star jasmine and frangipani, familiar smells in this alien environment. I wondered what she'd have thought of my global wanderings. She had died the year before, at ninety-four. She had been a rebel in her time – five feet nothing in stockings, feisty as the devil and tough as leather. I liked to think I had inherited some of her gritty determination.

'Hello, you two!' It was Doug's wife, Gina, framed in the front doorway. Tall and elegant, in spotless white tapered slacks and a black knitted top, she could have been a diplomat's wife welcoming foreign dignitaries at an embassy.

'Come on through.' She led the way into the living room. I took several steps onto the deep-pile cream carpet and paused, open-mouthed. The vast room could have been a Hollywood film set. Plate-glass walls on the western side gave views on to a floodlit tropical garden. Low-set glass coffee tables with chrome legs stood between deep cane armchairs with mock-zebra-skin cushions. Metre-high silver table lamps threw a muted glow over the room, and high on the walls, huge Gauguin murals depicted languid Tahitian women in a sensuous floral paradise.

Just then, three fresh-faced and beautiful young girls came into the room to be introduced. 'These are our daughters – Penny, Prue and Pippa. Girls, this is Mr and Mrs Henderson.' The girls all had long hair and wore jeans and long-sleeved T-shirts. They smiled demurely. Penny was in her early teens, Prue looked a couple of years younger, and Pippa was about nine, and they all looked so healthy I could imagine them as models for some up-market skincare product.

'Come and sit down.' Gina motioned towards the cane armchairs.

I perched on the edge of a chair, hoping none of the dirt on my jeans would rub off on the cushions, while Doug strode in and headed for the drinks cabinet. 'What'll you have? We've got most things.'

'I'm a whisky man – a Scotch, thanks.' Win had settled into an armchair, his builder's eye taking in every detail of the architecture. 'This place is an absolute gem. What's the story?'

'It was built by the millionaire pilot who founded Air Gabon.' Doug poured the drinks. 'A guy named Jean-Claude Brouillet. He was a daredevil flyer, and as you can see, he had a passion for the South Pacific. We're just renting here: we're building a place of our own up the beach in a suburb called Tahiti.'

A tall, slim Gabonese man wearing a pink apron came in carrying plates of savoury snacks and placed them on a coffee table. '*Merci, Louis-Marie,*' Gina nodded and smiled at him.

'*Merci, madame.*' Louis-Marie looked briefly at us and a hint of a smile played around his mouth. Gina made the introduction. '*Voilà Monsieur et Madame Henderson, Louis-Marie.*' He nodded shyly, '*Bonsoir, M'sieur et 'dame.*'

'Louis-Marie is employed by the company to help me with the cooking and housework,' Gina said. We had been plunged into a post-colonial world of incredible luxury and privilege, where African staff filled the same roles as they had before independence – except that now they earned decent wages and the country belonged to them again. I smiled at him. '*Bonsoir, Louis-Marie.*'

If I had drunk whisky, I would have fallen asleep. I opted for a fruit juice and eyed the food on the platters: boiled eggs with savoury filling, biscuits with spread, cheeses and nuts. It was the first food we had had in twenty-four hours, and I had to restrain myself to eat slowly and delicately. We hadn't enjoyed the luxury of an egg since London. I rolled each mouthful around on my tongue.

'Doug tells me you two crossed the Sahara.' Gina and the girls turned expectant faces towards us. 'We want to hear all about it.'

I lost track of time, but a couple of hours must have passed while we exchanged stories. The Hunts had lived all over the world – the US, Central America, Europe – wherever Doug's work had taken them.

Eventually the conversation turned to business. Doug was employed by Bethlehem Steel of Pennsylvania, the managing partners in the SOMIFER consortium, in which the Gabonese government held a fifty-one per cent share. Other partner countries included France, Germany and Romania. Doug had poured Win another whisky and I watched them interact: already they had a strong rapport. I listened as they discussed Win's long building career in Australia, Papua New Guinea and England. Doug was clearly impressed – this was not just another knockabout carpenter he had stumbled on.

Doug began by outlining what Win's role at Belinga might be. He needed a fully equipped wood machine workshop set up and single men's quarters built urgently. After that, an entire camp had to be constructed – expatriate housing, a geology laboratory, offices, a health clinic for the Gabonese families, furniture for the village houses, and anything else that cropped up.

'What's the country like up there?' I cut in. I wanted a clear picture of what we would be agreeing to if we accepted the job.

Doug's expression softened, and his voice mellowed. 'It's magnificent. The camp is sited at 700 metres altitude. It's cool most of the time with regular breezes – so cool that we need a fire in the dry season. The camp overlooks forest in every direction. There are ferns and vines and plenty of wildlife. I just love being up there.'

I took a deep breath and braced myself to take a tough stand. 'I'm really concerned about the biting insects. It was a nightmare for us driving down through the forest. We were bitten all over and the itch drove us crazy. If that's what we're in for, I wouldn't be a starter.'

'Okay. Let me try and reassure you. There *are* insects. The ones you're talking about are *fourreaux*. But we've found that after a few weeks, people develop an immunity to their bites and no longer feel them. By the way, you're on malaria prophylactics, aren't you?'

I nodded.

'Good, because that's endemic through here. The other main thing you need to be aware of is filariasis. That's spread by the bite of a red fly, the *mouche rouge*. They lay their eggs in human flesh and the eggs hatch into long white worms that can accumulate in joints, causing swelling and stiffness. They can also cause elephantiasis. You've probably seen pictures of people with grossly swollen legs? That's it. So you'll need to go on to prophylactics for that too.'

I listened in silence.

'There are also tsetse flies and *ghiques*.'

'What are *ghiques*?' Small pricks of revulsion moved in waves along my skin as I listened to this entomology lesson.

'*Ghiques* live in the ground. They burrow into the soles of your feet and create a blister-like bubble that encloses a long thread-like worm. It's not a major problem. You can kill them by covering the blister with vaseline to cut off the worm's air supply. Once it's dead, you can cut round the edge of the blister with a razor blade and pull it out.'

Oh, a doddle, I thought – I cut my skin with razor blades all the time! It was like reading some nineteenth-century African explorer's diary.

'The main thing to remember,' Doug continued, 'is never to go barefoot.' I was sure I'd have no trouble remembering. He hastened to reassure me further. 'It's not all bad. There's a hospital in Makokou, 100 kilometres downstream. The company would provide all your food, and there'll be a couple of other wives arriving in a few months' time. And there could be an opportunity for you, too, if you wanted it.'

I brightened up. 'What did you have in mind?'

'Well, with your French, you could tutor the expatriate children.'

'I'm not a teacher, you know.'

'No, but the opportunity would be there. You'd have plenty of time on your hands.'

By this time, I could see Win had already made up his mind. He could hardly wait to get up there. From his perspective, the job had everything he could wish for – challenge, excitement, wilderness and more money than he had ever earned. Back in Brisbane, US$30,000 equalled a doctor's earnings. If we accepted, our worries about visas, money and accommodation would be over. I could feel myself relenting.

Doug looked from me to Win. 'So, you're happy for me to set the wheels in motion to appoint you, Win?'

'Yep. Go for your life.'

At that point I abandoned any thoughts of resistance. I would just have to handle the insect onslaughts as best I could.

'Okay. I'll telex France and the States tomorrow and seek their go-ahead for a six-month, no-strings-attached contract. But you both need to understand the camp is extremely isolated. There's no entertainment, and it'll be pretty rough going for a while.'

'It couldn't be worse than the Sahara!' Win's wry smile appeared again.

Doug moved back to the cocktail cabinet. 'Come on, Win. Have another drink! This is something to celebrate!'

'Oh, no thanks,' Win said. 'I've had quite enough, really.'

'Oh, go on,' Doug pressed. 'Just one more.'

It was late, and fatigue, lack of food and the strain of recent weeks had taken a toll on us both. But our new boss was offering hospitality and Win felt obliged to accept. Doug must have refilled the glass to the top.

We sat back in the armchairs and drifted into a drowsy late-night reverie. Eventually, I looked at my watch. It was after ten. We needed to go, but neither of us had thought about where we would spend the night – events had completely overtaken us.

But when I looked across at Win, his face had turned a pale grey and his eyes were glazed. The next moment, he lurched forward in the armchair, vomited copiously on the deep-pile cream carpet and fell unconscious to the floor.

I leapt out of my chair and dropped to my knees beside him. My first-aid training came flashing back: get the patient into the prone position so they don't inhale their vomit. I rolled him on to his right side. He was breathing steadily, but out to it. 'Oh well, that's killed it,' I thought. 'How to impress your new boss: vomit all over his shag-pile carpet.' It was another first: I had never seen Win drunk. The only time I had seen him vomit had been on a rough voyage out to the Barrier Reef – we'd both been sick, side by side over the rail.

'You're a good little mother.' It was Doug, squatting beside me.

'I'm so sorry,' I murmured. 'We don't normally do this. If you have some spare towels, I'll clean up.'

Gina was unfazed. 'Don't worry. Louis-Marie will take care of it.'

Now I had another problem: with my automatic driver's licence, I couldn't drive the Kombi and Win was unconscious. We weren't going anywhere.

'We're going to have to sleep here overnight in the Kombi, I'm afraid,' I said. I couldn't remember ever being more embarrassed. The Kombi was parked in the Hunts' driveway, shielded from the road by shrubs and trees.

'Come on,' Doug offered. 'We'll carry him out between us.' He took Win's top end and I lifted the legs – eighty kilos of dead weight between us. We shuffled out of the living room, through a hallway and into the warm night, the stench of vomit fresh in our nostrils. Crickets sang in the bushes. In the background, the Atlantic lapped on the shore. I unlocked the sliding door and cleared everything off the bed. We lifted him onto it, then stripped his clothes off down to underwear. I bathed his face with a damp cloth.

'He just needs to sleep it off,' Doug reassured me. With a sheepish grin, I thanked him for everything, apologised again and said goodnight. I lay awake for about an hour, my mind a rat's nest of jumbled thoughts. It had been the most bizarre day of my life and I couldn't imagine what the next day might bring.

Win woke in bright sunlight, with a blinding headache and a raging thirst, rubbed his eyes, pulled on a pair of shorts and slid off the bed. 'How did I get out here last night?'

'We carried you, Doug and I.'

'What a disaster! I suppose all we can do is go in and apologise, then get the hell out of here.' We dressed, washed our faces and walked up to the front door, ready to face the embarrassment.

But a note fluttered from the door signed by Gina: 'Good morning! Hope you slept well. Your breakfast is waiting in the dining room. Help yourselves to a hot shower. See you at lunch.' We looked at each other, mouths agape, eyes wide, and laughed with relief.

The whole family was out, but Louis-Marie ushered us to an iron-lace dining table beside the plate-glass wall and brought fresh fruit salad, toast and jam and tea. Just outside, flowering hibiscus and bougainvillea painted the garden purple, blood red, burnt orange and buttercup yellow.

We ate slowly, looking out beyond the garden to the coconut palms, the only sounds the rustle of palm leaves and the whirr of insects. Once again, I felt like an actor on a film set, playing out a fantasy that would soon end. After a second cup of tea, I sat back and tried to picture what our life at Belinga would be like, and how it would feel being the only white woman in a forest that stretched for thousands of kilometres into the Congo. My idea of the camp oscillated between an African Eden and an insect-plagued frontier, a place of isolation and hardship.

I could hardly wait to shower – my hair was caked with salt, and I felt sticky and unclean – and was grateful when Louis-Marie returned and led the way to the bathroom. It turned out to be a cabana perched on a timber walkway that snaked through the coconut palms. Inside, twin copper-lined shower recesses glowed in the soft light, and above them, Gauguin prints decorated the walls. That sense of unreality overwhelmed me again. We were dreaming – we must have been.

***

At midday, the whole family returned. 'You slept well?' Gina's graciousness carried no hint of what had happened the night before.

'Look, I want to apologise,' Win said. 'I'm absolutely mortified. It was just a case of too little sleep and too much alcohol on an empty stomach.'

They both made deprecatory gestures. 'Don't give it another thought. It didn't worry us at all. In fact, we'd like you to join us for dinner tonight.'

'What dish have you missed most on your trip?' Gina asked.

'Well, we have felt a steak deficiency,' Win said.

'Then steak it will be.'

Our Australian addiction to steak had suffered two years of neglect while we lived in London, where only the rich could afford it. I tried not to look overeager. 'That sounds terrific!'

'Getting down to practicalities again, though,' Win said, 'we still don't have anywhere to camp. Is there somewhere you can suggest?'

'Actually, there is,' Doug said. 'Our new house site at Tahiti adjoins some land occupied by the French Aviation Tennis Club. In between, there's a strip of land you can use. It's out of the way and no-one will bother you.'

'Great – how do we find it?'

'Look, why don't you come back late this afternoon and I'll take you there?' Gina offered. 'Let's say five-fifteen?'

We spent the afternoon relaxing at the beach and driving around the city to get the feeling of it. At sunset Gina took us down to the camping place. The white, deserted beach was fringed with the ubiquitous coconut palms.

Apart from the tennis courts and clubhouse, there were only a couple of bungalows visible through a stand of trees: the spot was out of sight of officialdom and away from the haunts of Sunday picnickers and would-be burglars.

That night, over a dinner of juicy Rhodesian steaks and cauliflower with cheese, Doug was expansive. 'Well, I've had a telex back from the States, Win, and they're happy for me to put you on staff on the basis we discussed. But I don't expect you both to accept sight unseen. The company will fly you up to Makokou next week and take you up to the camp to have a look, on a no-obligation basis. If you change your minds once you've seen it, there'll be no hard feelings. How does that sound?'

Win was still incredulous at the whole offer. 'It sounds fine, but I'm a bit concerned that I can't provide you with any evidence of my credentials. Normally people want references or proof of some sort. How do you know that I am what I say I am?'

Doug's quick wit produced an instant retort: 'Oh, look, anyone who can hold their liquor as well as you can must be good!' We both erupted in laughter. It was the best one-liner I'd ever heard. I decided that working for Doug was going to be a riot.

'I've booked you on Monday's flight to Makokou,' he said. 'You'll have two nights in the camp and fly back on Friday. You can park the van in the company's compound in town. It'll be safe there.'

Despite myself, I felt mounting excitement. In less than a week we would be transported to the absolute heart of Africa, to an area we could never have reached by ourselves.

Slowly I began to accept that what lay ahead just might be something rare and wonderful.

For the next five days we camped at Tahiti Beach, and relaxed more fully than we had since leaving London. We had made it through every trial from Morocco to the equator – half the length of Africa – and now we were poised for another colossal leap of faith. I wrote letters and postcards home, washed clothes and sat for long periods under the coconut palms staring out at the grey-green Atlantic. In the afternoons, Gina brought the girls down for visits. We swam, built sandcastles, laughed and played.

It seemed to me that life could not get any better, but one day it did. We were sitting drinking tea and looking out on the ocean when a Frenchman with steel-grey hair and a whimsical smile appeared from behind the tennis club and introduced himself. '*Bonjour! Roger Bonnet.*'

'*Bonjour, monsieur!*' I shook his hand and introduced us both. 'Won't you join us?'

'*Vous parlez français?*'

'*Un très petit peu!*' I said, feigning modesty – a very little bit. He pointed at the map on the side of the Kombi. '*Vous avez fait ces voyages-là?*' I nodded and told him we had recently crossed the Sahara.

'*Mais vous parlez très bien!*' he insisted. The van, our travels, and my French seemed to intrigue everyone we met. 'What are you doing in Libreville?' he asked.

'It's a long story,' I said. 'Would you like some tea?' He fetched a chair from the tennis club and settled in to listen to the saga of our desert crossing. Like everyone who heard, he was spellbound.

'We're moving up to Belinga soon,' I said. 'Win will be in charge of designing and building the camp for SOMIFER.'

His eyes widened. '*Ah bon?*' It was the French way of expressing surprise. I guessed he was thinking something like, 'These Australians don't waste time – down and out one day, off to the jungle to work the next!'

Roger and I chatted for two hours. He was Win's age and height, looked fit and was excellent company. He had lived in Gabon many years and worked as a communications engineer with ASECNA, the organisation responsible for the installation and maintenance of aviation beacons throughout the country. I also discovered that he shared two of Win's passions – aircraft and gourmet cooking. Despite Win's lack of French, as soon as I relayed this to him his friendship with Roger was sealed.

'How are you managing for showering and washing?' Roger asked.

'Not too well, I'm afraid,' I said. 'We're bathing out of a bucket, and washing clothes in a plastic basin.'

'That's no good! Come and use my place – I'm on my own at the moment. You can come and go as you please. It's just over there.'

His open-hearted offer stunned me. 'Oh, that would be *wonderful*,' I breathed. He led us to a low-set white bungalow surrounded by the signature plants of Libreville – coconut palms, flowering hibiscus and bougainvillea. Brightly coloured birds swooped and flitted through the garden; a porch at the front of the house held a table and chairs that faced the ocean.

'Here's the laundry and bathroom,' he said. 'Just make yourselves at home.'

***

We spent long hours with Roger in the days that followed, learning about Gabon and enjoying his zany tales of life in Libreville. On Sunday, he even invited us for a celebration lunch before our trip to the camp – five courses, served alfresco. An onshore breeze rattled the palms. On the beach, a lone African boy wearing only shorts picked his way gingerly along piles of scattered okoumé logs, and slowly twirled a long thin stick in the air. Okoumé is the most famous cabinet timber of Gabon, and these logs had broken free from rafts on the Ogooué River and been washed up on the beach. Again I felt like we were characters in a film – perhaps *South Pacific*, with Roger as the planter played by Rossano Brazzi. I still could scarcely believe the colossal reversal in our fortunes. We were not just rid of all our troubles, we were riding an unprecedented wave of excitement and privilege. A beneficent fate seemed to have enfolded us. Suddenly everything was falling into place.

Over cheese, coffee and Cointreau, we discussed the details of the journey to Belinga – a flight to Makokou on Monday, then a pirogue trip upriver on Tuesday.

Roger smiled, a little indulgently. 'Wait till you see the forest from the air. It just looks like a sea of green cauliflower.' Africa from the air – I could hardly wait.

chapter three

To the Mountains

The terminal was stuffy with the mingled smells of sweat, cooking oil and oversweet toiletries. This was our first taste of a Gabonese airport. Throngs of local women and children milled around in the departure lounge, their baggage consisting mainly of rolls of bedding tied up with rope and wicker baskets full of chickens. A handful of European businessmen stood in the background, looking hot and fed up. The floor of the lounge was laid with grimy vinyl tiles, and the few rows of plastic seating looked as though they hadn't been cleaned in years.

My thoughts galloped as I stood looking out towards the tarmac. This was the beginning of our new life: we would soon be part of this pulsating, chaotic world. We had a purpose in the country, and we were bound for a wilderness that even most Gabonese would never see. My heart thumped and I felt like shouting to the crowd, 'This is a huge moment for me!'

Beside me, Win was silently taking everything in, his eyes never still. I knew he was as excited as I was, but his stoical Scottish genes ensured that he hid it well.

When the boarding call came over the loudspeakers the passengers surged forward in a tight mass, converging on the narrow doorway that led to the tarmac. We were jostled and propelled along by the throng towards the door, then, in a single movement of compression, squeezed through it like squashed insects. A fine chain bracelet I was wearing was ripped off my arm by the force of people pushing past, and as I bent down to retrieve it, risking being knocked over, I paused to wonder at the apparent desperation of the passengers to reach the plane. It wasn't a refugee flight. Later I would learn that the concept of queueing was foreign to most parts of Africa.

Our aircraft was a mini-jet, an F-28 that did the mail run up to Bitam in the north, then on to Makokou. As we climbed and banked, I looked out the window and saw the coastline, then the swamps behind Libreville. We were flying just under a blanket of dry-season cloud. Soon we were over the forest. Roger's description of the view had been perfect – it looked like a giant field of green cauliflower, divided by the snaking brown lines of streams. My pulse raced, and tears sprang to my eyes. I was overwhelmed by the splendour of Africa. We were bound for a dot on the map far to the north-east, close to the Congo border.

I wondered whether Mary Kingsley had felt as I did – breathless with anticipation, impatient for her encounter with the unknown. I found it difficult to sit still in my seat, with the steady vibration of the aircraft under me carrying us forward to our new life. Once again I wanted to stand up and shout that we were on a mission, going to the frontier to further a great enterprise. Nothing I had ever done felt so exciting.

We had been flying for perhaps two hours when I noticed a thin, ochre-coloured line snaking through the dark green of the forest like Ariadne's thread. It was the main road south from the border with Cameroon, the one we had battled a fortnight before – the one that had almost defeated us. 'Road' was too good a word for it.

I thought back to the towering blue peaks and luxuriant forest of Cameroon, the patchwork of plantations, the clear, rushing streams, and our visit to the high country, where we'd sat on bleached hippopotamus skulls in front of the old sultan's ruined palace at Foumban. Cameroon had been our reward for crossing the Sahara and surviving. I had never seen such beauty anywhere – so exquisite it almost hurt. But Cameroon was special to me for another reason too, one that I could not have predicted. There I had held my first great ape – a tiny chimpanzee infant with a pink face and liquid brown eyes. We had been passing through a village on a track to the beach when a man had stepped out from behind a hut and waved us down, holding the baby in his arms. I had never seen a chimpanzee outside a zoo before. It had displayed no fear, and appeared well cared for.

'Do you want to buy it?' the *Camerounais* asked in French. In my entrancement, I didn't stop to wonder how he had come by the infant. I shook my head. What would we do with a baby chimpanzee?

'Would you like to hold it?' My whole body instantly turned to jelly – would I? It was like asking if I would like to win the lottery. I reached out, grasped the tiny body and cradled it in the crook of my arm. Its black hair smelt clean and sweet as it snuggled into my chest. I couldn't take my eyes off its expressive face, its alert gaze, its mobile lips. I wanted to hold it forever. All I could think was, 'They are so like us.' I believe that that was the moment when my encounter with wild Africa really began.

On the descent into Bitam, we recognised the airport buildings adjoining the immigration post that we'd passed through on our way to the coast a fortnight earlier. As the jet's tyres touched the dirt runway, a cloud of red dust hurled itself into the air and drifted back onto the two or three hundred upturned African faces pressing against the barrier fence. The stopover lasted about twenty minutes. Some passengers left, and a few boarded. Among them was an engineer from the Dutch company, Van Splunder, building a new bridge over the Ivindo River at Makokou, who chatted with us for the rest of the flight.

It was almost four o'clock when we touched down at Makokou. At the cabin door, I paused to take it in. Out behind the aircraft, a dust-brown haze hovered over the runway; overhead, the low cloud was still unbroken. A crowd waited in front of the terminal, and a cluster of parked vehicles bore the official logos of companies operating in the area: Land Rovers from SOACO and the Commissariat of Police, a Peugeot from SOMIFER, a utility from Van Splunder and an assortment of battered Citroëns.

We descended the boarding ladder and walked across towards the building. In front of the crowd, a group of Gabonese gendarmes stood looking important. Behind them clustered several Europeans including a priest and a couple of Gabonese religious sisters. Around them waited a group of local men, women and children. Some stood, but most sat on the ground next to their battered suitcases, holding half-eaten pieces of some grey-coloured food wrapped in banana leaves.

One of the gendarmes thrust disembarkation cards into our hands, so I pulled a pen from my bag and filled them out in French – 'SOMIFER staff, visiting Belinga camp' – and handed them back. Then a short, rotund man approached us, extended his hand and said in a gravelly voice, '*Bonsoir! Monsieur et Madame 'Enderson? Émile Kruger.*' Kruger was SOMIFER's man in Makokou. He looked around sixty, with steel-grey hair brushed back from his face, and wore creased shorts, a short-sleeved cotton shirt and work boots. His stocky build and florid complexion suggested a love of food and drink. Brusquely, he instructed a Gabonese chauffeur to take us to our lodgings; he would remain behind to collect our bags and the SOMIFER mail, food and freight.

The drive into town led past supply depots for companies, hardware yards and prefabricated huts, sprawling behind high wire fences on dusty, featureless land. Closer to town, we started passing decaying colonial residences set back from the road behind clumps of palms and bougainvillea, their painted shutters warped and peeling.

Makokou was the main town in the province of Ogooué-Ivindo – a vast, largely uninhabited region drained by the Ivindo River and its tributaries. The town felt like a frontier outpost, and the presence of the priest and religious sisters reminded me that missions, along with trading posts, had been the earliest white institutions to penetrate the interior.

I thought again of Mary Kingsley, who had lodged at missions on her expeditions through the country. Makokou seemed little changed from that time one hundred years earlier, except for the aircraft and motor vehicles.

The car turned into the driveway of one of the old residences and pulled up beside the kitchen door. The house was built of concrete, painted dark maroon, with shuttered windows set in Spanish-style arches. Clumps of taro and other native plants grew wild in a long-neglected garden.

The chauffeur led the way inside, suggesting we make ourselves comfortable in some well-worn cane chairs. Within the hour, Kruger arrived with our bags, explaining that the house was known as the Roux house – SOMIFER used it as a guesthouse. In the dim interior, the flagstone floor shone with the patina of years. Kruger introduced the African domestic staff – Roger the cook and Boniface the housekeeper, then gave us a tour of the house. A massive refectory table dominated the dining room. In the bedrooms, a musty smell hung in the air, and the ancient double bed sagged deeply in the middle. The legs wobbled when we sat on the edge; strange cylindrical pillows that stretched the full width of the bed promised certain discomfort. Before he left, Kruger invited us to his home for an aperitif: the chauffeur would collect us. As I moved from room to room taking in every detail, I felt I was stepping back in time, as if traces of those who had gone before lingered in the still air. Despite its decay and neglect, the house set my imagination alight and I felt excited to be there.

Two hours later, the chauffeur pulled up outside the kitchen door in a dusty Peugeot. A few minutes later, we swung into a driveway beside a large sign that read, 'Concession SOMIFER'. Kruger's house lay in the middle of the company's spacious compound, set high on a hill overlooking a bend in the Ivindo River, and surrounded by a high chain-wire fence. Kruger met us at the door and led us to his living room, motioning to two large armchairs.

The room resembled a museum. On tomato-red walls hung a startling collection of masks, statuettes, bronze castings and well-worn traditional African drums. I turned slowly in a full circle, taking in every detail. Back in London, I had spent many lunch hours poring over artefacts from Central America, the South Pacific and Africa at the Museum of Mankind in Old Burlington Street, just three blocks from where I worked. But this was different. Kruger's collection proclaimed a long life spent in remote Africa, an expatriate world of meaning that was now all he knew.

My eye was drawn to a tall, elegant wooden mask with faces on all four sides, exquisitely carved, and painted black and white. 'What's that, Monsieur Kruger?'

Kruger's face registered no change of expression. 'That? That's a Bakota dance mask from a village out on the road to Okondja.'

'And that walking stick?'

'Ebony.' His laconic answers somehow matched the surroundings perfectly. I dropped into one of the roomy armchairs and Win settled into another, while Kruger poured three glasses of Ricard, the cloudy white drink the French often sip at sundown.

I wondered if he would be more forthcoming about the Roux house. 'Who were the Roux?'

Kruger raised tired-looking eyes from his glass and focused on some point beyond the ceiling. As he spoke little English, he answered in French.

'Old Roux was a prospector. Came in after the gold. He was a young man then. Came to Africa to seek his fortune.'

'Was there much gold around here?'

'Not here. Up the river.' He inclined his head towards the Ivindo. 'He struck it rich – alluvial gold. Went panning for it up on the Nouna River near the Congo border, and around Camp Six. Made a fortune, they did.'

'Who are "they"?'

'He and Carmen.'

'Carmen?'

'His wife.'

'Where did she fit in?' His brief responses gave little away, but I sensed a good tale.

'Carmen? Well, there's a story! What a woman! Beautiful! Still is.'

'Go on.' Getting him to elaborate was like pulling teeth.

'Roux had been here a few years on his own. She was back in France. It was all arranged that she would come out and marry him. But he got leprosy. So he wrote to her, breaking the news and telling her not to come, that he was dying.'

'And still she did?'

'Couldn't stop her. Said she'd agreed to marry him and marry him she would. Came out here, a young girl. They got married, and in the end he was cured by Albert Schweitzer. She worked with him in the business – remarkable woman. Learnt all the dialects, knew the Gabonese by name, handled the money. Old Roux died a millionaire. She's back in France, but she comes here sometimes for a visit. It's her house you'll be sleeping in tonight. We rent it from her, but it's old now . . .'

Before we'd planned our African trip I had never heard of Gabon, but I had heard of its most famous historical figure, Albert Schweitzer, at primary school. Schweitzer's mythological status in western civilisation, as a musician, doctor, theologian and philosopher who had sacrificed his comfortable European life for a struggle with tropical diseases in the swamps of Lambarene, had been unassailable for decades. He had won the Nobel Prize in 1952. In later life, he had had his critics as colonialism met its demise, but the fact that his leprosy hospital at Lambarene still operated impressed me as a heroic achievement. Listening to Kruger, I had the sense, just as I'd had at the Roux house, that we were being drawn into a time warp where little had changed in decades. Kruger lived alone.

'How long have you been in Africa, Monsieur Kruger?'

'Thirty-four years. I'm one of the old hands.' He spoke in a monotone, barely moving a muscle of his heavily veined face.

'What did you do in the beginning, before you came up here to SOMIFER?'

'I was in the timber camps. There was only timber in those days – Gaboon wood, okoumé – it was big business, till the bottom fell out of it.'

'And after that?'

'Oh, I knocked around.' He must have been getting fed up with my questions.

'How long have you been in Makokou?'

'Six years now. Too long.' There it was – his confession of boredom and frustration. This was the man who would be our link with the outside world once we moved to Belinga. I wondered how that would go.

Win was only following snatches of the conversation. I

tried translating, but it proved clumsy and ruined the flow of the stories. He told me not to worry, he'd try and get the gist his own way.

Even though I didn't particularly like the aniseed taste of Ricard, I accepted a second glass: I wanted to prolong the encounter. Kruger had a repertoire of anecdotes of African life, and once he realised I had an insatiable appetite for them, he loosened up.

'What about traditional beliefs and practices, Monsieur Kruger? Does much of that survive today?'

His face twisted into a wry grimace and he told me another story. There was a Gabonese army officer who had three wives, a man of some ability who had prospered under the French command and risen to a senior rank. But he had one major problem – he was impotent. Notwithstanding his western education and professional position, the officer consulted the local witchdoctor, who counselled him to eat the genitals of a Pygmy. Accordingly, he ordered the secret killing of a Pygmy and went through with the ritual.

I couldn't comprehend that such beliefs had survived into the present, but that was only my naivety. It turned out that the officer's crime had been discovered and he was 'rotting in Makokou jail' (as Kruger put it) as we spoke.

'And where did this happen?' I asked.

Kruger's face remained impassive. 'Just one hour up river from where you will be living.'

If he was trying to shock me, he had succeeded. So that was the environment we were going into – a place where superstition and witchcraft still held people in their thrall. More and more it seemed, as I listened, that little had changed since Mary Kingsley's time.

Kruger grasped a solid bronze object from a shelf and handed it to me. 'Here, feel this.' I took it and almost dropped it because of the weight.

'What is it?'

'They're called slave bracelets. The women used to be forced to wear them around their ankles to stop them from escaping.' The bracelet was a broken circle with a bulbous knob on each end. I estimated its weight at three kilos. When I put it on my wrist, my arm dropped like a stone and I could barely lift it.

'Do the people around here still make traditional artefacts?'

'Not much. Not like the old days. The missions stopped most of that, as far as they could. When they came, they collected all the objects linked with tribal religion and witchcraft and buried great piles of them in the forest, then set about trying to convert the people. The missionaries were the only ones who knew where the things were buried. The story goes that years later, traders from the Middle East came through and paid off the missions to sell them the stuff, then quietly smuggled it out. That's Africa, Madame 'Enderson!'

I looked at my watch and saw that it was nearly eight o'clock. 'We must be going,' I said, edging out of the armchair. 'What are the arrangements for tomorrow?'

'You will leave at nine-thirty: I'll send the chauffeur around to collect you. The pirogue will be ready and you'll each have a life jacket. You can ask Roger and Boniface to prepare you a picnic lunch. It'll be a long ride because the river's low, so you'll get hungry. I'll see you down at the *débarcadère* – the landing stage. There'll be bread and fresh food for the camp to go up with you.'

Kruger got up and walked us to the car. As we rounded the corner of the house, an outside light was burning. He stopped, bent down and picked something up, cursing. Straightening up, he held out his hand to reveal a black rhinocerous beetle the size of a small bird. Screwing up his face, he hurled the beetle at the concrete wall and it fell stunned to the ground. Then he picked it up and threw it into a plastic bucket to join dozens of its deceased relatives.

Back at the Roux house, Roger had prepared soup, steak and salad, followed by cheese and fruit. After dinner, we explored the sanitary facilities. There were two showers and two toilets. Running water and handbasins had been installed, but Boniface had forgotten to light the fire under the triangular flat-iron hot-water tank – and there was little firewood anyway – so we settled for a cold wash and crawled into the sagging double bed.

Mosquitoes whined around our heads, and muffled singing and shouting reached our ears from somewhere in the town. I finally dropped off to sleep thinking about Carmen Roux, leprosy and rhinoceros beetles.

Next morning, slits of pale grey light showed through the gaps in the bedroom shutters, and the rise and fall of African voices passing under the window brought us to full consciousness. It was just after eight o'clock and out in the street, groups of people had gathered to talk. Given the noises we had heard the night before, I wondered when these people ever slept! After breakfast, we left Roger and Boniface to prepare our lunch while we went to look for Kruger.

From the verandah of Kruger's house we looked out on the bend of the Ivindo River: Makokou lay on its western bank. It was still early morning, and a leaden sky blocked out any warmth from the sun. The river lay brown, glassy and deserted. Along the banks the forest stretched, forming a green corridor. Wisps of morning fog hung in the air, filmy wraith-like patches, low over the water and drifting through the branches. Kruger wasn't at home.

The *débarcadère* was a steep clearing on the riverbank, where a group of pirogues bobbed in the shallow water. A rusty iron barge lay beached nearby in the mud. Part-way up the slope, a corrugated-iron shed with a padlock and chain on the doors provided storage space for outboard motors and fuel.

Gabonese men ran in all directions, people were shouting orders, but no-one listened because everybody spoke at once. Children bathed and played in the shallows. Women washed clothes in the river. Flies buzzed. Men in white hard hats loaded lengths of timber into a twelve-metre pirogue, along with drums of outboard fuel, spare motors, and bundles of local food wrapped in banana leaves. All the company's Gabonese staff wore hard hats with SOMIFER printed across the front. They came up in turn to greet us. Their calloused hands felt like old rope as they gripped mine.

Kruger stood astride a petrol drum, amidships in the pirogue. He appeared to be having a rough time of it, and I sensed that now was not the moment for small talk. He came ashore, shook hands briefly, and after barking a few more orders in the direction of the boatmen, disappeared to keep a radio liaison with Belinga back at the office.

We returned to the house and settled down to wait for the chauffeur. Instead, about ten o'clock, Kruger himself pulled in near the kitchen door, red-faced and agitated. He loaded our bags hastily into the car and announced that we'd be sharing the pirogue with the *sous-préfêt* (the deputy district governor) and a trade union representative, who were making a routine trip to Belinga. When we climbed in, he reversed out into the street and gunned the accelerator, sending clouds of red dust into the air.

At the riverbank, the frenzy had abated. Our luggage and the iceboxes of fresh food were stowed, then there was a last-minute flurry to find enough life jackets and folding chairs for all of us, and position them in a line down the middle. Finally, everything was ready. We climbed in and took our places, the *sous-préfêt* at the front. The huge black pirogue slid quietly backwards into mid-stream. At the stern, the *pinnassier*, the boatman, sat grave-faced with his hand on the tiller. At the bow, the navigator peered intently into the water. Then the outboard shuddered into life, and with a last-minute warning from Kruger not to make any sudden movements or we could tip over, we were off, sliding through the tea-brown water and watching the hill of Makokou grow smaller and smaller behind us.

For the first hour no-one spoke, and the only sounds were the thudding of the outboard and the swish of the bow wave past the gunwales. We were seated one behind the other on the folding chairs, with no room to move in any direction. A long corrugated-aluminium canopy stretched over our heads almost the full length of the canoe. We might have been a set of the carved ebony figurines sold in the markets, sitting motionless and bolt upright in their carved ebony boats.

The great forest slid by on either side, massive walls of jungle that were reflected back in the water, so that it was hard to tell where the forest ended and the reflections began. Here and there, clearings with small groups of mud huts dotted the riverbank. A tiny pirogue occasionally emerged from one of these, under the shadows of overhanging vines. I breathed in the sights and silence, conscious of a profound peace settling into my mind. I thought again of Mary Kingsley and how she had travelled up the mighty Ogooué River in a pirogue nearly a century before. Now I was here.

Around midday, we opened the lunch boxes and had cold beer, crusty French rolls filled with garlic salami and tomato, and fruit and biscuits.

The *sous-préfêt* and the trade union representative had made no effort at conversation during the morning and still kept to themselves. The *sous-préfêt* was evidently a keen hunter, judging by the shotgun slung across his knees. I had noticed his request to sit in the front seat, where the canopy just stopped short of the bow. In the early afternoon, when we were becoming drowsy, he said something fast in dialect to the *pinnassier*, who immediately cut the motor. We drifted silently and the *sous-préfêt* stood up in the bow, sighting his barrel at the forest. I spotted his prey just before he fired – a colobus monkey, distinctive against the solid green of the forest with its long black hair, white-ringed face and striking white dorsal 'cloak'. In the silence the shot cracked out deafeningly, and the monkey's contorted body plummeted from the branch into the depths of the understorey. The *sous-préfêt* turned to flash a triumphant smile in our direction, his chest visibly bulging, but I wasn't about to acknowledge him. I struggled to hide my disgust, and stared fixedly at my feet.

I wouldn't have minded if he had needed to kill it for food, but to me this was barbarism. No-one spoke. I sensed

Win tighten, but there was nothing to say. This was my first intimation of what might lie ahead for us as we entered the world of African hunters.

Towards two o'clock, the outboard suddenly spluttered and stopped, and the *pinnassier* retrieved a large wooden paddle from the bottom of the pirogue and slowly steered us towards the riverbank. When the bow was securely settled on the mud, everyone climbed out and sat on the bank while the *pinnassier* tinkered with the motor. It would have been easy to fall asleep. We were nowhere near any village, and I wondered idly what would happen if the motor could not be coaxed into life. Finally he decided to give up on that motor and fit the spare one. With everyone back on board, we moved out again into the middle of the river.

We watched, half-mesmerised, as the reflected images of jungle slid past. Ahead, the river stretched as far as we could see. I had begun to doze off when the *pinnassier*'s low voice roused me: '*Madame! Madame!*' I jerked upright. He pointed dead ahead and upwards to the east. 'Belinga!' he said, nodding vigorously and smiling. It took me a few moments to realise what he meant and to focus on the distant point he was indicating. Then I saw it – far on the horizon, a long blue-green hump of mountain that rose above the intervening ridges like some giant slumbering beast. 'Belinga! Belinga!' he kept repeating. Excited, I twisted around to look at Win: 'That's it, sweetheart! Can you see it?' His whole face had lit up, his eyes fixed on the horizon as he nodded acknowledgement. I tried to focus on the hazy image as it hung there, high and distant. From the river, it looked utterly inaccessible. A burst of adrenalin coursed through my veins. Up there our new life awaited.

After a while, the river took a turn and the mountain

vanished. The day began to close in and a sharp chill descended. It was hard to believe we were just one degree off the equator.

Throughout the day we had peered at the forest for signs of wildlife, but apart from the colobus monkey, there had been none. Now, just on dusk, we caught sight of a large brown and white shape perched in a dead tree: a fish-eating eagle of the type common to Africa. We said nothing, hoping the *sous-préfêt* would not notice it, but his hunter's eye picked it up almost immediately. He ordered the *pinnassier* to halt, and without even waiting until the canoe had fully come to rest, he took aim and fired. The fish eagle's body fell like a stone into the canopy below.

I wanted to shout out that the magnificent bird was precious, that its death was a tragedy, but I was powerless to speak. He was a senior official, and I was a visitor in his country with no official status. Heaviness settled on my chest. Back in Australia, I had known nothing of the world of hunting. My encounters with animals had been mainly in zoos and wildlife parks. Now I had had my first experience of the way many Gabonese viewed wildlife – as bushmeat or hunting trophies.

As we moved off into the gathering dusk, the walls of jungle on either side began to throb with the insect chorus – faintly at first across the water, but quickly rising to a cacophony. The air had grown bitingly cold, and the river took on an eerily mysterious quality in the fading light. At last the outboard was cut and the pirogue drifted slowly towards a muddy embankment. In the last vestiges of daylight, I made out the silhouette of Doug waiting for us at the water's edge, and groups of figures clustered in the background.

We pulled into the bank, and climbed out. Doug came forward and shook our hands. 'You took your time!' His laid-back humour was never far from the surface. For me, it was an enigma that he could remain relaxed running a project like this.

The river journey had taken eight hours. We were now deep into the remote interior; a village called Mayebut lay a short way back from the water's edge. The only speck of western civilisation within reach was our camp on the mountain. Several Gabonese men wearing hard hats came forward and shook our hands.

Behind the clearing, a dirt track led away from the river, and a four-wheel drive utility and a truck stood nearby. A seventeen-kilometre drive up into the mountains lay ahead of us before we reached the camp. The men unloaded everything quickly – the iceboxes and our luggage into the utility, the timber into the truck. Win and I squeezed in beside Doug in the cabin of the ute; the *sous-préfêt* and the union representative would travel in the truck. Doug took the wheel and we moved off into the darkness.

For a time the ascent was gradual, and we moved quickly through the tunnel between the forest walls. Then, abruptly, the track began to climb steeply and snaked into a series of tight hairpin bends.

Suddenly an animal ran across the track. It was about the size of a fox, with cream-coloured fur and stripes. It paused briefly in the glare of the lights. Doug didn't recognise it, but I cast my mind back to our wildlife atlas and picked it for a genet, a low-slung cat-like mammal. It ran off towards the undergrowth and disappeared.

The utility was so heavily loaded and the climb so steep that it was slow going, and the engine stalled on one of the bends, but eventually we reached the crest of a ridge where the route levelled out. Rock outcrops and fern-covered banks jutted out on to the narrow track; branches brushed at the sides of the vehicle. Part-way along the ridge, Doug parked, climbed out and walked over to a gap in the line of trees.

'Come and have a look!' Win and I jumped out and stood beside him for our first sight of the camp. Off to the east, in a sea of blackness, a tiny cluster of white lights twinkled.

'That's where we're headed.' Belinga camp, perched in the vastness of the forest, looked like a spaceship adrift in the cosmos. The site was even more remote than I had imagined. My heart thumped. I could hardly wait to get there.

Twenty minutes later, we turned the final bend in the track and climbed the approach road into camp. Lights blazed out of a row of louvre windows on the hillside, and the silhouettes of human figures appeared framed against the light. We swerved up a steep incline and turned in a circle before a long, rough-stone building with a tin roof.

The first sound I heard was the throb of a generator on the hillside above us. In the stillness of the night, it seemed unnaturally loud. As we climbed out of the vehicle, an immaculately groomed olive-skinned Italian man speaking impeccable French, and accompanied by a German Shepherd dog, strode towards us with his hand outstretched.

As I grasped his hand and greeted him, conflicting emotions jostled within me. On the one hand, I was intoxicated with the romance of being there. On the other, the practicalities of the situation pressed in on me. How would I handle the isolation? How would Win cope building a camp with French-speaking workers when he spoke only English? What would our daily life be like? They were imponderables: I would find out soon enough. Behind me, Win stood in silence, scanning the scene to take in every detail. I squared my shoulders and walked towards the lighted doorway.

chapter four

First impressions

Mario Zanetti's Sicilian smile enfolded us in a burst of Mediterranean bonhomie. '*Bienvenue à Belinga, Madame Henderson!*' He reached out and shook Win's hand vigorously. 'Come on in!' Mario looked around forty. Behind his glasses, his dark eyes projected a mischievous sense of humour. His brown hair had been neatly cut, and the smell of aftershave came from his face. The dog, Lupo, stood calmly at his side. Mario looked at Win apologetically and explained with a wry grin, 'Me, no English!'

'That's okay,' Win laughed. 'Me, no French!' They both shrugged while Doug and I looked on grinning. I knew instantly what my initial role in the camp was likely to be – translator/interpreter.

Inside the low-set stone building, two Gabonese men in aprons waited to be introduced. I found it difficult to guess their ages, but they could have been in their late thirties. 'This is Nganga Étienne,' Mario said, indicating the taller, slimmer one, 'and this is Samba Bernard.' We shook hands. 'Étienne and Bernard take care of the cooking and housekeeping.'

From its appearance, the building might have been a hunting lodge. A glowing log smouldered in a four-sided stone fireplace in the middle of the large central room. Geologists' picks, yellow rain jackets and hard hats hung from the stone chimney. A worn sofa, some shabby armchairs and a timber coffee table occupied one corner, while at the far end, a long wooden dining table with twelve chairs had been set for dinner. Above a wooden sideboard against the end wall, an official portrait of President Bongo in full regalia hung in a fancy frame. On either side, the louvre windows were bare of curtains. Large black-and-white aerial photographs of the camp hung around the walls, and two wooden desks were strewn with files and maps. One held a bulky army field radio painted khaki, with a receiver on a hook and an array of dials. A posy of flowers in a glass vase at the centre of the table was the only feminine touch.

Over pre-dinner drinks by the fire, Mario explained that the building was known as the guesthouse, and formed the hub of the camp. He slept in a bedroom at one end. At the other, a large kitchen gave onto a bathroom and toilet.

Shortly afterward, Étienne announced that dinner was ready. '*C'est prêt, patron.*' '*Patron*'? It was the first time I had heard the term, meaning 'boss' or 'master'. I hoped my slight flinch had gone unnoticed.

Mario insisted that I, as the only woman present, should sit at the head of the table. The food and wine could have placed us in any good Italian restaurant, and Étienne served the three courses with a grave gentleness of manner that I warmed to instantly. Mario was in high spirits throughout, laughing and joking. He seemed delighted to have some company during a meal. I tried to picture what his life over the previous five months in camp had been like, as the only expatriate, trying to do the job of several men. I began to understand why he had brought his dog, Lupo, with him.

After dinner I walked out to the porch and stood in silence, trying to imagine what our life up here would be like. The chill air carried the earthy fragrance of the forest. The insect chorus and the throb of the generator played off each other in a syncopated rhythm, and the faint smell of smoke from the fireplace hung lazily about the building. All my senses told me I was going to love it.

We woke to a cold morning and the voice of Mario outside, giving instructions to a group of labourers. Dry-season cloud blanketed the sky. Bernard had stoked the fire and the table was set for breakfast.

My first view of the camp in daylight was through the louvre windows on the back wall. Abandoned banana and manioc plantations covered the hillside; beyond them, the forest canopy formed a patchwork of undulating green. Here and there, giant emergent trees spread their crowns against the sky. The mountains in the distance, grey-green in the pale morning light, were cloaked in unbroken forest. The sound of African voices reached me: men leaving on foot for work, and women setting off to tend their food gardens.

Doug had the day planned out for us. He would take us on a tour of the camp during the morning, and after lunch would brief Win in detail about the construction program. Over breakfast, he gave us a history lesson.

'Bethlehem Steel established this camp in 1960. The exploration phase ran for about seven years before the camp was shut down. This building dates from that era. In those days, there were French biologists based here as well, studying gorillas, birds and bats. We're at 670 metres altitude here. That's why it gets so cold.'

'How does the supply system for the camp work?' I asked.

'We bring everything up river either in the pirogues or on the company's barge. The fresh food is flown in to Makokou in iceboxes twice a week and the mail with it, in a locked canvas pouch. Fuel comes up in 200-litre drums. Most of our timber and cement comes from Makokou. We coordinate everything by radio.'

'What's the situation with the power supply?' Win asked.

'At the moment, we have a 110-volt Perkins diesel generator that we start up at six in the morning and shut off at ten at night. But once our mechanic is on board he'll be installing the new one, which will give us 240-volt power.'

I finished my toast and jam and drank a second cup of coffee, laced with thick tinned milk, and then we were ready for the grand tour.

Doug led the way to a padlocked corrugated-iron shed. Inside, rows of shelves were stacked with cans of vegetables and fruit, tins of coffee and evaporated milk, bags of sugar and flour, sacks of potatoes, rice and onions, and stocks of light bulbs, plastic dishes, cleaning materials and mousetraps. Just outside, a triangular flat-iron water tank was positioned over a fireplace to provide hot water for showers at night. Beside the guesthouse was a long open shed with a concrete floor and a tin roof on bush poles, empty and deserted.

'That was the old sample shed,' Doug explained. 'We're going to convert it into accommodation and offices.'

A short drive up a dirt road brought us to three corrugated-iron sheds with concrete floors which served as a carpentry workshop, vehicle service bay and a warehouse. The carpentry workshop lay empty except for a few timber saw stools. The two carpenters currently in camp worked with the most basic tools – claw hammers, chainsaws and hacksaws. 'That's where we want the wood machine shop to be, Win!' Doug said. 'State-of-the-art machinery to produce prefabricated housing and offices.'

Win took it all in without comment. I could imagine what he was thinking, 'Where do you start from a base as low as this?' Later he told me in private, 'I feel for the carpenters, trying to do good work with chainsaws. The first thing I'll do is get them some decent tools.' The large warehouse next door had chain-wire walls, and housed vehicle spares, lubricants, hard hats, building materials, fuel supplies, tools, and rations for the Gabonese workforce and their families.

At the next stop, further down the hill, we came to another shed with a tin roof on bush poles and a concrete floor.

'This is going to be our single men's living quarters, and the first occupants will be our four surveyors, due in ten days' time,' Doug said. 'Come and meet Bruno and Joseph.'

Mehendje Bruno and Andang Joseph, the two carpenters, were wielding chainsaws on panels of plywood and bush poles when we arrived. When they saw us they straightened up, switched off the motors and wiped the sweat from their foreheads. Doug introduced us and explained that Win would be their new boss, in charge of the whole construction program. They each shook his hand, '*Bonjour, patron.*' There it was again, that word. I knew Win would want them to be on first-name terms with him. He couldn't stand formality.

'Monsieur Henderson doesn't speak much French yet,' Doug told them, 'but he'll learn pretty quickly.' Bruno and Joseph smiled and nodded genially. Like most Gabonese, they knew no English. Another job for me, I thought.

The final stop on the tour was the terraced workers' village, set on a steep slope surrounded by forest. A line of rectangular mud huts with corrugated-aluminium roofs stood on the topmost terrace, facing down the hill. At the far end of the row, a lockable tin shed with a hinged panel at the front served as the village shop, known as the *économat*, where people could buy clothing, toiletries, batteries, soap powder and other items.

The sound of women's voices laughing and joking reached us from a lower terrace, where a line of new huts was being built. The women worked in teams of two, applying a slurry of ochre-coloured clay to latticework sapling frames with their bare hands. We drove down and got out to watch. They seemed to treat the work as a game, giggling and teasing each other. As one applied the mud, the other kept up the supply by stomping in a large mound of it with her bare feet. Several had babies strapped to their backs. From time to time, they swung the infants around to the front and breastfed them, barely pausing in the rhythm of slapping on the clay. Each team of women earned the equivalent of US$21 per hut, which kept them in pipe tobacco, machetes to till their food gardens, and *pagnes*, the lengths of printed cotton cloth which they wrapped around themselves like sarongs. Doug had a joking relationship with them, throwing out comments to which they responded with great hilarity. He turned to us. 'We've drawn our workforce from a wide area. They've all had to leave their home villages, so they have to establish themselves here from scratch. That's why we provide them with food and other rations.'

Back at the guesthouse, tantalising aromas were emanating from the kitchen. Lunch consisted of pasta with herbs, onion and tomato, and a large loaf of hot crusty French bread.

'Where did the bread come from?' I asked, astounded. Mario smiled indulgently and patted his stomach. 'It's Bernard – he bakes it every day in the old bush oven.' I called out my approval to Bernard, who put his head around the kitchen door to acknowledge me, embarrassed and coy.

The conversation between Mario and Doug over lunch focused on work issues. I tried to follow Mario's rapid-fire French sentences, but they were littered with words I had never heard. Each time one cropped up, I cut in and asked what it meant. *Contraplaqué* was plywood, the *groupe électrogène* was the generator, *béton* was concrete, and a *manoeuvre* was a labourer. Doug spoke in a quaint amalgam of French and English, but somehow managed to communicate the essentials.

At the end of the meal, I realised I hadn't had a single insect bite since we arrived.

'Why aren't there any *fourreaux* here?' I quizzed Mario.

He smiled mysteriously. 'Ah, that's because I've been fogging.'

'Fogging?'

'I fumigate the area around the guesthouse three times a week with a machine called a *swingfog*. It pumps out insecticidal fog that keeps the insects at bay and makes life a bit more comfortable.' I'd never heard of a fogging machine. That took care of my chief concern about moving to the camp.

In the late afternoon, Étienne lit the fire under the water tank for our showers.

'Drinks on the porch in half an hour,' Mario announced. The covered porch ran the full length of the guesthouse. Clusters of armchairs along its length faced up the hill and towards the forest. Once showered and dressed, we sat out there with cold beers and watched the light fade. The insect chorus began, chill air settled around us, and cooking aromas filtered through the windows.

As if on cue, a flock of iridescent blue birds the size of pheasants, with bright yellow beaks and red markings on the head, landed on the exposed branches of a fruiting umbrella tree nearby and began calling 'Coo coo coo coo crooooh!' as they cavorted in a spectacular ritual.

Mario saw the delight on my face. 'The Gabonese call them *faisans bleus*, blue pheasants,' he said. 'They come every evening. It's the mating season – that's why they're behaving like that.' We watched them, entranced. It was as if Belinga was turning on a final glorious burst of wildness in case we hadn't already made up our minds to move there. I couldn't imagine anywhere on earth being more beautiful.

The correct name of the birds was giant blue touracos. I would learn in time that they were the most exquisite species in the forest.

Win and I didn't need to discuss how we felt about the place. From the moment we arrived, we felt we had been moving through a dreamscape. Everything about the camp and the great forest resonated with us so powerfully that at that moment I believe we would have agreed to work there just for food and lodgings. After dinner, we gave Doug our decision, and told him we could hardly wait to start.

We left early next morning for the river trip back and Doug came with us in a six-metre pirogue. The level in the river had dropped further and the journey took most of the day. I found being on the river exhilarating. It was like entering another world, and this time we didn't have the trigger-happy *sous-préfêt* for company. We hadn't seen the *sous-préfêt* or the union representative since we arrived; they had stayed in the workers' village, presumably pursuing some official business.

chapter five

GEARING UP FOR THE MOVE

We arrived back in Makokou at dusk. At the Roux house, Doug, Win and I sat in the hot front room in weathered cane chairs with stubbies of cold Regab – the local beer – in our hands. I couldn't explain it to myself, but for the first time in my life I had a sense that a vital role awaited me, a role that would call on all my skills and resilience.

'There's one important person you still have to meet,' Doug said. 'The bloke cutting the road through the forest. I'm expecting him in for dinner. You'll love him.' Doug and Gina had mentioned Eamon Temple to us back in Libreville over dinner. We were on our second drinks when he pulled up outside the kitchen door and strode into the house wearing laced-up jungle boots and baggy knee-length shorts, his loose, short-sleeved cotton shirt hanging out. He was tall and wiry, around sixty, with tousled grey hair and arms and legs streaked with sweat and mud. Doug stood up and placed a hand on his shoulder. 'Eamon, meet Win and Annette Henderson.'

A firm hand gripped mine, and Eamon's steady gaze met my eyes uncompromisingly. 'Glad to know you.' His face creased into an exhausted smile. He spoke quietly with a mild Midwestern American accent, choosing his few words carefully. A glint of humour played around his eyes as he lowered himself slowly into an armchair.

Eamon was a native of Columbia, Indiana. He'd played a key role in the original establishment of Belinga, and he and his wife had raised their family there. Bethlehem Steel had brought him back for this second tour of duty because he knew the place better than anyone. He'd even known Schweitzer well. I was unaware then of Eamon's status as a living legend. In the 1950s, when the Belinga ore deposit had been first explored, he had surveyed the route of the proposed Trans-Gabonese Railway from the coast to Belinga through hundreds of kilometres of swamps and forest, on foot – twice. For this, he had been awarded the Star of Gabon medal. All I could see in front of me that night was a man, no longer young, haggard and drawn from his battle with the terrain, whose whole being was invested in the task before him.

He'd based himself at a rough forest camp on the banks of the Djadié River, a tributary of the Ivindo. He and a team of Gabonese plant operators were carving the route through to Belinga with Caterpillar D8 and D9 graders and dozers. Fifteen Gabonese – men, women and children – headed by Biété Benoît, a local powerbroker, shared his camp. Eamon had come into town that night to pick up cigarettes and whisky for the men.

I watched and listened as he recounted the litany of problems associated with the work to Doug over dinner. Machines had broken down, parts were difficult to get, and the mountainous terrain was crisscrossed by rock outcrops that required lengthy detours. They were under pressure to finish before the onset of the next wet, and in time for a ceremonial road opening planned by the government. Once the road was through, Eamon would become *chef de chantier* or chief of works at Belinga, which would put him below Doug, but above Win, in the hierarchy.

On the flight back to Libreville, Win's lack of French and the daunting task ahead of him occupied my thoughts most of the way. He had no aptitude for foreign languages, yet the job he faced would be a major challenge even without a language barrier. The tight project timetables would not allow much time for settling in.

Back at our beach campsite, there was little we could do towards our preparation until the shops opened on Monday, so we had the weekend free. After breakfast on the Saturday, I made my move. 'I think it's time I taught you a bit of French,' I declared, fixing Win with my most assertive look. His glum expression told me what I already knew – this would be a battle.

'Sit down here, and try to concentrate. Do you know what a noun is?'

'Remind me.'

'A noun is the name of something. For example, "table" and "chair" are nouns.'

'Right.'

'Okay. All nouns in French are either masculine or feminine. For example, "table" is feminine.'

'How can a table be female? That's bloody stupid!'

'It doesn't mean that it's a woman – it's just the way

French grammar works. You simply have to accept it.' Already his face was flushed crimson with irritation and I could feel his resistance building. I moved quickly on to forms of address.

'Now when you're speaking to people, it's crucial that you use the correct form of "you". When you're addressing people of high status, people you don't know well, or other men's wives, you must use the word *vous*. That signifies respect and formality. The other form, *tu*, must be used only for close friends, children or your spouse. If you use the wrong one, you risk giving major offence to the person you are addressing. For example, if you use *tu* to someone else's wife, it'll be assumed that you're having an affair with her.'

'How bloody childish!' The words exploded into the air. He stood up abruptly, shook his head and strode off down to the beach, swearing under his breath. I was left holding an exercise book and pen in my lap, with nothing written on the page.

Roger dropped by that morning, eager to hear every detail of our week *en brousse* (up country). He'd never been as far inland as Belinga. As I talked, his eyes shone.

'I'll help you prepare any way I can,' he said. 'You'll need a short-wave radio up there so you can get world news. You'll be able to receive Voice of America and BBC World Service, as well as Paris and South Africa. There's a shop where I get ten per cent discount. When you're ready, I'll take you there.'

The plan for our departure had been agreed with Doug during discussions at the camp. Following our week of preparation in Libreville, we would travel in the Kombi up to Makokou, where we and the van would be transported upriver on the company's barge. Initially, we would continue to live in it, but take our meals in the guesthouse with Mario and the surveyors. As time permitted, Win would convert part of the old sample shed into a flat for us. Doug had authorised us to buy linen, crockery and appliances before we left, and enough non-perishable food for three months. We had just five days to organise everything.

Our first call was to an import agency that dealt in heavy machinery. Win needed to choose machines that would equip the wood machine shop for every foreseeable task. They would have to come from France. The agent was courteous and keen to do business, but spoke no English. As I had no technical French and no knowledge of timber processing, it loomed as our first big test.

The agent motioned us to two armchairs and placed an armful of illustrated machinery catalogues, all in French, on a low table before us. An hour later, with the help of gestures, imitated sound effects and roughly sketched diagrams, we settled on a multi-function wood processing machine called a *combinée*. The price tag was US$40,000 – eight million Central African francs (CFAs). It would be delivered in two months and the machine weighed one metric tonne. We also ordered a breaking-down saw and a drop saw, which the agent could supply immediately from stock. He handed us colour brochures and a detailed quote and we left then to drop them off at Doug's office.

That afternoon, we began our survey of the hardware stores. Win needed to equip himself and his crew with a full set of tools each, and order enough hardware, toilet suites, plumbing and electrical fittings and louvre windows to build the first three sets of mini-apartments. There were no plans or specifications for the dwellings: Win would be both designer and builder.

The manager of the third hardware store we visited spoke good English. When he realised the scale of our order, he suggested Win return after closing time, when they could compile it together. One evening stretched into two, and two into three. In the end, the order filled six foolscap pages.

Our days, meanwhile, were filled with myriad other practicalities – having blood tests for filariasis, stocking up on stationery and toiletries, filling prescriptions at the pharmacy and buying furnishings for the flat. We also called at the Banque Nationale de Paris, ever hopeful that our money had arrived from London, but it hadn't. Last thing on Friday afternoon, I went with Roger to an electrical retailer and selected a Philips transistor radio with short wave.

Roger invited us for a farewell lunch with a group of his friends on the day before we left. He'd been cooking for three days and the five-course feast lasted all afternoon. Small groups of French expatriates arrived, wearing light summer clothing and talking volubly, and took their seats at the long table set under the coconut palms in his garden. They all seemed to know each other already and barely paused in their conversations when we were introduced. None of them seemed too happy to be in Gabon, and they showed little interest in two Australians destined for *la brousse*. From their conversations, their lives seemed to be focused on just two things: their next period of home leave, and gourmet food. As I listened to them I thought that Win and I were the lucky ones – we would experience the wildlife and the forest and the indigenous culture, a world their sheltered urban existence would never encompass.

Roger gave up his double bed for us on our last night, because the Kombi was stacked to the roof with all our purchases. We felt deeply indebted to him. His friendship and hospitality had smoothed our path and made our time in Libreville unforgettable, and the three of us had formed a bond that would last many years, long after we'd all moved on.

We left early on 21 June, with all the jerry cans full in case we struck petrol supply problems again. But the trip passed without incident: the dry season was well advanced, and the route had dried out so much that we made excellent time, reaching Makokou the next afternoon. Already we had learned that in the vast interior of Gabon, the pattern of the seasons critically affected transport logistics on the ground, by river and in the air. During the long wet season from February to late May when the dirt roads through the forest became quagmires of orange mud, it was not uncommon for dozens of long-haul trucks to become bogged end-to-end up to their axles for weeks at a time. Escape was only possible once the long dry season had set in. This lasted from the end of May until mid-September. In the wet, the rivers quickly rose to foaming torrents; in the dry, they fell just as dramatically. During the dry, thick cloud blanketed the sky most of the time, making navigation difficult and dangerous for aircraft when aviation beacons were out of order. The short rainy season occurred from mid-September to mid-December, followed by a short dry which ran until the end of January. Then the whole cycle began again.

When we caught up with Kruger, he was full of gloom about our chances of getting the Kombi upriver on the barge. The water level was low and falling fast, so large rock outcrops were already exposed, which meant the barge could easily run aground on sandbanks or rocks. And there were other problems. The last time the barge had been used, someone had forgotten to put oil in the motor and it had burnt out. No-one in town could repair it, and no local suppliers had a new Volvo marine diesel engine available. But he'd devised a compromise solution: two twelve-metre pirogues would be lashed to the barge – one each side – with two outboards mounted on each. With nearly five tonnes of barge and cargo, we could count on an eleven-hour trip at minimum, and that didn't allow for breakdowns. There was no guarantee we would get there, either. Kruger had allocated his four best *pinnassiers* to the trip the next day. With these dire predictions in our ears, we retired to the Roux house and went to bed.

When we presented ourselves at the *débarcadère* at eight o'clock next morning, the pirogues had already been lashed to the barge, which lay at right angles to the riverbank. Two wheel ramps ran from the deck onto the mud, ready for the Kombi to be loaded. Kruger was pacing back and forth along the deck, barking orders and dodging groups of women and children, stacks of timber and a new desk for the office. He introduced the four *pinnassiers* – Soukabothe, Mobissa, Jean-Raoul and Jean-Baptiste. Soukabothe held a cow horn in his hand, with a short loop of rope attached to one end and a mouthpiece at the other.

By nine o'clock the Kombi was secured on deck and all was ready. The outboards chugged into life, and the barge reversed slowly out into midstream. Kruger stood on the riverbank waving half-heartedly, arms akimbo and legs planted firmly apart, his face set in a look of resignation. Soukabothe put the cow horn to his lips and blew hard into the narrow end, producing a blast of sound that would have been audible several kilometres away. Soon Makokou vanished from view.

The *pinnassiers* made it clear that they were tackling the trip under duress, and told me plainly that they weren't happy about doing the journey in one day. With hindsight, I realised that this statement was the precursor of a trick they would pull that afternoon. Mid-morning I boiled the kettle in the van to make mugs of tea for all of us, unaware that Gabonese never drank tea. We had one battered packet of duty-free Gauloises left: I gave them to Soukabothe to pass around. But in my attempt to be gracious, I was unwittingly breaking all the social rules that governed relations between management and workers in the country, especially white managers and African workers. I had lost their respect.

Nevertheless, the trip progressed uneventfully until the early afternoon. The warmth of the day and the steady throb of the outboards had a soporific effect, and after lunch we had climbed into the Kombi and dozed off. When we woke some time after three, the speed of the barge had dropped. With grave faces, the *pinnassiers* announced that, unhappily, we would now have no chance of reaching Belinga by nightfall, and would have to spend the night on the river.

Win was immediately suspicious, in view of their earlier comments. He walked down to the stern to investigate and found that only two of the four outboards were operating. I watched from a distance, but said nothing. This would be his first test of authority. He looked each of them in the eyes, grinned widely, and indicated that he wanted the two idle motors to be restarted. The *pinnassiers'* expressions fell as they moved slowly across to the starter levers. With a single pull, each motor turned over perfectly, and the barge picked up speed again. The *pinnassiers* retired to the bow looking sheepish and remained silent for the rest of the trip. Win had negotiated his first hurdle, and we were spared a cold night on the river. We could only guess at what lay behind their actions. In time we would learn the truth.

It was almost seven-thirty and dark when we arrived at Mayebut. Kruger's estimate had been close – the trip had taken over ten hours. As the barge edged slowly onto the bank, flickering light from cooking fires dimly lit the dilapidated huts in the village. A couple of skinny dogs roamed around, and a baby cried somewhere.

Despite the incident during the afternoon, we shook hands with the *pinnassiers* and thanked them, then Win edged the Kombi slowly down the ramps and onto the bank. Libreville seemed a world away already. No moon lit the forest, and night sounds surrounded us. We climbed in, took deep breaths, and set out on the long drive up the mountain.

chapter six

PLUNGED INTO FRONTIER LIFE

Cocooned in the Kombi, we tackled the steep ascent of the mountain. I had never felt more alert. My mind jostled with images of wildlife, men in hard hats, women building mud huts, and the welcoming warmth of the fireplace in the guesthouse.

Our life for the next six months would be played out in a minuscule clearing in the jungle just two hours from the Congo border, immersed in an unfamiliar culture and reliant on two-way radio for our only regular contact with the outside world. I believed I could handle it, but I couldn't be certain. I had nothing to go on but blind faith and my confidence that together, Win and I were capable of tackling almost anything.

Tiny brown shapes flitted across in front of us in the headlights. 'Bats,' Win murmured. 'Those lovely little fawn ones.' Moist branches and giant ferns slapped against the windows, and the sweet earthy smell of the forest came to us on the cold night air. The Kombi laboured under its load up the steep inclines and Win drove cautiously, ready to brake if an animal darted out ahead of us. It was after eight-thirty when we rounded the last bend and the guesthouse came into view, flooded with light.

Mario strode out. 'You made it! Come on in – we've waited dinner for you.' There was no time to reflect on the challenges ahead, as the guesthouse was crowded with new faces.

'Annette and Win, meet the surveyors, Nigel, Andy, Colin and John!' The four men, all in their twenties, had been in camp just four days. The team leader, Nigel, with red hair and a ruddy complexion, came from Newcastle-on-Tyne; Andy was a tall, stocky, fair-haired Yorkshireman; Colin came from Scotland; and John was from southern England. Only Andy spoke any French.

'I see you've already made the acquaintance of the *fourreaux*,' I quipped, looking at the livid insect bites covering their forearms.

'Yeah, they're driving us nuts,' Andy grimaced.

'Sorry to have held you up,' Win said. 'The barge trip took over ten hours, and we'd still have been out on the river if I hadn't noticed the *pinnassiers* had cut two of the outboards while we were asleep.' We didn't know it then, but the *pinnassiers* regularly worked small rackets on these journeys if the opportunity arose. A favourite was selling off small quantities of the company's fuel to people in the riverside villages to power the outboards on their miniature pirogues; afterwards they would top up the 200-litre fuel drums with muddy river water. There appeared to be no way of stopping it. We could only speculate, but this informal village commerce may have been the reason behind their ploy to spend a night on the river.

During dinner, I sensed an atmosphere of unease

around the table, and it didn't take me long to work out why. Partly, it was the language barrier: Mario and the surveyors could barely communicate with one another. Also, the surveyors had been unable to do any work – all their equipment was still in transit from England, and there was no vehicle for them to use until the new mechanic arrived and could fix up an old Land Rover for them. To cap things off, their living quarters still weren't finished. They had bedrooms, but no toilets or showers, so they had to share the one in the guesthouse with Mario. They'd spent their first four days playing cards, listening to football on the radio and trying to escape the *fourreaux*. They had nowhere to relax but in the guesthouse, which wasn't designed for so many people. It hadn't been a promising start. It was little wonder everyone was edgy.

It struck me then that the project timetable seemed out of kilter: the surveyors' arrival should have been put off until things were ready for them. But I had a lot to learn about remote Africa.

Before bed, Mario had some exciting news: 'We have a distinguished visitor arriving tomorrow – Peter Telfair, the managing geologist from the old days. He'll stay overnight.' I looked forward to meeting him. It would give me an opportunity to learn some more of the camp's history.

Win had parked the Kombi near the old sample shed, close by the guesthouse, where we could use the bathroom. In the morning, we erected the canvas annexe to give ourselves some privacy and somewhere to dress and undress standing up.

After breakfast we had the camp to ourselves. Mario was at the *débarcadère* waiting to meet Peter from the morning pirogue, and the labourers were out in the forest cutting survey lines – narrow swathes through the underbrush to give the surveyors straight lines of sight for their measurements. The lull in activity gave us a perfect opportunity to explore the parts of the camp we hadn't seen before.

The day was hot and steamy with little cloud. We set off on foot, taking the dirt road past the surveyors' quarters and beyond, to the site of the old expatriate houses. The area had been cleared in the 1960s, but the vegetation had since grown back, and shoulder-high grass covered much of the ground. We pushed our way through it and came to the remains of the houses – bamboo structures rotting in the sun. The thatched roofs had partially collapsed, and chinks of sunlight glinted through the perished slats on the walls. The abandoned gardens had been smothered by wild flowers and vines, but mature avocado trees still stood tall, laden with ripe fruit. Brilliant butterflies danced through the air and lighted on blossoming vines. We didn't speak, reluctant to break what felt like a spell. I could almost feel the spirits of the people who had lived, suffered and toiled there.

Nearby, a stand of bright pink waxy flowers, each as large as a human hand, stood stiffly on tall straight stems that reached over my head. The blooms looked like giant waratahs, except that the petals were glossy and hard as china. I stood on tiptoes to smell them, but they had no fragrance. I ran my fingers over the stiff petals. They seemed like a creation of science fiction, out of place in the forest. It turned out I was partly right: I learned much later that they were *roses de porcelaines*, natives of Martinique, Costa Rica and other Caribbean countries, but Gabon had adopted them as its national flower.

We skirted the porcelain roses and came to a cracked cement floor and waist-high concrete and tile benches that must have been part of the old geology laboratory. At our approach, a black-and-yellow-striped snake sunning itself on the benchtop moved lazily away. Flocks of rainbow bee-eaters whirled and called overhead.

But for the bird calls and the insects' drumming, everything was still – the place lay in a kind of sleep. I thought to myself that once this new exploration project was complete and everyone had left, the forest would do the same thing again – grow over it all as if it had never existed.

Mario arrived back with Peter Telfair just before lunch. I was washing clothes in a plastic basin when a Hemingway-esque figure in cream stovepipe denims and matching jacket climbed out of the Toyota, nursing two bottles of Scotch. He looked about sixty, with sparse grey hair and a weather-beaten face.

'What's this? A white lady! How long've you been here?' The accent was American, east coast.

'G'day, I'm Annette. We got here yesterday.'

'Peter Telfair. Glad to know you! Come on in for a drink.' He walked into the guesthouse, stood by the empty fireplace and scanned the room, taking in every detail. His gaze lifted to encompass the view through the louvres out over the blue-green expanse of forest. I watched the emotions play across his face. He took a deep breath and let it out slowly, swallowed hard and strode towards the kitchen.

'*Étienne! Bernard! Bonjour! Comment ça va?*'

'*Patron!*' they gasped. '*C'est bien vous?*' As he shook their hands, tears sprang to their eyes. Shared history had bound them together, but it was almost a decade since they had last met.

Over lunch, conversation ranged across many topics, but one practical matter dominated. Mario said, 'We've got a major problem with the water supply. The pressure's suddenly dropped to half. I've tried to find a diagram of the old system in the files, but there doesn't seem to be one.'

'How about I take a look at it?' Peter offered. 'I can still remember how it works.' Later we learned that he was the person who had designed it.

'I'll come with you,' Win offered. 'One of us should be familiar with it.'

I decided to tag along as well, out of curiosity. Accordingly, after lunch the three of us trudged up the hill beyond the edge of the camp to where a concrete cistern about four metres square had been built into the hillside. A galvanised-iron pipeline laid in a narrow V-shaped gully fed it from a spring further up. We scrambled up the gully to the top, looking for the water take-up point.

'This is it,' Peter said. A small concrete drain fed the water from the spring into a 200-litre metal drum via a pattern of holes in the lid, which filtered out leaves and stones. On the downhill side of the drum the pipeline led to the cistern, having deposited any sediment at the bottom of the drum. The system was brilliantly simple, but the drum needed to be cleaned out regularly – a point neither Mario nor Doug had realised.

Leaf litter had built up on the lid: Peter raked it clean then lifted the lid off. Inside, the drum was choked with silt. He rolled up a sleeve and grinned at Win. 'How long's your arm?' They knelt down, one each side, and plunged their arms into the water up to the shoulder, hauling out fistfuls of mud. I watched for twenty minutes as they flung the mud out into the forest, until finally they could feel the bottom of the drum.

'That should do it.' Peter replaced the lid and stood up. We walked back a different way, following another pipeline from the cistern to the surveyors' quarters. About halfway along, we found water seeping from a joint in the pipe into a deep puddle.

'There's your other problem,' Peter said. 'Mario will need to get on to that. In the old days someone used to check the water lines every day.'

After dinner, Mario and the surveyors retired early, leaving Win and me by the fire with Peter. It was the opportunity I had hoped for to ask him about the history of the camp.

'How was iron ore discovered here?'

Peter drew an old map from his bag and smoothed it out on the coffee table. 'An old French *piste militaire* – an army track – used to run between these two villages here – Mekambo to the east, near the Congo border, and M'Vadhi on the banks of the Ivindo, about an hour's journey upstream from here. In the 1890s, a French soldier walking the track came across a group of people using forged iron spearheads. It was such an important discovery that he made a report to the colonial government. When systematic geological exploration started around here in the 1950s, we used their old records.'

'So what does "Belinga" mean?'

'It's the local Bakota word for iron.'

'And how did this camp start?' As I asked the question I could see he was reliving it all, his mind snapping back as if it were just a week ago.

'We sited and established it in the late 1950s. I was the managing geologist, responsible for everything. Over the years, we employed more than 300 Gabonese workers on the exploration program. We blasted tunnels into the mountainsides to sample the ore and cut eighty kilometres of tracks through the forest.'

I told him we had seen the old split bamboo houses that morning.

'Ah yes, they worked well on the whole, but they were so open that a leopard wandered into someone's living room one night.'

'Was anyone hurt?'

'No, not that time, but people here can tell you stories of leopards taking their relatives from inside a house. Just ask Étienne.'

'What about the research scientists who worked here?'

'We had lots of people working in different fields – birds, bats, monkeys and so on – but mainly with the western lowland gorillas. There was a French primatologist, Annie Hion, who hand-reared eight of them here. One of them was called Arthur; he was like a member of the family. When we used to sit around having a drink at the end of the day, Arthur would be there with us, sitting on a chair, drinking beer out of a glass. He was included in all our social gatherings.'

I sat transported, trying to imagine how that must have been.

Peter's face softened and he smiled. 'People used to carry Arthur around on their backs while they worked. And one of his favourite pastimes was friendly wrestling. Some of the men used to wrestle him while everyone else watched. He loved it.'

My knowledge of gorillas was minimal, but these stories of Arthur fascinated me. We talked until almost midnight, by which time the fire had burnt down to a pile of ashes and we were all ready for sleep.

To Mario's relief, the water pressure had returned to normal in the morning. I shook Peter's hand as he prepared to leave for Makokou after breakfast.

'It's been a joy talking with you,' I said. 'I won't forget.'

'You're a strong woman, Annette. Make the most of your time here. You won't find another place like this.'

I watched him climb into the Toyota with Mario and drive off for the *débarcadère*, and thought about what he had said. I had already fallen under Belinga's spell just as he had all those years ago.

Our night encounter with the leopard came just days after Peter had left. As I recounted the episode to the surveyors over breakfast the following morning, I thought of Peter telling me a leopard had come into one of the old bamboo houses in the early days. Little had changed in the intervening fifteen years. Belinga was still a place where people and animals met in an uneasy relationship.

During that first week, I took every opportunity I could to learn from Mario about how the camp operated and who made up our workforce. The camp and the whole project had captured my imagination, as they had Win's. With everything I did, I had to know the detail – a general impression was never enough. In addition, I was determined to be accepted as a useful member of the camp team, not simply a young wife along for the ride, and that meant fitting into a man's world. So I asked endless questions, and I wrote up my diary every evening.

The company employed fifty-seven men from three different tribal groups – the Bakota and Bakwélé formed the majority, and there were a small group of Fang and two Pygmies. They all spoke French, but it was a distinctively African form of French, with sounds and speech rhythms unfamiliar to me.

The names of mountains in the SOMIFER exploration area had been officially recorded when the first geological surveys were carried out. The peaks surrounding the camp were called Bakota North, Bakota South, Mombo and Bakwélé. The whaleback ridge we had seen while travelling up the river was Babiel, which was the Bakota word for eagle. Babiel North and South contained the main body of iron ore.

Some of the old survey points had names, too. The crest of a steep rock escarpment close behind camp was Grand Crête Un or Belvédère (Great Crest 1 or Viewpoint), so called because it afforded a view right out over the forest into the Congo. I decided that one day, when the old tracks had been cleared, Win and I would drive up there so we could see that view for ourselves. Everywhere the forest had been cleared for roads or buildings, the red laterite soil was exposed. The texture varied from gravel in some areas to fine red dust in others, the product of countless aeons of weathering of the underlying ironstone rock.

Work at the camp was based on a six-day week, Monday to Saturday, and workdays began with *appel* – rollcall. The men assembled outside the guesthouse to have their hours of work for the previous day recorded, and to be allocated tasks for the new day. Work began at seven. The workforce consisted mostly of labourers, with a small number of carpenters, plumbers, electricians and masons – more men would be recruited as soon as sufficient houses had been built. Jacques Poussain, a French mechanic, was due to arrive in several weeks' time with a team of Gabonese mechanics. The conditions of employment were regulated by the government, under an agreement which bound all mining companies, specifying classifications of workers and their pay levels. Labourers earned the equivalent of US$140 a month for a forty-hour week; specialists received more than double that. Mario calculated the wages, and the men were paid monthly in cash by Mbunda Fidèle, a small, serious man employed as bookkeeper and payroll clerk who also managed the *économat*.

A basic clinic, known as the *infirmerie*, occupied a rough plywood hut opposite the surveyors' quarters. There a male Gabonese nurse attended to a constant stream of women and children, and dispensed medications sent up by the French doctor in Makokou.

Every second Friday was ration day, when each family received an allocation of dried salt fish, processed manioc, block soap, salt, paraffin and palm oil, according to government regulations. Preparing for ration day was a complex exercise that took all morning. Bulk supplies of all the items were issued from the warehouse early in the morning and delivered to the ration shed, a long concrete-floored pavilion with a tin roof. The 200-litre drum of palm oil had to be heated over a fire to melt it, the block soap had to be chopped into portions with machetes, and the drum of paraffin had to be fitted with a hand pump.

The manioc came in cylindrical portions about thirty centimetres long called *bâtons*, encased in banana leaves and bound with vines – each weighed a kilogram. Mario travelled up the river every Wednesday to buy the manioc from the local villages. It was prepared from the roots of the cassava plant, which were pounded to a powder then soaked in water for a week to leach out the cyanide.

The company aimed to provide every man with twenty *bâtons* of manioc a week, but this depended on the availability of supplies: when local stocks were short, rations were supplemented with rice.

On ration days, there was a fixed routine. The women walked in a long line up the hill from the village to the shed, balancing large enamel dishes on their heads. They sat on the floor in a semicircle, with their dishes, empty bottles and flagons in front of them, facing fifty-seven identical piles of rations set out along the floor. Mbunda Fidèle presided. When he called out each worker's name, the man's wife came forward to collect her pile of salt fish, soap, manioc and salt, then took her empty bottles to be filled with paraffin and palm oil. As each woman completed her round, Mbunda marked off her husband's name in an exercise book. The first time I witnessed this fortnightly ritual, I realised just how difficult it was for families to leave their home villages and come to an unfamiliar place where they had no direct access to their normal means of survival.

Their diet wasn't all manioc and salt fish, of course: SOMIFER also employed two local hunters to provide fresh game meat for the workforce daily. There was an established routine for this as well. Early each morning, Mario issued them with shotgun shells – *cartouches* – from a locked cupboard in the guesthouse. They hunted all day in the forest, and presented the carcasses outside the guesthouse for weighing in the late afternoon. If their kill was too heavy to carry, Mario sent the Toyota out to bring it in. Mostly they shot monkeys, and duikers – small antelopes – and sometimes they took wild pigs. Mario weighed the meat on a set of rusty scales and noted each man's daily total in a book. They were paid by the kilogram at the end of the month.

Because the weigh-in took place just metres from our annexe, I often watched. Most times, the sight of slaughtered animals did not distress me, as I knew that this diet replicated what people ate in villages, and generally the animals the hunters took were plentiful. But one day was different. They had shot two great apes. They'd hacked off the limbs and left the heads and bodies in the forest. I stared at the hands, the long powerful fingers curled in death, the calloused feet, the thick black hair. I wasn't sure whether they were chimpanzees or gorillas, but the same horror filled me as when I had watched the *sous-préfêt* on his shooting spree. Gorillas were protected animals. Killing them was illegal. I decided at that moment that I couldn't stand by and allow their slaughter. Somehow I would try to bring some influence to bear, though I wasn't sure how yet.

I often sat in the guesthouse listening in while Mario conducted the morning and afternoon radio links. It gave me an added insight into how the camp was run and what issues were current. Sometimes the static was so bad it drowned out the voice on the other end in a sea of hiss and crackle, forcing Mario to guess the bits he missed or reschedule the session to a later time. When he saw how interested I was, he showed me how to operate it.

'There'll be times when I can't be here,' he explained in French, 'and it'd help enormously if you could cover for me and take any messages.'

'I'll do my best,' I grinned, 'but I've never done anything like this before.' As he demonstrated the steps of switching on, calling up Makokou or Libreville, and ending each burst of speech with *à vous* or 'over to you', the remoteness and romance of our situation at Belinga bore in on me yet again. This bulky khaki metal box with the hand-held receiver on a hook at the side embodied that remoteness. I had only ever seen such devices in war films, yet here I was learning how to operate one. The wellbeing of everyone in camp depended in large measure on the communication that passed across the airwaves each day. The radio was a lifeline, and, in a strange sense, proof that a world existed outside the camp. I could not have guessed how soon my nascent radio-operating skills would prove vital.

A violent electrical storm hit the camp on the morning of 1 July. Solid black cloud hung low over the forest, blotting out the sky. Mario quickly unplugged the radio aerial to avoid the possibility of a lightning strike. Next morning, he had urgent matters to attend to down in the workers' village and asked me if I would handle the radio link. Win and I had barely been in camp a week but I was the only one able to do it, so I had no choice. At nine-thirty, I switched on the set to find Kruger already trying to raise us.

'*BE-ling-a! BE-ling-a!*' The static was bad, but I could just hear him shouting over it. '*Il y a un avion tombé dans la région de Belinga! Avez-vous compris?*' What I thought I heard chilled me: 'There is an aircraft down in the Belinga area. Do you read me?'

'*Répétez s'il vous plaît*,' I shouted into the receiver. 'Please repeat.' Again, it came through, chopped up by the crackle: '*Avion . . . tombé . . . région de Belinga*.' Moments later, Mario walked through the door. I whirled around in my seat to face him and blurted out, 'Kruger says there's a plane down somewhere in this area. He wants to know if we've heard anything.'

The colour drained from Mario's face. He stared at me, mute for some moments until the implications sank in. Étienne had heard Kruger's urgent call, and stood at the kitchen door, his face creased with concern. Mario started pacing up and down and fumbled for his packet of cigarettes, his eyes darting here and there as he tried to decide what to do. Meanwhile, Kruger was holding on at the other end of the line, waiting for some kind of response. Minutes later, I watched as Mario's demeanour switched in an instant to commanding decisiveness: 'Tell him to come on air at five o'clock this afternoon and we'll let him know.' As an afterthought, he added, 'Tell Bernard I won't be in for lunch, will you?' Grabbing a fresh packet of cigarettes, he strode out the door. I had no time to ask him what he planned to do. As I relayed his message to Kruger, I heard the tyres of the Toyota ute churning up the loose gravel as Mario gunned the accelerator and swung around the loop of road heading for the *débarcadère*.

He was gone for the whole day. Confined to camp, Win and I felt helpless. We had food, bedding and drugs in abundance if only we knew where the plane was and how to reach it. Was it a commercial passenger plane, a cargo carrier, a light plane? In this wilderness of mountains and forest, what chance would any survivors have of being found and rescued? I tried to picture the scene, but my mind recoiled from the horror.

Mario arrived back in the late afternoon, and Win and I ran out to meet him. 'Did you find out anything?' I pressed. His sombre expression could have meant he had, but he shook his head, '*Rien!*' He'd driven straight to Mayebut and despatched a reconnaissance pirogue downriver to ask at all the villages. Then he'd travelled upstream as far as M'Vadhi in another small pirogue to enquire there, but no-one anywhere along the river had seen or heard anything. At the radio, he conveyed this to Kruger, who signed off quickly to go and relay the news to the authorities. Mario poured drinks for the three of us and we sat in silence out on the porch in the gathering dusk, weighed down by our impotence and this brutal reminder of human vulnerability in this unforgiving terrain.

We were unaware as we sat there that a sequence of events was unfolding in Makokou with Eamon Temple at its centre. It had begun when one of his earthworks machines at the Djadié River had broken down. Work had halted while parts were sourced in Makokou. Late in the day of the electrical storm, Eamon had driven in to Makokou to collect the parts. On arrival, he'd been informed that a Cessna on private charter to Van Splunder, the Dutch company building the bridge at Makokou, had gone missing in the region earlier that day with six people on board. The French pilot had overshot the airfield at Makokou during the storm. His last radio message had indicated he was coming below the clouds to have a look. After that, all radio contact had ceased.

It was to be a week before we heard the details of what followed. Kruger had not been forthcoming about it over the radio; Eamon himself recounted the aftermath to us when he made a brief visit to camp after it was all over. I was shocked at the change in him. His eyes seemed hollow in their sockets, and his gaze appeared fixed on some far distant horrific reality. He revealed little detail, and as he spoke I thought he looked like a man newly returned from a theatre of war.

At Makokou on the night of the crash, a representative of Van Splunder had approached Eamon, convinced he knew where the plane had gone down and could lead Eamon to it if he agreed to take part in a search. There was no search and rescue service to call upon, and Eamon knew that part of the country better than anyone. It was characteristic of the man we later came to know that Eamon didn't hesitate. He was, after all, the man who had surveyed a route for the Trans-Gabonese Railway twice, on foot, years earlier, an epic feat covering more than 600 kilometres from the coast to Belinga through thick jungle, swamps and rugged mountains. Eamon was at home in the Gabonese forest, and accustomed to putting his own wellbeing last.

That night, he and the Van Splunder executive drove to the Djadié camp, and at first light next morning set out on foot to cover as much ground as they could. They walked all day in ever-widening circles, some thirty-five kilometres, but found nothing and only returned to camp at dusk. By then, almost forty-eight hours had elapsed since the plane had come down. They drove back to Makokou immediately to report in to the authorities, by which time the Gabonese army had been placed on standby to assist.

The provincial government put Eamon in charge of the search operation. Next day, he set his men at the Djadié camp to work cutting a heliport in the forest. Meanwhile, although it was the dry season, heavy rain had fallen all day, making flying conditions too dangerous, and costing a precious day. Three days had now gone by, holding out little hope of finding any survivors alive. On the fourth day, Eamon conducted an aerial reconnaissance in a military helicopter flown by an army pilot. Within an hour, he had located the wreckage, all too obvious from the air. In its fatal descent, the Cessna had cut a swathe through the trees, shearing off its wings before ploughing into a mountainside and bursting into flames.

In a combined operation involving Eamon's men and a party of Gabonese military personnel, a track was cleared from the Makokou road to the crash site. A scene of unspeakable tragedy awaited them when they reached it. Two of the six people had survived the crash and managed to crawl away some little distance to escape the fire, but had perished along with the others in the days that followed. Four Van Splunder executives were among the dead, together with a seventeen-year-old girl, the daughter of one of the men, who had been visiting Gabon on holidays.

Eamon's head sunk to his chest as he told us, 'I knew that pilot well. He was one of the best in the country.'

The bodies were brought out on stretchers through the squelching mud, to be transported back to Makokou in an army truck. The only question I felt able to ask Eamon was why that experienced pilot had overshot the airfield at Makokou. Why couldn't he have been guided in by the navigation beacon? Eamon looked me in the eye, his face ashen, and said, 'The beacon wasn't working that day because they'd run out of fuel for the generator.'

For days afterward, I tried to get my mind around the senselessness of it, this brutal extermination of life in the most stupid of circumstances. And I wondered, pointlessly, what we might have been able to do in time had we known the crash was only twenty kilometres from Belinga. For me, the tragedy proved a stark introduction to life in this frontier region where safety nets seldom existed.

Our supplies of fresh food, mail and other items arrived on Tuesdays and Saturdays. The iceboxes – *glacières* – usually contained an assortment of vegetables, meat, cheeses, yoghurt and fruit, originally from Paris or Johannesburg, but purchased at Mbolo supermarket in Libreville. The vegetables often arrived perished from being in transit too long. Small articles of hardware came up in padlocked tin trunks called *cantines*, which shuttled constantly back and forth on the aircraft, trucks and pirogues.

The consignment of builder's tools we had ordered in Libreville took a fortnight to arrive. When the shipment came in, it was time for Win to begin work. I accompanied him in the Kombi up to the carpenters' workshop – the *atelier du bois* – for his first encounter with the men. Bruno and Joseph, the chief carpenters, were there, along with another carpenter, several labourers and some trainee masons.

Win bounded out of the driver's seat and greeted them with a beaming smile. '*Bonjour!*'

'*Bonjour, patron! Bonjour, madame,*' they chorused.

'*Bonjour!*' I smiled around at the group, then stood back and waited to see how Win would handle the next five minutes. I had made no progress in teaching him French, and I knew I was unlikely to succeed, however long I tried.

He picked up an offcut of plywood from the floor, drew a felt pen from his pocket, and wrote his name on it in capital letters. He held it up to the men. 'My name is Win, Win Henderson.'

The men who could read looked disconcerted and shifted their weight from one foot to the other. Those who could not looked on with blank stares. Bruno and Joseph spoke up, telling Win it was fitting that they should address him as '*patron*'. He was their boss, and that was how things were done. It was a term of respect.

'You'd better listen to them,' I said. 'We're the outsiders here.' He thought for a moment, then grinned his acquiescence to the circle of faces. 'Okay, okay!' He motioned everyone to follow him over to the Kombi, where the boxes of new tools lay open – electric drills and circular saws, German hammers, leather carpenters' aprons, measuring tapes, spirit levels and dozens of other items, many of which the men had never used before. Their eyes lit up, and a hubbub of approval broke out. '*C'est bien, patron!*' They looked from one to the other, smiled and nodded as if they had never expected such a windfall. Through me, Win explained that each man would have a full set of tools, and everyone would be responsible for his own kit, to be kept in a lockable wooden box. I left them shortly afterwards, crowded around Win while he made the first toolbox as a demonstration. The introduction had gone better than I expected. I could see that the men already respected him, and his sense of humour and energy more than compensated for his lack of French. I told Win that in the early stages, I would spend half an hour in the *atelier du bois* each morning interpreting where necessary.

In the weeks that followed, Win instituted a program to teach the men modern building methods and safe work practices. He led by example, demonstrating techniques first, then supervising as each man tried them. I sometimes watched from the sidelines. They communicated so well it was almost as if no language barrier existed. The men taught him words for tools and types of timber, which he picked up quickly, laughing readily at his own mistakes. He slotted into the role seamlessly, so I gradually withdrew as interpreter and left them to it.

The initial building priorities were to finish off the toilets and showers in the surveyors' quarters, double the floor area of the *atelier du bois* to take the *combinée*, and convert the far end of the old sample shed into an office for the surveyors. Once the *combinée* had arrived, house frames and roofing beams would be pre-cut in the workshop before being transported down to each site, halving the time taken to complete each dwelling. As there was no spare vehicle, the Kombi quickly became vital to the building program. By day it transported materials, men and equipment around camp. By night we slept in it.

On Sundays, Mario sometimes drove down to the river to fish, using a line with a piece of soap on the end. We had been in camp just two weeks when he made the catch of his life. He pulled up in a cloud of dust in front of the guesthouse, hit the horn and shouted to Étienne and Bernard to come quickly. We ran out to join them, peering into the back of the Toyota utility. A colossal fish, over a metre and a half long, lay motionless on its belly. Its smooth skin was dark grey and white with no scales. Whiskers protruded from either side of its broad, flat head. It had no dorsal or ventral fins, and its tail tapered off like an eel's. To me, it resembled an exhibit from a natural history museum. I had never seen anything like it.

'A catfish!' Win cried.

Mario nodded vigorously. '*Oui, oui – c'est ça*.'

Win turned to me, knowing I'd never seen one before. 'They're bottom feeders. They spend their time on the riverbed, cleaning up everything that builds up on the silt.'

I ran to fetch the camera and insisted Mario let me take his picture with it. He beamed in triumph and struck a pose that reduced me to helpless giggles. Then Étienne and Bernard grabbed one end of the fish each and staggered into the guesthouse, where they dropped it onto the kitchen table. I heard their voices through the window: '*C'est bien, ça! Bien à manger!*'

'They're good eating, those catfish,' Win said to Mario.

'*Oui, oui – ils sont délicieux*.' Étienne and Bernard had already begun skinning and gutting it and cutting slabs of the flesh for freezing.

'Leave some out,' Mario called through the window to them. 'We'll have it for dinner tonight.'

That evening afforded Win and me our first taste of Gabonese wild food. Mario had told Bernard to prepare the fish in an Italian sauce of herbs and tomato, served on a bed of boiled rice. The flesh was moist and sweet, with a delicate flavour that belied the fish's life as a bottom scavenger. Mario kept a good cellar: we drank one of his light white wines with it. The meal created a festive atmosphere, and I could see that a day away from camp had lifted Mario's spirits.

The following week, Doug made one of his regular visits, and sounded me out about a job. His original idea that I might teach expatriate children had been overtaken by subsequent events, as the family in question would now be based in Makokou. Instead, Doug wanted me to take over some of Mario's more routine administrative duties in running the camp. We sat out on the porch over morning coffee and he outlined it to me.

'How would you feel about a part-time job supervising the hunters and the distribution of rations, monitoring the movement of supplies, doing the ordering and accounting for the *économat*, and gradually taking over the radio operation? We could pay you US$300 a month.'

'What do you mean, supervising the hunters?' I said. I was sure they didn't need me to tell them how to shoot monkeys.

'It would just be a case of issuing them with their ammunition and weighing and recording the meat each afternoon – that's all.'

'And what's involved in monitoring the movement of supplies?'

'Well, we need someone to keep track of what's been ordered, where it's coming from, whether it's been delivered, and making sure it's locked safely into the warehouse – all that sort of thing.'

'Mmm,' I mused. 'Sounds like a lot of work for US$75 a week.'

'Oh, it sounds more than it really is. Once you get into a routine with it, you won't find it takes much time.' I gulped down some coffee and chewed on a biscuit while

I thought about the practicalities. My technical vocabulary was still weak, but I liked the prospect of having something definite to do. From the company's point of view, it made sense. Mario was overloaded, and my French was under-utilised. From my standpoint, there was another thing in its favour too. It could give me an opportunity to influence what animals the hunters shot.

'I'll make a deal with you,' I said, because I knew I was in a strong position. 'I'll take on the job if you instruct the hunters that they are not to kill any more gorillas, and if they do, they won't be paid for the meat.'

Doug screwed up his eyes, sat back and regarded me with mock seriousness. 'You're a hard woman, but I think we can do that.'

'Good! So you'll tell the hunters tonight, will you?'

'I will, and I want you to be there when I do.' He was as good as his word. The hunters listened gravely while he spelt it out – no more gorillas to be killed. They took it on the chin. I had the impression it didn't matter to them what they shot.

Doug was delighted that I had agreed to the job.

'I'll have the office draw up a contract for you as soon as I get back. We'll probably have to designate you as a bilingual secretary. Then, as soon as that's approved by the government, your salary will start going into the bank.'

'You realise it'll take me a while to master the radio,' I warned him. 'I've listened to Mario handling Kruger sometimes and it's not beer and skittles.'

'I've got no doubt you'll be equal to it,' he replied. 'In a few weeks you'll be giving them heaps.' I wished I could be as confident as he was, but I welcomed the challenge and would give it my best shot.

My new duties commenced immediately. At six-thirty next morning I heard the hunters calling to me from outside the annexe: '*Madame! Madame!*' I stumbled out of bed, pulled on some jeans and stuck my head out the door.

'*Bonjour, madame. Les cartouches s'il vous plaît, madame.*'

'*D'accord. Attendez.*' They waited in the chill air – woollen hats pulled down over their ears and ragged pullovers covering their flimsy shirts – while I went to the locked cupboard in the guesthouse and counted out the day's quota of shells.

'*Voilà!*' I placed the shells in their calloused hands and wished them good hunting.

At nine-thirty, I sat beside Mario at the radio and tried to follow the rapid bursts of French coming from Kruger in Makokou and the staff in the Libreville office, through the dry-season crackle. I realised how much colloquial French I had yet to learn. Kruger's laconic way of speaking didn't help either, and I guessed, knowing his style, that he wouldn't be making too many allowances for my inexperience. I'd put myself on a steep learning curve accepting the job. Time would tell whether, as Doug had predicted, I was equal to it.

chapter seven

Frontier woman

The first six weeks in camp tested my mettle, both emotionally and in my job. Mario was only too pleased to pass on some of his tasks to me. The strain of the previous six months, during which he had managed the camp by himself, had begun to show, and he was often edgy and distracted. In the early stages, I had no concept of the sorts of problems he faced daily. By mid-August, my initiation would be complete.

Not long after I started work, I accompanied him on a river trip to buy manioc.

'That's M'Vadhi up there, on the bluff.' Mario pointed to a cluster of huts in a clearing, high on the southern bank of the Ivindo, as our pirogue rounded a bend in the river. We had travelled upstream for an hour through the still, cool morning. The surface of the water was like brown glass, the only ripple our gentle bow wave. I'd wanted to go to M'Vadhi ever since I'd first heard about it from Kruger and Peter Telfair. Now I had a good reason: Mario came here every Wednesday to buy supplies of manioc for the workforce. Since I would be supervising the distribution of rations, I decided it was important for me to know where the manioc came from and how we acquired it.

It was now several weeks since Win and I had moved into camp, but the sense of wonder was still fresh, and being in the heart of Africa still had the power to overwhelm me. On the river, I had one of my 'pinch me' moments, not quite able to believe I was really there. Joy, wonder and awe all mingled together – and I felt too small to encompass them. I wanted to make these intense moments last, to carry them with me always, because nothing in my life before could compare with them.

M'Vadhi was the furthest settlement on the river, close to the Congo border. We glided towards a wide bank of white sand, left exposed by the drop in water level during the dry season. A flotilla of small pirogues laden with bundles of manioc and bunches of plantains lay beached on the bank below the village. A crowd of women and children watched as we pulled in. Dressed in their brightly patterned cotton cloth and headscarves, the women could have been a cluster of vivid butterflies, forming a mosaic of colour against the white of the sand and the red ochre of the bluff.

Mario greeted them with jokes and banter – they smiled shyly and giggled behind their hands while the children played and splashed at the water's edge. I greeted them in French, and shook hands with a few of the nearest ones.

I was eager to see what a traditional Gabonese village looked like, as the only one I had seen close up was Mayebut. I followed Mario up the steep dirt track. The bare, ochre ground had been swept clean of fallen leaves and debris. Pavilions with thatched roofs, open sides and bench seating formed the hub of the village; huts of puddled mud skirted the perimeter. Behind them vegetation rose in a green jumble of shapes. Several men were working in the open air, carving small objects and repairing traditional weapons. Small groups of older men sat in the sun, talking and smoking pipes. The view from there took in a panorama of river, a patch of savanna and distant mountains through a line of banana trees and palms.

We moved through to the far end of the village, where a cluster of hemispherical leaf-thatched shelters housed families of Pygmies. The shelters were made from thin sapling frames curved over and crisscrossed, then covered with a thick layer of enormous leaves.

'The Bakwélé here have taken the Pygmies as slaves,' Mario said matter-of-factly. Pygmy families sat dejectedly in the dirt, framed by the curved doorways of the shelters. They appeared poorly nourished and lethargic. To me, it was a sight of profound pathos. I knew how they had lived traditionally, that they hunted and gathered in small family groups, that they possessed intimate knowledge of the forest and animals. Their lives in the deep forest had been a celebration of freedom and harmony. They had sung and danced in the euphoria of an elephant kill. Now all that had gone. I thought back to the story Kruger had told us, about Pygmy genitals being used as a cure for impotence by the Bantu, and I wondered whether the murdered Pygmy had been one of their relatives.

I consciously steeled myself. I was powerless to change this situation, and hadn't yet developed the emotional resources to cope with it easily. As each day passed, I became increasingly aware that the juxtaposition of the glorious with the desperately sad was the essence of Africa, and that I had better get used to it.

On the way back to the riverbank we passed a woman with severe elephantiasis. Her lower leg was swollen to the size of a long fat vacuum cleaner bag. She couldn't walk, and sat on a wooden bench staring vacantly into space. Elephantiasis was one of the extreme manifestations of filariasis. Village people had no access to expensive prophylactics, so the disease was endemic throughout the interior. I tried not to stare, but my thoughts turned dark: in Equatorial Africa, it seemed idyllic village life didn't exist. There was always a dark underbelly of suffering.

Back at the riverbank, the women had unloaded their produce from the pirogues and arranged it in heaps along the sand. Each woman sat behind her own bundle. Each bundle of ten *bâtons* of manioc sold for 250 CFAs or about US$1. Mario had a briefcase full of cash under his arm; as he moved slowly along the line, each woman stated how many *bâtons* she had for sale, and he paid her in notes. Some women had taro and plantains as well.

'I always buy whatever they bring, as a mark of good faith,' Mario explained. I thought of the mutual dependence that this riverbank commerce embodied: the women produced something the company needed, while in turn, the needs of our workforce afforded them the chance to make some money without leaving their villages.

They loaded the bundles of manioc, taro and plantains into our pirogue until every spare inch of space was filled. Then Mario retrieved the lunch box that Étienne had prepared, and we sat down cross-legged on the sand looking out over the river to eat.

In the warmth of midday, a torpor had fallen over everything. There were no sounds from the forest, and the women and children had moved back up to the shade of the village to rest before returning to their own villages. Where the river met the bank, the clean white sand showed clearly through the tea-brown water. A gentle sun had broken through the dry-season cloud, and bathed the sandbank in soft light. We sat in silence, absorbed in our own thoughts – Mario the experienced Africa hand, I the novice. I wondered how many other white women had been so far up the river. Carmen Roux must have, in the days of the gold workings at Camp Six, but that was decades before. And Annie Hion, the primatologist who'd studied the gorillas in the 1960s, might have come here. But there couldn't have been many others. There were no missions, no trading posts, no reasons to come. I was convinced no other Australian woman had ever been here. That thought lodged in my mind as I ate the salami and tomato roll Étienne had made, and drank the cold Regab beer straight from the bottle. Could I ever have imagined myself in such a place as I grew up in suburban Brisbane in the 1950s? I hadn't been out of Australia until I was twenty-seven, and now I was here. I pinched myself again.

By the time we were ready to go, most of the women were preparing to leave too. I realised that these women were the linchpins of their families. They reared children, produced crops, collected water, carried heavy loads of firewood, cooked meals and transacted commerce, all in the most basic of conditions. And on these market days, they paddled their small, fully-laden pirogues with the grace and skill of elite athletes. All the way back I reflected on their lives of unremitting hard work, and was filled with admiration.

* * *

Jacques Poussain, the French mechanic, arrived on the barge early in July, bringing a small car with orange plastic bodywork and a black vinyl soft-top. The badge on the side identified it as a Citroën Méhari. It looked like a Mini Moke.

Jacques himself was dressed plainly in jungle boots, shorts and a short-sleeved cotton shirt. He looked to be in his late forties, tall, with light brown hair and fair skin. His reputation had preceded him. He was a first-class mechanic, an expert on Caterpillar earthworks machines, and a veteran of the camp's previous epoch.

During his long working life in Gabon, Jacques had worked in the timber industry and at the manganese mine. He and Eamon were so close from their years at Belinga that they were like brothers. I shook his hand on the riverbank. 'This is my husband, Win,' I said. 'He doesn't speak much French yet.'

'*Et je ne parle pas anglais – rien du tout!*' he replied. The two shook hands. They were about the same age, and each had a depth of experience that put them on an equal footing. I hoped they would get on.

With Jacques' arrival, we now had eight expatriates in camp of four different nationalities – Italian, Australian, British and French. Two spoke no English and five spoke no French, leaving me as the only one who spoke both.

Jacques moved into a room in the surveyors' quarters. His wife and daughters would live in Makokou, and he would commute there at weekends. In the months ahead, Jacques would teach me much about the wildlife of the Gabonese forest. My first lesson came one night during dinner when a penetrating sound from the forest cut through our conversation. It began as a low insistent murmur, then quickly rose in pitch, volume and tempo, until finally it erupted in a prolonged piercing scream that made my flesh crawl. I put down my knife and fork to look across at Win: we had heard this sound once before while camped in a forest in Cameroon, and were convinced then that we had heard someone being murdered.

I turned to Jacques, wide-eyed, hoping he could identify its source: '*Qu'est-ce que c'est?* What's that?' With his long experience, I felt sure he would know.

'*C'est un daman,*' he said calmly.

'A *daman*? What do they look like?' Jacques described a small, brown, tree-dwelling animal that resembled a guinea pig, hard to see during the day, but active at night, calling from the treetops. When I translated for Win, he recognised the description immediately: 'Ah, a tree hyrax!'

Jacques nodded vigorously: '*Oui, oui, c'est ça!*' I marvelled that an animal of that modest size could make such a terrifying sound, but was relieved that at last I could put a name to it. That night was the first of many when the tree hyraxes punctuated our evenings with their screams. Months later, I realised that these vocal displays had ceased, and guessed that they had been a seasonal phenomenon connected with territories and mating.

We shared the guesthouse with a family of geckoes that lived behind the sideboard and the framed photographs on the walls. Each night as we ate, they crawled out and positioned themselves to wait for insects that congregated near the lights. To me, the geckoes' delicate translucent cream bodies and large chocolate-brown eyes were exquisite, and I never tired of watching them launch themselves at moths so big that their small mouths seemed barely able to hold them. When they had gobbled their prey whole, they retreated to lie in wait for more. I expected them to make the clicks and chirps that their Australian and Asian relatives do, but they were always silent.

Jacques slotted back easily into the place and his work. I struggled to pick up the threads of my own job: I felt I was dealing with an iceberg. The part above the waterline was what I knew, but underneath was everything I needed to know and didn't. There never seemed to be time for a proper briefing. Mario would explain a task, then be called away to deal with some urgent matter, leaving me with the words 'but how . . .' on my lips.

I soon discovered there was no system in place to track orders for materials. There was no such thing as a 'normal' turnaround time between ordering and receiving goods, and I didn't know who was responsible for what in the chain of command. Communication between the three company locations occurred in a kind of staccato pattern: people fired off requests, complaints and directives like pellets from a peashooter. From where I stood, things seemed to happen in a vacuum, with me in the middle. I gleaned snippets of information piecemeal, mainly on the run.

I learned that our fleet of pirogues consisted of two small ones and two large. The large ones – *grosses pirogues* – were twelve metres long and over a metre wide in the middle. They could carry twelve 200-litre fuel drums at a time, or two tonnes of cement in bags, or several hundred sheets of aluminium roofing, or a large quantity of sawn timber. The two six-metre pirogues were used for lighter cargoes. We also had the barge, which could carry vehicles and large quantities of materials, but it was limited by the height of water in the river – fully laden it could run aground in the dry season, and there would be no way to free it until the rains came.

The radio links gave me some of my most testing times. Win and Jacques were working to critical deadlines, and the timely receipt of supplies was vital. Some mornings they would stride into the guesthouse for the nine-thirty radio link sweaty, grimy, red-faced and pumped up with anger.

'Ask Kruger where my load of timber is!' Win would bark. 'It should have been here last week.'

'Where are my Land Rover parts?' Jacques would shake his head in despair. 'Tell him I can't go any further till I get them.' I would relay the queries to Kruger and sit back to wait for his terse replies. I could hear him bristling.

'The orders have been placed, Madame 'Enderson. This is Africa. Nothing happens quickly.'

Even worse for me were the occasions when Win and Jacques would hand me lists of things to order urgently, by radio, while they stood beside me flushed with frustration. Their enigmatic scribbles on scraps of dirty paper or pieces of plywood meant nothing to me. Jacques' lists were in French, Win's in English. I think they both overestimated my competence with technical French.

Later, when I looked back on these episodes I could laugh, but at the time there was no humour in them.

'I don't know what you're asking for!' I'd glare at Win. 'I'm not a bloody builder! Explain it slowly, and I'll try and convey it to Jacques so he can tell me what it's called.' The three of us could have been characters in some comic play. Win would try to explain the function of each item, often with sound effects, or draw a diagram. In turn I would struggle to explain to Jacques so he could tell me the correct

French word. Meanwhile, Kruger would be at the other end of the radio breathing hard.

'It's a nightmare!' I complained to Doug after a few weeks of these exchanges. 'I don't know what I'm doing. I need some sort of reference book.' He must have heard the desperation in my voice, because the next time he visited camp he handed me a technical dictionary in French and English, with drawings of tools and hardware, each one labelled in both languages. I kept it on the desk beside the radio, and it saved me much anguish in the months ahead.

To monitor deliveries of supplies when they finally arrived, I needed to be available whenever trucks came in from the *débarcadère* to accompany them up to the warehouse. Deliveries always had to be attended to straightaway to eliminate the risk of pilfering. And they came in at all hours – during meals, at night and in the early morning. The work brought me into close contact with M'Poko Lucien, the *magazinier* or storeman. He was tiny – half a head shorter than I was – and spoke softly, with a gentleness of manner I liked immediately. He always wore a white hard hat and carried a clipboard.

We would usually watch the truck drivers unload together: every item on the dockets had to be checked against the load to make sure nothing was missing. But if M'Poko had finished work for the day, I would check the goods into the warehouse myself and lock up afterwards. The loads were usually mixed – timber, cement, hardware, rations, hard hats, mattresses, drums of fuel, stocks of clothing for the *économat* and drugs for the *infirmerie.* The unpredictable delivery times meant that I never knew when my meals would be interrupted or my evening leisure time cut short. Living on site, glorious as it was, meant I was always accessible. It was just one of many pressures that would threaten to bring me down as I tried to adjust to life in camp.

While we spent our days scurrying about, deadline-driven, rattled and frustrated at the chaos, the life of the forest continued around us in timeless rhythms. In the camp, thwarted human endeavours held sway; on its periphery, the peace and order of the natural world prevailed. I'd felt this dichotomy almost from the outset – the yin and yang, the interplay of opposites. While urgent tasks demanded my energies much of the time, whenever I walked outside I felt the pull of the forest, a yearning in my spirit to connect with the wildness.

The awe and wonder I'd experienced during our first visit to the camp, when we'd watched the flock of brilliant blue touracos cavorting on the umbrella tree near the guesthouse, had never left me, and in the weeks since we'd moved into camp, an awareness of what lay just beyond the clearing permeated my thoughts night and day.

Of all the wild creatures we would come to know, the giant yellow-casqued hornbills gave me some of my greatest bursts of joy. They were the most visible and dramatic of the birds we regularly saw, and they made me laugh with their raucous exuberant calls. Win and I had first seen them when we'd camped in a rainforest clearing in Cameroon. Initially we couldn't work out what was making the swishing and whirring sound high above the canopy, which grew louder the nearer it approached to us. Then we saw them – three large black and white birds with massive down-curving beaks like toucans, and startling bony projections like centurions' helmets on their heads and upper beaks. They flew in line, slowly, one behind the other, their powerful calls echoing through the forest. When I'd looked them up in our wildlife atlas I'd learned they often followed bands of monkeys as they travelled to feed. At Belinga, these giant hornbills with personalities to match were never far away, and for me the sight and sound of them became synonymous with Belinga. Often as I walked around camp, I would watch them flying from treetop to treetop, calling constantly, always moving in the same direction – west to east. The sound of their swishing wings lodged in my memory, elements in a soundscape whose meanings were growing clearer with each passing day.

In the late afternoons, Mario, Jacques, Win and I often sat on the porch with a cold beer or a whisky, and allowed the peace of the closing day to enfold us. Sometimes bands of colobus monkeys would appear, playing on loops of vine at the edge of the clearing, leaping and swinging like acrobats on a trapeze. The tufts of fluffy white hair on their faces, backs and tails stood out against the grey of ancient tree trunks and the tangle of foliage. Watching these wild primates cavorting as though we weren't there, I felt hugely privileged – a spectator on a secret world – and I marvelled at the bizarre events that had brought us to this place.

chapter eight

FÊTE FEVER

In mid-July, our supply chain from the coast suddenly collapsed. Air cargo destined for the camp failed to arrive in Makokou, and our fresh food was off-loaded in Libreville several times.

'What the hell's going on down there?' I yelled over the radio to Doug one morning. 'Hardware we can wait for, but food we need now.'

'It's this confounded *fête*, Nettie. We've got no control over government requisitions on cargo space. If it doesn't improve, I'll charter a plane to get your food up there.' At times I wondered if the Libreville staff really understood how it felt for us being at the end of the line, at the mercy of every glitch in the transport system.

'We'll hold you to that,' I replied tersely. I'd had complaints from all the expatriates about the lack of fresh vegetables for dinner and mail from home.

All the supply problems stemmed from the fact that festivities for *la fête* – the anniversary of independence, celebrated annually on 17 August – would focus on

Makokou that year. The preparations for it would distort commerce and transport in our region for a month.

On the radio one morning, Kruger explained the details. An accelerated building program was underway in Makokou to complete several major projects, including a multistorey hotel, a television station, a sports stadium, paved roads and the town's first street lighting. Every square metre of air-cargo space out of Libreville had been officially requisitioned, and planeloads of materials, labourers, colour televisions and luxury furniture were arriving in Makokou at the rate of three per day. Against this backdrop, the cargo destined for Belinga had been assigned a low priority.

There was another problem, too. As part of the celebrations, the new road through to Belinga was to be officially opened. Doug came on the radio one morning to tell Mario we could expect a visit from President Bongo by helicopter on the day of the opening. I watched Mario's face as the implications hit him. He lit three cigarettes in quick succession and paced around the room, his eyes wild with panic. We'd need a helipad, but we had no earthworks machines to create one. A flat area of ground opposite the warehouse would have to be cleared of forest with chainsaws and machetes, and an approach path created adjacent to the guesthouse.

He set teams of labourers to work immediately felling trees and clearing secondary growth. It would be slow work and time was short. I watched from the doorway as the first of the forest giants crashed to the ground.

On the second day of clearing, I was alone in the office. Win and Mario were at the *débarcadère*; the labourers were working nearby, unsupervised. I heard the high-pitched whine of a chainsaw, followed by the ripping of branches and vines as a tree plunged down through the forest, then a thunderous crash as it hit the earth. All the lights went out in the guesthouse, and the fridge and freezer motors fell silent. There was a moment of absolute silence, then a burst of riotous laughter from the labourers as they realised the tree had fallen on the powerlines.

I strode outside, furious, to find them still doubled up at what they regarded as a huge joke. I stood rigidly facing them, and tried to make myself look as authoritative as I could. 'This is a big problem for us,' I shouted. 'All the meat in our deep freezer could go bad, and now the radio won't work!' The men stopped laughing and stood silently in their hard hats, staring at me blankly. Electrical power and freezers meant nothing to them.

I marched up the hill to the mechanics' workshop and broke the news to Jacques. '*Merde!*' he muttered, wiping his greasy hands on a lump of rag. It would be his job to repair the lines, and he had more than enough to do already. I walked back down to find the men planning their next move. The massive tree in their sights was perilously close to the guesthouse. If they felled it to the left, it would take out the washing line, the stores shed, and possibly our annexe. To the right, it would completely block the road into camp. I had to do something.

I breathed deeply, braced myself, and yelled, 'Stop! No more!' They froze, looking at me, then at one another, with wide staring eyes. They must have thought me mad. They were only following Mario's instructions. What was I on about? But they stopped. When Mario and Win returned, the men had been standing idle for an hour, Jacques had inspected the damaged cable, and Étienne and

Bernard were preparing lunch. Next day, Win took over supervision of the tree felling, but still disaster never seemed far away. An even bigger tree narrowly missed the kitchen roof and two of the labourers on its way down. I had given up watching. I hated the destruction, and I had no stomach for the potential disasters involved.

It was just a week after the helipad had been completed, and we had celebrated this milestone, that we received the news: the president wouldn't be coming after all. The opening ceremony would take place at a location out on the new road.

At that moment, I felt for the first time that we were locked into some endless farce, powerless to mitigate the chaos engulfing us. Mario grew more disaffected as the days went by, blaming the management for many of our problems. I watched as his normally buoyant manner disappeared little by little and was replaced by a moody cynicism. Then one day he told us outright, 'I'm planning to resign. I'll stay for the *fête*, but no longer.' No-one was surprised. We all understood what had driven him to the decision. Still, none of us could imagine how the camp would run once he had gone.

The pressure-cooker atmosphere was further heightened by the dry-season shortage of bushmeat for the workforce. The hunters found it more and more difficult to locate the usual prey animals, as they gravitated towards the river during the dry. Many of the men complained of 'meat hunger', rubbing their bellies and assuming a pained expression when they saw any one of us. In response, we increased the issue of dried salt fish on ration days, but they regarded this as a poor substitute. As each day passed, I felt increasingly under siege, and I began to lose sleep.

In the midst of all this, there was one positive development: the *combinée* arrived at last, heralding a new and streamlined phase in the building program. Win could barely contain his joy.

We had been there a month when Dr Werner Krol, the ninth member of our expatriate team, arrived. It was the end of July and we were battling the pre-*fête* chaos. I hadn't known what to expect of this Bavarian geologist. Perhaps he would be aloof and self-important, I had speculated. He had a PhD, and I had only met one other person with such a high qualification. What would he think of our basic facilities? Would they be too down-market for him?

I need not have worried. The fair-skinned young man who stepped out of the Toyota walked towards us smiling, his hand outstretched. 'Hello, I'm Rodo.' He spoke perfect English. He had a scholarly face, but a ready sense of humour shone from the blue eyes behind his spectacles. His bald crown was fringed with light-brown hair.

'Hello, I'm Nettie.' I shook hands and beamed back. 'Welcome to Belinga! How was the trip up?'

'Well, it was a little slow, but that's okay.' He had a deep voice, made gravelly by cigarettes. I knew he was new to Africa and unmarried, so I had prepared a welcome pack for him with soap, a towel, a box of tissues and a few personal items. I wanted him to feel at home, as his contract was for two years and he had come straight from university.

'This is for you,' I said, handing over the parcel.

He blushed bright pink. 'Oh, thanks – that's very kind!' A hint of German accent coloured his English, and gave a musical rise and fall to his intonation.

For me, Rodo's arrival marked a new and welcome phase. He spoke four languages – German, English, French and Spanish – so I was no longer the only one with English and French. More than that, I had a colleague to share the daily crises with, someone new to Africa like I was, and the same age. Win came down from the workshop, covered in sawdust, to greet him, and I sensed he too felt relief that there was another English-speaker in camp.

I thought Rodo looked too vulnerable to be in remote Africa, though. He seemed too gentle, too shy, and I hoped that the pre-*fête* frenzy would not be too brutal an introduction for him.

'Your room is ready down in the *cas de passage*,' I said. 'You'll be near Jacques Poussain, our French mechanic. It's pretty basic, but it's all we have for the moment.' Mario had renamed the surveyors' quarters the *cas de passage* – vistors' lodge – since it now had a suite of single bedrooms as well as toilets and showers. It would accommodate visiting staff and contractors, as well as house all the new staff until their mini-apartments could be built.

'That's okay,' he assured me. 'It will be fine.' On that first day, I could not have guessed how closely future events would bind Rodo, Win and me together. All I saw was a sensitive, cultured young man, and I looked forward to working with him.

By the second week of August all of us were under pressure, and the crises had piled up as the *fête* drew closer. Our fresh food had been off-loaded in Libreville twice running. Kruger had moved out of his house in Makokou into a cottage and was supervising conversion of his old place into a guesthouse for the *fête*. Jacques needed to wire the camp for 240-volt power but couldn't get cables. Win had a deadline to meet for completion of the surveyors' office, but couldn't get timber. One of his labourers suffered from epilepsy and could no longer safely operate a concrete mixer, so had to be allocated other tasks. Mario had suffered a black eye and broken spectacles in an altercation with a militant Bakwélé man he had had to dismiss. When he called in the commandant of the Brigade de Gendarmerie at Makokou to quieten down the Bakwélé, the commandant threatened to burn their villages if they didn't settle down.

Teams of carpenters, masons and labourers worked noisily outside the guesthouse all day, and Étienne and Bernard complained daily that they wanted their wives to be brought up from Makokou. The surveyors' gear still had not been cleared through customs, so all they could do was cut brush and clear vegetation from around the old trig stations. Everyone's morale was at rock bottom.

In the midst of all this, the company was vigorously recruiting labour. More tradesmen and labourers were urgently needed to keep pace with expanding work schedules. New recruits arrived in twos and threes on every pirogue, and each man had to be issued with a basic kit of rations on arrival. This task fell to me, but in most instances, I had no warning. Usually, the first I knew was when the men presented themselves at the guesthouse door expecting to receive their woollen blanket, dried fish, rice, palm oil and paraffin.

Many of the new recruits were unaccustomed to frontier life, and expected that the consumer comforts they enjoyed in town – electricity, filter-tip cigarettes, record players and football boots – would be available in camp. My feeling of being under siege grew stronger each time a worker bailed me up outside the guesthouse with some new demand.

Our supply situation worsened daily as the *fête* approached. Stocks of hardware, timber and vehicle parts from retailers in Makokou were long since exhausted. The supply of manioc had also dried up, because all the manioc from every village in the region had been officially requisitioned to feed the influx of people in Makokou. We issued rice in its place, but this did nothing to appease the men's discontent. The whole camp seemed primed for an explosion.

During dinner each night, work problems dominated the conversation. Each person's tension fed on everyone else's, so the atmosphere around the table grew increasingly poisonous. After several weeks, Mario reached the limit of his endurance. One night we sat down to dinner to find an empty tin can on the table with a hole punched in the top.

'That's the fine tin,' he announced. 'Anyone who mentions work during a meal incurs a fine of 1000 CFAs.' It proved to be an inspiration. Dinners became occasions for riotous laughter when people momentarily forgot the rule and everyone else pounced on them and forced them to pay up.

Still, by day I struggled with my role and tried to suppress a growing sense of despair – but I had no privacy, nowhere to go to escape. Our Kombi and the annexe were in the most public area outside the guesthouse, surrounded by noise and activity day and night. When I needed to cry – something that happened more and more often – there was no refuge. I felt like a caged animal. One day the tears welled up in the middle of the morning. I didn't want anyone to see that I was unravelling – I had too much pride for that – so I left the desk strewn with papers and headed up the hill to a cleared area behind the generator shed. I sank to the ground, leaned back against the corrugated-iron wall, and let wracking sobs take over.

I was discovering exactly what Doug had warned me about. 'It'll be pretty rough up there for a while,' he'd said. I doubted even he could have known how rough it would become. But I didn't regret our decision to come here. I just had to work my way through the bad patch and hope things improved.

Win could see I was struggling, as I slept poorly and was emotionally brittle. He wanted to help, but there was little he could do, and he had his own battles to fight. I made up my mind I wasn't going to give in. This was the biggest test of my life, and I had no intention of failing it.

My confidence received a boost on 11 August, when I conducted an entire radio link on my own for the first time, without Mario hovering in the background. I had won my six-week battle with French idiom, unfamiliar procedures, bad reception and unrecognisable French voices coming from the Libreville office. It was not a moment too soon – Mario's departure was only days away.

In the village, the week before the *fête* passed in a haze of palm wine. Kruger sent up dozens of cartons of the government's commemorative cloth, printed with President Bongo's portrait and proclaiming the fifteenth anniversary of independence, and overnight, everyone in the village seemed to be wearing a dress or a shirt made from it. A small contingent of our workforce was going to Makokou to take part in the formal celebrations, but even this became contentious. Every man felt he should be one of the ones to go. The verbal battle between Mario and the men over who would be chosen lasted for days. The men also lobbied for extra spending money, extra days off, whisky and free beer. *Fête* madness gripped the whole village, to the point where hardly anyone wanted to work. The government evidently expected trouble in Makokou, too, as a convoy of military vehicles was mounted from Libreville, carrying 600 gendarmes to keep order in the town during the festivities.

The government had set Saturday 16 August as the date for the official opening of the new road. A pavilion would be erected near the Makokou end of the route, and representatives of SOMIFER's shareholders would assemble there to await the arrival of government dignitaries by helicopter. The only problem was that the road was not yet finished at the Belinga end. Eamon and his men were still out in the forest on Friday the fifteenth, working on the final section.

We had expected Eamon and the men to arrive in camp that morning. When there was no sign of them by mid-afternoon, the suspense got the better of Mario. 'Let's go out and find them!' he cried.

Jacques, Rodo and I climbed into the Méhari with Mario at the wheel, and headed out along the ridge of Bakota South, where the old track from the 1960s had been partly cleared. Branches of giant trees overhung the route. Loops of thick liana straddled the spaces, and families of monkeys leapt screaming and chattering through the canopy. I had only come this way once before.

About twenty minutes out, we came on three of Eamon's men walking along the track with their shotguns, framed by the massive bulk of a Caterpillar grader in the background. Eamon wasn't far away, they said. We left them to their hunting and soon reached a fork in the track. One of the paths was freshly cut. A stack of chainsaws and jerry cans littered the ground at the junction. We followed the new track to the bottom of a steep incline: a massive tree, newly felled, lay across it.

Mario cut the engine. 'Listen!' he whispered. The low rumble of heavy machinery sounded through the forest. We climbed out and followed the direction of the sound. Fallen trees strewed the ground. Oozing mud sucked at our boots. As we breasted the next rise, the rumble became a roar. Below us, a gully sloped sharply, and we caught sight of the huge bulldozer halfway down, moving ponderously on its tracks back and forth on the hillside, Eamon sitting stiffly at the controls.

When he changed direction, he suddenly caught sight of us. He inched the dozer up the incline, drew level with us, and stopped with the engine still running. The noise of the engine made conversation impossible, but he climbed part way down the machine, and one by one we reached up and shook his hand. His gaunt body was streaked with sweat and mud. The sinews in his legs and arms stood out against the bones. Under the hard hat, his face was haggard and his skin the colour of putty; he managed an exhausted smile before excusing himself. The final bend in the route, just 150 metres long, had to be shaped before nightfall. As we watched him move off again, I wondered how long a sixty-year-old could punish his body and mind to that extent, and what drove him. Still, on the way back to camp, we all felt the euphoria of his achievement, fortunate to have been there to witness that final push.

The day of the official road opening began quietly in camp. No formal celebrations were planned for Belinga, but at the morning radio session Kruger informed us that some of the dignitaries wanted to come on to Belinga after the ceremony. That meant providing accommodation, meals and hospitality, but we had no specific information. As the opening ceremony was scheduled for early afternoon, we calculated we would have most of the day to prepare for their visit.

This sanguine view was abruptly shattered when, at 11.20 am, the thwack-thwack of a helicopter's rotor blade sounded over the forest. Mario, Win, Rodo and I dropped what we were doing and ran outside to peer at the sky, where the silhouette of a helicopter had emerged over the canopy.

'They're probably just sightseeing,' Mario said. But the helicopter traced a wide circle around the camp, then began its descent.

'Quick, quick!' Mario shouted to Étienne and Bernard, who stood on the guesthouse porch watching. 'Put a cloth on the table, and bring out the whisky and some glasses!'

The pilot had spotted the landing pad on the hillside and manoeuvred the helicopter over it, preparing to land. The Alouette touched down lightly – it was the type of aircraft the president used. We braced ourselves to greet him in our grimy jeans and T-shirts, but as the pilot climbed out, followed by several men with cameras around their necks, he called out, 'We need to get this one out of the way quickly – the big one will be here any moment.'

They were journalists charged with covering the road opening. We sprinted up the hill and helped to push the Alouette off the pad. Moments later, a bulky Puma jet helicopter lumbered noisily into view. Like a giant insect, it descended slowly, sandblasting us with fine laterite dust. The door opened and I counted the passengers alighting – fourteen in all – mostly men in business suits with open-neck shirts and sunglasses.

A heavy-set man in a chocolate-brown suit headed the delegation. He walked towards Mario, smiling broadly, and shook his hand. It was Vice-President Mébiame, deputising for President Bongo. His deep, resonant voice, speaking impeccable French, reminded me of Paul Robeson. 'Perhaps you would be kind enough to indicate to the pilots the direction we should be taking to the ceremony? I'm afraid we're lost!'

Mario didn't falter. 'Yes, of course. But perhaps you would care to join us for a drink first?' Win, Rodo and I hung back, waiting our turn to be introduced.

At that moment a group of about thirty women in bright costumes and headscarves appeared, moving as one up the red dirt road from the village. They danced, clapped and sang their way up until they reached flat ground, where they formed a tight block and shouted a traditional welcome, swaying and stamping their feet. They must have planned it beforehand and been ready to move as soon as the VIPs appeared.

The official party stood to watch, waved their acknowledgement, then slowly made their way down to the guesthouse. Étienne and Bernard had covered the old wooden bench on the porch with a spotless white cloth, and drinks were set out as if the event had been planned for months.

Mario introduced us to the vice-president and the minister of energy and mineral resources, Monsieur Edouard M'Bouy Boutzit, an older man in a powder-blue suit who walked with a stick. Much later I learned he was one of the most loved politicians in the country. He'd been cured of leprosy by Schweitzer as a young man, and still seemed to glow with the miracle of his recovery.

Mario moved among the visitors, pouring drinks and expounding on the life of the camp. Everyone agreed that the landscape at Belinga was breathtaking, and that they all wanted to return some day. I had never mixed with a vice-president or a cabinet minister before, but I had learned to expect that life at Belinga would be full of 'firsts'. The party stayed just half an hour, then filed back into the Puma to keep their appointment at the opening ceremony.

Doug, Gina, Eamon and the rest of the official party had been waiting for them at a ceremonial pavilion down on the new road. By the time the two helicopters finally reached them, the assembled dignitaries were on the point of going home. We heard no details of the opening ceremony, but Doug told us that another ceremony was held that afternoon in Makokou before a large crowd, and Eamon was decorated by the president once again for his outstanding contribution to the development of the country. I felt myself to be caught up in big events – the Belinga exploration project was the highest profile development in Gabon. But in the day-to-day frenzy of life in camp there was little time to reflect on that fact.

August 17 brought Mario's departure. As promised, he'd stayed just long enough to see out the celebrations. We were all in subdued mood as we drove to the *débarcadère* to see him off. Win, Rodo, Bernard and I stood on the riverbank to watch as his belongings were loaded into the pirogue. Lupo stood close by his leg, calm as always.

I remembered all the good times we'd had with Mario around the dinner table when we first arrived – the wine, the good food, the jokes. We'd all miss him. He shook hands with each of us formally. His last words to me were, '*Courage, Nettie!*' I would need it while the camp adjusted to this latest convulsion. Then he and Lupo stepped into the waiting pirogue and we watched as their silhouettes grew smaller and smaller in the distance. That night I lay awake for hours, wondering what lay ahead for us. My job was certain to grow, and I hoped I would be up to it.

In the week after the *fête*, Makokou's hastily erected infrastructure fared badly: the multistorey hotel closed down, the television station ceased to operate, the stadium track was flooded and partially washed away, and some of the street lamps fell over. Life in Makokou, and the whole province of Ogooué-Ivindo, then returned to normal.

chapter nine

My role mushrooms

The thunder of hooves pounding down the hillside nearby brought our planning meeting on the porch to an immediate halt. Men's voices, high-pitched with panic, shouted, '*Buffle! Buffle!*' – buffalo. The animal had bolted towards the village; if it stampeded through there, people could be killed. Doug, Jacques, Win, Rodo and I dropped our paperwork and ran down the slope. Madame Elizabeth, the senior woman of the village, joined in the chase, with several others trailing behind her.

We stopped at a fallen log and peered towards a patch of thick forest, where it seemed one of the hunters had cornered the animal with his dog – we could hear the beast thrashing about trying to escape. Then a single shot rang out and echoed around the hillside. In the silence that followed, we stood motionless, holding our breath. Then someone called out, '*Il est mort?*' Is it dead? No answer. '*Est-ce qu'il est mort?*' A small voice from the undergrowth replied '*Oui, il est mort.*'

We entered the forest in single file. In the dim light, our

eyes took a few moments to adjust to an unwelcome sight. A large, roan-coloured animal with white stripes across its back and face lay on its side. Although it was as large as a buffalo, it looked more like an antelope with long thick horns twirling gracefully back from its skull. It was in superb condition, its coat glossy even in the deep shadows. The shot had entered cleanly between its eyes. The hunter, Émile, stood transfixed in front of it, his eyes set in a glassy stare, his body bathed in a sweat of fear. He could barely speak. Augustine, the village chief, squatted nearby with his wife, Madame Elizabeth, staring at the beast's wide eyes.

I stroked its warm flank and felt the smoothness of the fine coat under my fingers.

'*C'est quoi, Émile?*' I asked. 'What is it?'

'*Nous ne savons pas, madame*,' he answered. 'I don't know.'

'It looks rather like a kudu to me,' Win said.

Jacques shook his head authoritatively: 'No, no. There are no kudus in Gabon. They're only found in the south, on the savannas.'

There was a silence. I looked at the faces of the group squatting in a circle around the carcass. There was no doubt what the expatriates were thinking: why did this magnificent – and apparently rare – animal have to die like this? But, try as I might, I couldn't interpret the stunned response of the Gabonese. In the middle of the dry season, that amount of meat would feed the whole village, I thought. Why aren't they rejoicing? Madame Elizabeth picked a handful of broad, glossy leaves from a nearby shrub and placed them gently over the animal's eyes. To me the gesture seemed reverential: perhaps an acknowledgement that the animal had a spirit. After a time, we all stood up, still silent, and walked away.

The animal's rare status was confirmed in our wildlife atlas. A colour illustration showed exactly what we had seen – a bongo antelope – and its conservation status: 'Rare, seldom seen in the wild'. Reading that, I felt even sadder. I would never get used to such killings. Other species of antelope were abundant, and I could accept that they were important sources of protein for the people, but the bongo's death struck me as a tragedy.

Following Mario's departure, Doug had come up to sort out the reallocation of administrative tasks. Under the new arrangements, I would also take over running the guesthouse and ordering food. I would continue to operate the radio, and be responsible for ordering supplies generally.

Our domestic staff now numbered four. The two recent arrivals – Mambo Bernard and Mohibi Léon – had both worked at the camp in the 1960s, were fully trained and knew Eamon and Jacques well. I was to be their new supervisor. In addition, I would continue to oversee stock control and cash flows at the *économat*, and supervise M'Poko Lucien at the warehouse. With these increased responsibilities, my salary of US$300 per month seemed meagre, but the company was feeding us, and once our flat was ready our housing would be provided too, so I didn't make an issue of it.

'Some good news, though,' Doug said. 'Eamon's found a man to look after rations. He'll weigh and allocate the game meat, purchase the manioc and supervise the distribution of rations. He'll be reporting to you.'

'When's he coming?' I asked.

'He should be here within the week. He comes from the Makokou area.' It was welcome news, even though it meant I would have seven men to supervise instead of six. I grinned at the irony of being in charge of the domestic staff. I had never run a home, and my cooking was indifferent. Worse, I didn't know how to go about it, how strict I should be, or what the norms were. I couldn't imagine what I could teach these men who had been doing the job for so long.

'I want to go down to Makokou to see what foods are available in the shops there,' I told Win the next day.

'How about we go down together?' he suggested. 'It'd be good to get out of this place for a couple of days.'

'Damn it, you guessed,' I laughed. 'I do need to escape for a while, but I've got a good excuse. If I'm going to be ordering food, I need to know what we can get locally.' We arranged to go the following day.

The river trip was slow and difficult, as the water was at its lowest level for the year. Giant rock outcrops loomed above the shallows, and we had to walk the pirogue through several stretches of rapids. We arrived in the early afternoon and Kruger drove us to the Roux house.

Makokou had just two general stores – Kaczmarek and Loupin. I decided to try Monsieur Loupin's establishment first, as I'd heard he had a better range. We arrived at the shop mid-afternoon. I was especially interested in small luxuries like bacon, poultry and fruit preserves, because I believed that interesting and varied meals were essential to boost everyone's morale.

The force of Monsieur Loupin's personality hit me the

moment I stepped through the door. He was short and wiry, in his late fifties. His pale-blue eyes were bloodshot, and his short grey hair stood straight out from his head. He wore the standard bush uniform – shorts, lace-up khaki jungle boots and a short-sleeved cotton shirt – and spoke in a harsh, rasping whisper. I'd seen him briefly when we first visited Makokou two months earlier. He was also the Air Gabon agent in town, and looked after ticketing, passengers and cargo.

When I introduced myself and explained why I had come, his eyes lit up at the prospect of substantial ongoing custom. He spun around to face the door to a back room and emitted a screech like a startled cockatoo: 'Lisette! Lisette!' His wife, a thin woman with wispy hair, appeared in the doorway. Her dry and wrinkled skin bore the mark of too much tropical sun, and a look of resignation was etched into her face. She took up a position behind the counter, and Loupin turned back to give me his full attention.

He ushered me to a dimly lit corner of the shop where a bulky deep freezer took up half the floor space, and opened the lid with a flourish. 'Look at this! Is it not magnificent? A home-grown guinea fowl, raised and slaughtered by my own hand!' The frozen bird had been plucked and dressed, ready for cooking. 'Madame, just look at these: snails, partridge, rabbit, quail! What more can you desire?'

'Look at this!' he urged, gesturing at a stack of frozen jars, small beads of saliva forming at the corners of his mouth. 'These jars contain completely pre-cooked meals I prepared myself. I keep these always on hand in case of guests. People come to Makokou to visit and I say, "Come! Eat with Loupin!"' I started to understand why Madame

Loupin wore a resigned look. Loupin was a showman – he must have been exhausting to live with.

We moved on to inspect the contents of the shelves. Loupin waved extravagantly towards the jams. 'Jams? How many do you want? Plum jam, cherry jam, pineapple jam, loganberry jam, Eng-lish mar-ma-lade jam! Which one do you want, madame? Madame, tell me, what is it you want? Anything you need, Loupin will find it! You like tea? Come with me!'

I was starting to wilt under the onslaught, but he grasped my elbow firmly and marched me to the other end of the shop. 'There!' He swept his arm along the display: 'Assam, Darjeeling, Jasmine, Breakfast, Lapsang Souchong, Herbal . . . take your pick! You see the brand? Jacksons of Piccadilly. That's one thing the English do know, how to drink tea!'

I tried to marshal my thoughts about exactly what we needed. As I reeled off the items, I watched his face fall – our menu at the camp was never going to encompass quail and partridge. To him, the list was disappointingly mundane, and his face told me there would be no excitement for him in my custom. In an attempt to placate him, I launched into an explanation of how conditions were at Belinga.

'Belinga! Don't talk to me about Belinga! Nobody knows it better than I do! I once lived there, you know!'

'I didn't know that,' I said.

'*Mais oui!*' His voice dropped into the bass register, conveying his incredulity that I hadn't already heard. 'I've worked for SOMIFER, and I've worked for Roux. Twenty-four years I've been in Gabon, madame, twenty-four years! You will still be in Makokou tonight?'

'Yes, of course.'

'Good! You must come to Loupin for an aperitif. Oh, I can tell you so many things . . .'

'That's very kind of you, but . . .' I began.

'So, it's settled then. You come at six-thirty tonight! *Bien!*'

Win and I arrived at the appointed time, and as Loupin ushered us into the living room, Lisette appeared silently from the kitchen with a tray of savouries. I still hadn't heard her speak. Loupin settled us into two worn armchairs and poured us a glass of Ricard each. We still hadn't developed a taste for this aniseed drink, but we took the glasses politely – it was a French tradition, and we wanted to at least appear to fit in.

Loupin wasted no time in embarking on his repertoire of stories.

'I was paymaster for old Roux at the gold workings at Camp Six,' he began. The abandoned gold camp stood on the banks of the Ivindo, within walking distance of Mayebut. We'd heard about it from Kruger. Loupin pointed to a gold nugget displayed on a shelf. 'That comes from there. Belinga was wild in those early days. We used to have leopards coming right up to the house. I shot one once just a metre from my front door, and then a week later another one in exactly the same place.' This tallied with what we'd heard from Peter Telfair, so I knew it wasn't just bravado.

'They still come in,' I said. 'We had one prowling around our annexe one night.'

Next, Loupin launched into a string of stories about

traditional tribal practices, throwing in anthropological terms here and there. Anthropophagy (cannibalism) and necrophagy (eating of the dead) featured prominently. I think he was trying to shock us. Then a cat entered the room, backed up to a wall, and sprayed the paintwork with its urine.

Loupin's face turned purple with rage. He grabbed the gold nugget and hurled it at the terrified animal, shouting a tirade of abuse. The nugget hit the wall like a cannonball and the cat bolted for its life. Win and I could only watch in silence, mouths agape and eyes wide. When he had calmed down, he stood and beckoned us to follow him out the back door.

He stopped before a spacious cage, where a breeding pair of fish-eating owls and their chicks fixed their luminous eyes on us from a high perch. They were the most exquisite owls I had ever seen, with delicate fluffy feathers the colour of coffee cream. Loupin entered the cage, calling to each one by name, and we watched, bewitched, as they flew down and perched on his arm.

In a nearby enclosure, he kept a tree-climbing primate which he called a cuscus. The shy animal looked down at us warily with wide, forward-facing eyes. Its thick fur was a rich gold, and its prehensile tail gripped the branch tightly. Months later, when we saw one at Belinga, I learned that this animal was in fact a rare golden potto.

Seeing our joy in the animals, Loupin continued the tour: 'Now watch this,' he said. Beside a fenced yard he called to another of his charges. 'Bismarck! Come here, Bismarck!' An enormous whiskered hog emerged from the semi-darkness, minced gently up to the fence, and coyly rolled over on the ground to allow Loupin to scratch its belly. The hog had prominent fleshy pads protruding from its cheeks, fringed with light yellowish hair that curved around like a fan. Its huge ears also bore long fringes, which dangled at right angles to the ground. Its coat was patterned russet, black and pale yellow.

Loupin's pride shone from his face. '*Un potamochère*,' he explained. 'Go on, touch him. He doesn't bite.' Bismarck was a red river hog. I had never seen one before and thought him one of the strangest looking creatures I had ever encountered, but his sweet temperament won me. I made appreciative noises and tickled the coarse hair behind his ears.

We had to cut our visit short at that point, as we were expected back at the Roux house for dinner. I extended my hand to Monsieur Loupin and thanked him for an evening I knew I would never forget. Win followed suit: although he hadn't followed much of the rapid-fire French, he'd loved seeing the animals, and he appreciated a genuine eccentric when he met one.

That night, I pondered the hugeness of Loupin's personality. Was it Africa that had made him into such an overblown character? Was that how he had survived life in remote camps? I guessed that his eclectic interests were now what kept him sane amid the mundanity of life as a shopkeeper and airline agent in a place like Makokou. Expatriates had to create their own micro-worlds – there was nothing else for them.

Next day, we shared the pirogue back to Mayebut with Mendoum Dominique, the new man Eamon had recruited to look after rations. He was tall and articulate, with polished European manners. I put his age at around fifty. I was relieved that Eamon had found someone so quickly because it would lighten my workload.

chapter ten

THE CAMP MATURES AND THE WET ARRIVES

On the afternoon of 1 September, a convoy of five heavy vehicles thundered into camp down the new road – a grader, two bulldozers, a Caterpillar tractor/loader and a Unimog, a high-set army-style truck. Eamon had broken camp at the Djadié, and he and his men and their families had arrived to live in camp.

That day marked a turning point: more people and more technology in camp brought increased noise and greater complexity. Eamon assumed his role as *chef de chantier* – camp boss – and moved into Mario's old bedroom in the guesthouse.

The next fortnight became a race against time to push the maximum volume of supplies through on the new road before the onset of the next wet season, which would last three months. There was no bridge at the Djadié River, and the crossing would be submerged once the rains came. Doug hired a fleet of trucks to speed up the process, and consignments of timber, vehicle parts, cement and hardware arrived at the rate of a truckload a day. The deliveries included all the toilet and basin suites for the two houses and six apartments, along with crates of glass louvres for the windows. Mixed in with the hardware were bulk supplies of rice and salt fish to tide us through the wet season.

M'Poko Lucien and I spent entire days checking everything in to the warehouse and updating the inventories – it felt as though we were stocking up for a siege. As we worked together day by day, I came to appreciate M'Poko's quiet sense of humour and his calm, methodical approach more and more. Often the craziness of the situations we faced would leave us shaking our heads, then we would dissolve into laughter and everything would seem all right.

Down in the village, construction of an area of specialist workers' housing was underway. Rodo had the sensitive task of allocating the housing. The position of a man's house on the hillside would reflect his status and qualifications: the highest sites carried the most prestige. Rodo made a series of plan drawings showing which houses would be allocated to whom, and what furniture would be issued. All the houses needed beds, tables, benches and cupboards, which had to be manufactured on-site. With the total population in the village now close to 500 and the demand for furniture relentless, Win allocated four carpenters full-time to the task of furniture production until the needs of every family had been met.

Paydays were also Rodo's responsibility. Each month, on a Saturday, he would spend an entire morning calculating the pays and preparing the 100 pay packets. In the afternoon, he would set himself up at a table outside the guesthouse, where the men would assemble to wait for their names to be called. The calculation of pay was complex –

many men had received advances against their salaries during the month, and accordingly received only the balance remaining on payday. Each time, some would have forgotten about their advances and want to dispute the amount they received. The ensuing palaver always meant that payday stretched out to occupy an entire afternoon. Win and I would watch from the guesthouse and marvel at Rodo's patience and good nature in the face of harassment. When it was all over, we'd invite him to join us for drinks on the porch to recover. In the village, pay nights were celebrated with large amounts of homemade maize and palm wine. These potent drinks quickly banished inhibitions, and outbreaks of violence were common.

With Belinga now a substantial settlement, the workers and their wives increasingly expected the *économat* to stock items they used to buy in town – clothing, babywear, toiletries, double foam mattresses, bicycles, perfume and cooking equipment. Every day people would come to me with new requests, and as fast as stock arrived at the *économat*, it sold.

Meanwhile, Mendoum Dominique needed to establish himself in his new job and keep the workforce fed. On his first day I sat with him and explained the ration system. He understood immediately and was eager to begin, but he'd arrived at a difficult time. The women who produced the manioc out in the villages knew that Mario had left. Unaware of Dominique's appointment, they were reluctant to produce large quantities in case the company closed down and their market evaporated. So they had cut back production.

Accordingly, for the first few weeks, Dominique's manioc-buying trips yielded no more than 400 *bâtons* a week, whereas we needed at least 1200. Compounding the problem, it was around this time – the end of the dry season – when the women worked on their maize and manioc plantations, preparing the ground before the onset of the rains. This left them less time for processing manioc. Dominique had to rely on taro, plantains and rice to make up the shortfall.

In time, the situation improved. Dominique negotiated verbal contracts with the women for set quantities of manioc each week, and built up their trust week by week until they were supplying 1500 to 2500 *bâtons* a week. Since each *bâton* weighed a kilo, the company was buying, transporting and distributing at least a tonne and a half of manioc every seven days.

Bushmeat was still scarce, and the men kept up their mock-serious routine of rubbing their stomachs, assuming a pained expression and declaring, '*Patron*, I'm suffering,' at every opportunity. I wasn't sure who was looking forward more to the arrival of the wet – they or we.

The surveyors' equipment finally arrived in late August. They had lost almost two months of work time because of the delays, and now had to try to catch up. Jacques had resurrected two old Land Rovers for their use, and teams of labourers had worked steadily slashing secondary growth along the old tracks to give them access.

I felt sorry for these four young Englishmen: their job was the most physically demanding, and the terrain they had to map presented endless obstacles. Once out in the forest, they did most of their work on foot, climbing up and down muddy or rock-strewn mountainsides all day with no footholds except roots. They worked in all weathers and endured the incessant onslaught of biting *mouches rouges* and *fourreaux*, along with the ticks and *ghiques* that dropped or crawled inside their clothes as they struggled through the undergrowth. They also faced the ever-present risk of meeting deadly Gaboon vipers or hooded cobras. They had to place every step carefully, as the snakes concealed themselves in leaf litter. To cap off their miseries, the two old Land Rovers regularly broke down, as the rough terrain found their every weak point.

Often I would see the surveyors pull up outside the guesthouse at the end of a day's work, their faces haggard, their clothes torn and drenched in sweat, and their skin covered in pink welts. Their morale grew chronically low and they suffered constant exhaustion. The only one who could still manage to smile and enjoy a joke was Andy, the big Yorkshireman with the curly hair. Whenever I could, I stopped to chat to him, and every few weeks I cut his hair on the porch while we exchanged stories.

During September, Jacques resurrected a third old Land Rover, this time for himself. He christened it the *familiale*, because it seated nine people. The Méhari was passed to Rodo, who shared it with me because he spent so much time in the office. At last I could deliver stock down to the *économat* myself and move around the camp quickly on other tasks. I loved how small and light it was, and I mastered the gears passably well after a couple of lessons from Jacques.

Rodo and I occupied a desk each in the guesthouse. His faced up the hill overlooking the workshops; mine looked out over the old plantations and the forest. After he had conducted rollcall and allocated the teams of labourers to the day's tasks, we often had coffee together at the dining table.

It was only after we had settled into this pattern for several weeks that I realised what a difference his presence in camp had made to me. I had a congenial colleague with a ready sense of humour to share the daily trials with, and he spoke English. Before, I had battled a sense of isolation; now I had a comrade in arms. In the evenings and at weekends, Win, Rodo and I spent time together talking, swapping stories and listening to music on the cassette player. The three of us grew closer and closer with each passing week.

Eamon's store of local knowledge and memory for detail constantly amazed me. He seemed to know things almost before they had happened. If someone's mother-in-law had died in a remote village, if the buffalo were running near M'Vadhi, if the Fang and the Bakwélé were shaping up for a scrap, he would know. He knew where most of the men were born and who were their half-brothers, cousins and enemies. If he wanted to recruit a man who lived in a distant village, he would simply notify that man's best friend, sister or uncle. Soon the grapevine would do its work, and the man – or a message from him – would arrive in the camp. When dealing with the men, he used the tactic of hints and rumours to great effect. A word here or an oblique warning there could be assured of reaching its target with no loss of face to anybody. It was a rare talent. He knew how the men thought, and they would do anything for him.

Eamon and Jacques, for all their toughness and resilience in the work environment, were gentle men off-duty, and their frontier humour was never far from the surface. Around the dinner table each night I took every opportunity to ask them about the old days, especially the wildlife – they had lived through extraordinary times when the camp was in its infancy.

Jacques had given me my first lesson on gorillas back in July. 'Gorillas are calm and unhurried,' he had said. 'They approach their food delicately. In captivity, they are capable of great affection for humans, and often show a powerful need to be cuddled and touched. There have even been cases where gorillas in captivity have died of grief when separated from their long-term carers.' I had listened with awe. How I longed to experience what he had.

He'd said that, in contact with humans, gorillas faced many health risks, and were especially vulnerable to lung complaints. In the wild, gorilla infants were raised with lavish care, and remained clinging to their mothers for two or more years. They didn't breed until they were about eleven years of age. Mature males became 'silverbacks' when the hair on their back turned white, and some males lived to forty or fifty. His emotional account of these gentle giants, who had been maligned and misunderstood for so long in the western imagination, whetted my appetite to see them for myself.

'Tell me more about the gorillas,' I begged Eamon and Jacques after dinner one night. Both men's faces softened, and a tenderness came into Eamon's voice as he spoke.

'Well, we had eight of them here in camp for a long time. Dr Annie Hion was studying them. They became part of the family. We used to play with them and they came everywhere with us. They're so intelligent.'

'What about Arthur?' I prompted.

Eamon laughed, his blue-grey eyes twinkling and his mouth turning up at the corners. 'Arthur's favourite thing was friendly wrestling. He just loved us to wrestle him. He was so powerful we reckoned he was five times as strong as our biggest man, who stood at six feet four. The only way to break loose from Arthur's grasp was to go completely limp all over, then he would know the game was over and he would loosen his grip. Oh, he did love it!'

'What happened to the gorillas in the end?'

Eamon's face clouded. He took a deep breath and sighed, 'Ah well, that's a different story. Annie had been looking after them and studying them for some years. Then there came a time when she had to return to France for a year, so she arranged for them all to be cared for while she was away. But when she came back, every one of them had been killed.'

I sat stunned. I tried to imagine it – the gentle animals who had come to trust humans, slaughtered, in all probability, for their meat. I didn't press Eamon any further. The pain, even after all the intervening years, showed in his face.

The onset of the short wet, on 10 September, afforded a spectacle more awe-inspiring than anything I had ever seen. The clouds had been building up since early morning, and by three o'clock the sky had turned green-black and a solid storm front hung in the north-east. The air seemed to crackle with electricity. Rodo and I left our paperwork and stood side by side on the porch looking out, as a colossal anvil-shaped cloud mass swept towards the camp from the Congo.

Long before it arrived overhead, we heard the roar and drumming of rain on the forest. Ahead of the front, giant trees tossed their crowns wildly, battered by the force of the wind. Some were bent double. A solid curtain of water – silver-grey and opaque – advanced towards us and pounded the forest at the edge of the clearing. Then, just before the storm hit, violent wind gusts tore through the camp, ripping off roofing iron and throwing plastic chairs about like scraps of paper. The wind howled and shrieked through the guesthouse like a living thing, and a murky green light enveloped everything. We watched, transfixed.

Then the air overhead exploded in a thunderous crash, sending shock waves through us, and at once, the sky cracked open and disgorged its load on the camp. We sheltered in the doorway, dumb before its fury. Torrents pounded the corrugated-iron roof, and spouts of water gushed from the end of each corrugation, gouging holes in the red earth where they hit the parched surface. Within half an hour, the dry season's layer of fine red dust had become a coating of greasy red mud.

When the storm had passed, the rain settled to a steady downpour, whipped up now and then by gusts of wind. By nightfall, it had eased. Waterfalls were crashing their way through the forest and down the hillsides. That night, as Win and I lay in bed in the Kombi, we heard the sound of a slow ripping and tearing from the nearby forest, followed by a mighty crash. The ground shook and the Kombi rocked on its tyres. The sound of a forest giant losing its grip on the sodden soil and plummeting to earth was something we would hear often in the weeks that followed. In our tiny clearing in the forest, it made us feel as insignificant as matchsticks.

The rivers rose quickly. The ford at the Djadié was rapidly submerged, so that the new road could only be used by setting up a meeting of two vehicles, one on either side of the river, at a pre-arranged time, and ferrying passengers and cargo across in a pirogue. On the Ivindo, the rapids, sandbanks and rock outcrops were soon covered by a metre of muddy water, allowing us to reach Makokou once more in just three hours.

In mid-September, the carpenters finished the new kitchen and a recreation area in the *cas de passage.* Here, Samba Bernard and Mohibi Léon would keep house for the surveyors and any visitors.

With the growth in size of the camp, maintaining supplies and servicing equipment had become major tasks. In some weeks we used 12,000 litres of diesel fuel, and Jacques now had a fleet of twelve vehicles to maintain. Fortunately, despite the wet, Eamon set the earthworks machines to grading and widening the road to the *débarcadère*. When the work was complete, the old forty-five-minute trip to the *débarcadère* became a thing of the past; it became possible to do the trip in just seventeen minutes.

Win and I were having coffee in the guesthouse one day when Rodo walked in carrying a dead cobra.

'Do you want to have a close look? The surveyors got it out on Bakota South.'

I left my paperwork to peer at the metre-long reptile dangling limply from a stick. The head had been mangled, so the fangs and eyes were just a crushed mass. Étienne and Mambo Bernard put their heads around the kitchen door. They were usually quick to appreciate game meat, but they greeted the snake with silence. I knew many of the people ate snake – even regarded it as a delicacy – so I asked them whether this one would be good to eat.

They shook their heads. 'No, madame! We do not eat that.'

'Oh?' I said. 'Why? Because it's poisonous?'

'No, madame, it's not that—'

'But some people eat them, don't they?'

'Yes, madame, some do, but we don't.'

I wasn't about to give up, as traditional beliefs and practices intrigued me. 'Don't you like it?'

They looked at each other in silence, then back to me, shrugged their shoulders and repeated that they just didn't eat it. Rodo handed it to them, and we watched as they made much of throwing it onto the fire and watching it turn black.

Win looked on with intense interest. He'd often handled snakes back in Brisbane: one of his sons had kept a collection of them in cages in the backyard. For Win, they were beautiful and fascinating, whereas for me they were creatures to be feared and avoided. My childhood understanding of them had been shaped by my grandmother's stories of her early married life 'out on construction' at Oakey on the Darling Downs in Queensland when the western railway line was being built around 1906. The surroundings of their bush home, overgrown with shoulder-high grass, harboured many venomous snakes. Her tales of a deadly red-bellied black curled up under the back stairs or a king brown sunning itself near the clothes line filled my child's mind with terror. Snakes were to be killed, I was taught – a belief that most Australians held as I grew up. Only when Win began educating me about them did I start to see them differently. 'They're more afraid of you than you are of them,' he would tell me in our early days. 'They'll usually get out of your way; they'll only strike if they think you're threatening them.' His respect for them, as for all wildlife, meant that he would never kill one.

I had occasion to witness Win's comfort around snakes just weeks after Rodo had brought the dead cobra into the guesthouse. The two of us were out driving along Bakota South when we spotted the graceful curves of a snake moving across the track ahead. As the sky was overcast and the air cold it moved sluggishly, then stopped altogether when it saw the Kombi. We pulled up just metres away, close enough to have a clear view of its distinctive black and yellow markings. 'It's a cobra!' Win said excitedly. 'See if you can get a shot of it. I'll get out and try to keep it still, but you'll have to hurry.'

The cobra was large – around two metres long – with a small neat head. We knew deadly hooded cobras were endemic to the Belinga area and assumed that this was one, although no hood was visible. Somewhat nervously, I climbed out with the camera slung around my neck. Win had positioned himself in front of the snake, blocking its path to the nearby vegetation. Confronted, it slowly rose up, extended the hood on either side of its head and settled into a ritualised motion of threat, swaying from side to side, its eyes fixed on Win.

'Now don't fiddle around,' Win urged. 'I'm not going to be able to keep it here for long.'

'For God's sake be careful,' I hissed as I fumbled with the camera settings, trying to compensate for the low light. 'They're not aggressive, you know,' Win assured me. 'I wouldn't be doing this if they were. Come on! Hurry up!' Each time I focused afresh the cobra moved and I had to start again, my concentration blurred by fear. The short depth of field dictated by a fully open lens only made the task more difficult. With each passing moment Win's impatience grew, and with it the snake's discomfort at being cornered.

'For pity's sake, get on with it!' Win shouted. 'What the hell are you doing?'

'Trying to get it right. What do you think?' I snapped.

In a languidly beautiful movement I wish I could have appreciated at the time, the cobra ceased swaying, sank to the ground, and began advancing towards Win's feet. He leapt backwards, cursing my procrastination, grabbed a handful of dirt and threw it at the glossy black head. Momentarily distracted, the cobra paused just long enough for me to click twice and retreat to a safer distance. No longer cornered, it changed direction and moved off to disappear into the cover of vegetation.

'Did you get it?'

'I got something, but I don't know whether it'll be any good.'

I had never photographed a snake before, much less a deadly one that was threatening to strike at my husband's legs, and it was not an exercise I was keen to repeat. 'Next time we won't be doing that,' I said tartly as we returned to the Kombi. I should have been used to Win's risk-taking behaviours by then, but they still had the power to annoy me. In contrast, Win was glowing with the excitement of his first cobra encounter. 'I wasn't in any danger,' he insisted. 'It was just telling me to move on.'

It was only months later when Win related the episode

to Eamon Temple that we were brought up with a jolt. Eamon sat poker-faced listening to the whole story, then in his measured Midwestern tones offered one of his heart-stopping retorts: 'You know there are spitting cobras round here, don't you? They can spit venom into your eye from a couple of metres away, and if they get you you're blinded for life. You're just lucky it wasn't one of those.'

There was little we could say at this news, but I hoped it might instil some caution into Win for future occasions. Eamon must have grimaced privately at the audacity of this newcomer to the African forest whose supreme confidence could have cost him so dearly. The ultimate irony was that when I had the film developed, I discovered the shots were grainy and out of focus.

I thought little about Étienne and Bernard's comments about the dead cobra until one day I was chatting to Jacques' plumber, Lougué-Lougué Marcel, about various types of game meat, and he told me he didn't eat a certain animal.

'And why is that?' I asked.

'Where I come from, we don't eat that.' I couldn't persuade him to tell me why. These food taboos – for that is what I believe they were – reminded me of something Mary Kingsley had written. She described a Gabonese custom whereby each person was allocated a forbidden food at birth or in infancy that they were prohibited from eating for life. The food differed from person to person; abstinence from it was intended as a sacrifice to the spirit governing the person's life. In Kingsley's day, most people adhered strictly to this custom, as any lapse could result in misfortune. The belief was widespread, and the consequences of breaking the taboo greatly feared. I could only speculate whether this custom underlay the two conversations I'd had.

I often chatted with Mendoum Dominique about subjects unrelated to work, as he was articulate and precise in expressing himself. If anybody could explain to me the intricacies of traditional beliefs, I thought, perhaps he could. So one day I decided to try. I began with some general questions about local belief systems. I had barely started when his eyes widened and he became tense and guarded. He took a step back, put up his hands and declared, 'Anyway, I'm a Christian, so it's no use asking me!' He repeated this several times, declaring that the Good Lord was his God and that he left all that traditional nonsense to others. I felt myself blush and changed the subject immediately. From then on I never asked people directly about their beliefs, and resigned myself to learning what I could piecemeal.

Not long after that conversation, Dominique received a large advance on his salary to cover the cost of his daughter's treatment by a traditional healer near Makokou. The girl was gravely ill. As she had not responded to western medical treatments, he had taken her to the healer, where she spent three weeks being treated. Dominique related all this to me on his return. I listened carefully but asked no questions. I guessed that the girl was considered to be suffering spirit possession, a paralysing condition that some of our workers had experienced. It made them lethargic, fearful for their lives and unable to carry out their normal daily activities. Under Gabonese law, spirit possession was an illness for which workers were entitled to time off to be treated. In these cases, western medicine had nothing to offer.

As time passed, we found that traditional beliefs often emerged unexpectedly in the midst of everyday situations. One day, one of the men asked to be driven out into the forest to bring in a leopard he had caught in a trap. We took the Toyota utility, and the man and several other hunters rode in the back. When we arrived at the spot, there was a large antelope with its leg snared in a *piège* – a wire trap – but no sign of a leopard.

'Where's the leopard?' I asked. The man looked sheepish, mumbled something and turned his head away – the leopard story had evidently been a ruse to persuade us to use the Toyota to save them carrying the carcass back on foot.

We stood at a discreet distance and waited for the hunter to kill the antelope. It bellowed in pain and fear as he twisted its head around to expose the throat for slitting, but then he froze, his face covered in sweat and his eyes wide. He remained bent over the animal for some minutes, paralysed, before calling to one of the other hunters to kill the beast for him. I turned away, unable to watch. When it was all over and the carcass loaded into the Toyota, I asked him why he had not killed the antelope himself.

'*Ma femme est enceinte*,' he explained – my wife is pregnant – as if that clarified everything. On the way back to camp, I mulled over what it could mean. Was it similar to the taboo the people observed on eating eggs? Eggs were never eaten but always fed back to the chickens. Was this about the sanctity of unborn life? Each time we witnessed these traditional beliefs in action, I realised afresh how little I knew about the world view of the people, and how little seemed to have changed since Mary Kingsley's time.

* * *

By the end of September, Win had finished work on our flat at the eastern end of the old sample shed. It was one large room with a shower and toilet to one side and a bare concrete floor. Along the northern wall, louvre windows revealed a view out over the old plantations to the forest and mountains. The flat was insect-screened and equipped with a stove, a fridge, a double bed and a wardrobe with a light bulb inside to prevent mildew growing on our clothes. We set up our camping table and chairs at the kitchen end and our radio cassette player on the bench, then unpacked all the crockery, appliances and linen we had bought in Libreville three months before. Our long-awaited privacy had come at last. I could escape from the daily chaos if I needed to. It was cause for celebration.

It was a destiny day for another reason, too – I had turned thirty. Rodo, in his characteristically thoughtful way, had made me a birthday card and secretly organised Étienne to bake me a cake. We'd invited him in for a celebratory drink in the flat that afternoon; when he arrived at the door, he held the cake high over his head and sang 'Happy Birthday' in his gravelly bass voice.

I hugged him hard, thrilled that he had gone to the trouble. Win put on one of our classical music tapes, and the three of us sat at the table eating the cake and looking out over the forest.

During the three months since we had arrived, I felt I had been in a crucible, tested at every turn. It was as if all the outer layers of myself that I had carried around for so many years had been stripped away, and I had come face to face with my inner self for the first time. I'd discovered I possessed a kernel of toughness. The more I had engaged with the challenges of helping to run the camp, the more my confidence had grown.

Although I didn't yet know it, on that landmark birthday, I was poised for the greatest change of my life, and the three of us – Rodo, Win and I – would be bonded forever by events that would unfold in the weeks to come.

chapter eleven

Josie

It was a Sunday evening early in October. Win and I had spent the day relaxing in the flat, relishing our new-found privacy and the space to spread out after living in the Kombi for six months. Win had listened to a Rachmaninov piano concerto while I wrote letters home to my family, trying to paint a picture for them of what our life in camp was like. I regularly wrote to all our friends back in Australia and England, determined to maintain the relationships despite our isolation. Letters from the outside world had assumed a great importance for us since we had arrived in camp: apart from the radio, they were all we had to connect us to everything we had known before. Back in Australia, Win had new grandchildren he had never seen. Each time the mail pouch arrived on the pirogues, we waited impatiently to see if there were any letters for us.

Rodo had driven down to Mayebut that afternoon for a few hours' respite from the demands of the camp. From our flat, we could see the final bend of the road that led up from the *débarcadère.* We had been watching for his return, and when he hadn't arrived by six o'clock, we became concerned. Then we heard the crunch of the Toyota hitting second gear halfway up the hill. Instead of driving straight down to the *cas de passage*, he skirted the guesthouse and braked to a halt outside our front door. We heard the car door open and the sound of his boots running on the laterite outside. Something was wrong. We both felt it.

We threw open the door just as he reached it. His face was white with shock. He said nothing, but motioned us to follow him to the car. When he opened the door on the passenger side and stood back, we saw in the half-light what had brought him to this state. A tiny black figure sat hunched up on the seat, cowering. I took in the leathery texture of its face, the roundness of the head, and the way its legs and arms were drawn tightly up to its body as if to protect itself. Although we had never seen one before, the features were unmistakable. It was a baby gorilla – and it was in crisis. Its body was wracked with tremors, and its filthy, matted coat gave off the stench of infection.

For some moments, all we could do was stare. Thoughts tumbled through my mind. How did it come to be here? What do we do? Then Rodo leaned forward to pick it up. As he did, the infant looked up listlessly, then stretched out its arms to him in a gesture of inexpressible pathos. He gathered the baby to his chest, where it clung with a desperation that moved us close to tears.

'What happened?' I managed to ask.

'One of the Bakwélé men at Mayebut tried to sell it to me. They shot the mother three days ago for raiding their banana plantation, and they've kept the baby in a hut ever since, tied up around the groin with a rough liana.'

'How could anybody bear to do this?' I thought. 'Have they no compassion?'

Win stroked the infant's head gently and tried to comfort it with soft crooning sounds.

'I didn't pay them,' Rodo said. 'I told them we'd talk about that later. I just wanted to get it out of there.'

We stood in silence. The three of us had talked about gorillas so often, about how much we wanted to see one, but we had never imagined it would happen this way. In the face of the infant's trauma, I felt helpless. We had no equipment, facilities or expertise to deal with the situation.

'We'd better check with Eamon to make sure he's happy for us to keep it,' Rodo said. 'It's a big commitment, and it won't be easy.'

Eamon lay stretched out on his bed reading. We walked in and stood silently at his door. Normally he would have smiled and greeted us with some quirky comment, but when he looked up and saw what Rodo was nursing, he jerked bolt upright. We waited for him to speak. He looked hard at the infant and shook his head. 'Oh my lord, where did it come from?' I saw the same sadness in his eyes I'd seen when he'd spoken about the gorilla deaths in the 1960s. He met Rodo's eyes and must have realised at once that he'd set his heart on caring for the infant. Eamon seemed on the point of saying something – I sensed he wanted to warn us to beware of caring too much. Instead, he nodded and simply said, 'Make sure you keep it warm.'

Our little orphan was a female, about the size of a three-month-old human child. Rodo set her down on the long wooden table on the porch, where a single light bulb gave off a dingy glow. She sat hunched up, her arms locked around her body, grinding her teeth. She had a tiny wizened face and a grip of iron. Her eyelids slowly opened and closed as though she was utterly exhausted. Win stroked her head and back, trying to reassure her.

'I want to get a good look at her and see where the septic smell is coming from,' Win said. 'I'll try rolling her over on her back, and if you two can keep her there, that'll help.' Our first attempt was not encouraging. When we laid her on her back she screamed, flailed her legs and arms, rolled herself back on to her belly and sat up.

'I don't want to stress her more than she already is,' Win said, 'but we've got to keep trying.' On the third attempt, Rodo held her arms against the table and I steadied her legs. She squirmed and struggled, registering her protests with a series of lusty screams. In spite of all she had been through, her spirit and strength seemed to be intact.

She was in a pitiful state. Her backside was smeared with dried excrement, and a deep wound, 8 centimetres long and 2.5 centimetres wide, ran the length of her left groin where she had chafed against her tether. The wound oozed pus and was matted with filth and twigs. Her skin and flesh had been sliced through to the hip joint.

'I'd say she's been tied up for much longer than three days,' Win said. 'It looks more like a week to me. And we don't know whether she has internal injuries either.' I had never been faced with an injured animal before. As we bent over her, the importance of our role in her life hit me. She wasn't just any animal, she was a great ape – so like us – and a member of a threatened species. Her survival probably depended on what we could do that night.

'We've got to do something,' Win said. 'If we wait to take her down to the vet in Makokou in the morning, it might be too late.' He looked across at me. 'Can you get our first-aid kit?'

It was almost seven o'clock, dinner time, but we had no thought of food. I arrived back with the first-aid kit to find Win peering at the wound. 'That's not going to heal by itself. It's just too big. It should be stitched.' Our comprehensive kit included sutures and a curved surgical needle. Win stared fixedly out into the darkness for perhaps a minute, then murmured, 'If you two can hold her still, I'll stitch her myself.'

The table on the porch became our operating theatre. We covered it with an old woollen blanket and put a pillow under her hips.

'How're we going to keep her calm and still?' I said. 'She's so strong, she's going to fight like hell.'

'Good question. We need a sedative of some kind.' Around us the insects droned. Flying termites hit the light bulb and dropped onto our heads. The isolation of our situation pressed in even more than usual.

'There is one possibility.' Win perked up. 'We've got plenty of red wine. A cupful just might do it.'

Rodo fetched a bottle of Bordeaux and a plastic cup from the kitchen while Win rummaged around in the first-aid kit to find the eye-dropper. As she lay on her back with the two of us bracing her arms and legs against the table, Win squirted the wine into her mouth, a few drops at a time. She shook her head from side to side and struggled to break free. Several times, she almost succeeded in biting on the eye-dropper with her sharp teeth, but each time Win withdrew it just in time. An hour passed before she swallowed the last of the wine and grew drowsy.

I filled a bowl with warm water and set out disinfectant

and cotton wool, then Win set to work swabbing out the pus and debris. The wound was the size of a fat cigar, and so deep that the bone of her hip joint lay exposed.

Win stared at it in dismay. 'I'm not even sure it's possible to stitch a wound this size without a clamp to hold the sides together.' The first step was to prepare the margins of the wound for stitching. I disinfected a pair of surgical scissors and Win trimmed away the thick black hair from the edges.

'I'm going to fill the wound with antiseptic cream to try and combat the infection,' he said. 'It's a bit unorthodox, but it's worth a try.' Then he threaded the curved needle with a suture and looked up at us both. 'Are you ready? Just hang on to her tightly now – we don't know how she'll react to the pain.' Rodo and I held our breath as Win used all his strength to push the first stitch through her tough skin. She was still conscious and her eyes open, but to our amazement and relief, she didn't as much as flinch. However a moment later she jerked her bottom suddenly to one side, causing the stitch to cut through the flesh and give way.

'That's okay,' Win said. 'I know now that it was too close to the edges. I'll go further in with the next one.' Meanwhile, he had worked out a way around the problem of holding the sides together without a clamp. He would space out the first eight stitches widely, then put additional ones in between to finish off.

It was painstaking and slow work. Each stitch was separately tied off. After an hour, just ten were in place. But our fears about inflicting pain on her proved groundless. She appeared to feel nothing. About nine-thirty, Eamon came out to watch. It must have been a bizarre sight – a builder sewing up a gorilla by the dim light of a sixty-watt bulb, showered with termites. Eamon's dry sense of humour was never far from the surface. In a quiet, deadpan voice, he quipped: 'Well, I don't suppose there'd be many folks back in Brisbane sewing up a gorilla tonight!' Despite ourselves, we dissolved into helpless laughter. Eamon stood watching a little longer, then, suddenly serious, turned to Win. 'I commend you for your compassion.' Then he went inside to bed.

By ten-thirty, the twentieth stitch was in place and the wound had been completely closed. Win had been bending over her for three hours. He straightened up, arched his back and massaged his aching muscles while Rodo and I released our hold on her arms and legs. We had no idea what to expect. Would she try to escape? Would she collapse from stress? As we watched, these fears melted away. She simply rolled over onto her belly, sat up sleepily, and wrapped her arms around her chest.

We had not eaten or drunk since lunch, and we'd been tending to her for almost four hours. Fatigue was beginning to take over, but our elation overrode it. Everything had gone far better than we had dared to hope. She hadn't gone into shock and there had been no bleeding. As Win stroked her head and back and talked softly to her, she relaxed and closed her eyes.

In those four intense hours we had bonded with her, and with each other even more strongly. If she made it through the night, we would try between us to give her whatever she needed to survive. Just before eleven, Rodo gathered her up in the woollen blanket and took her down to his bedroom.

I put my arm around Win's shoulders and kissed his cheek. 'I'm so proud of you, sweetheart. That took real courage, compassion and skill.'

With his usual modesty, he made light of it. 'Well, it remains to be seen whether she pulls through. Tomorrow should tell.'

Rodo carried our small patient up to the guesthouse in the morning in the bed he had created for her – a sturdy cardboard box lined with the red woollen blanket. Her eyes were bright and she seemed relaxed. I had just finished breakfast.

'Well, how was it?' I asked.

'You really want to know? I made up this bed for her and settled her into it. I thought she'd feel cosy and safe in it, but as soon as I turned out the light she got out and tried to climb into my bed. I put her back. We did this for about three hours, until she finally wore me down. As soon as I let her climb in beside me, she fell asleep. I woke up this morning to the find the sheets smelly and soaked with her urine.'

'How're you going to keep this up?'

'I don't know, Nettie. We'll just hope it gets better.'

He placed her in the box out on the porch, where the early morning sun gave some warmth. I pulled up a chair and sat beside her, marvelling at how much she had improved in just twelve hours. Already, word of her arrival had spread through the camp. All the surveyors came up to see her, then some of the carpenters and several labourers. I watched their faces light up with wonder when they saw her. She had an extraordinary effect on people.

Étienne and Bernard fussed over her like a new baby, and cut a small piece of sugar cane for her. She reached out and grasped it gently, turned it over and over, and explored its texture and smell. When she was satisfied it might be good to eat, she put it to her mouth and started chewing on one end. Then she systematically pulled off the fibrous outer layer of the stalk with her sharp teeth to reach the sweetness inside.

Despite Rodo's lack of sleep, his whole attention was focused on her needs. He asked Étienne's advice about how best to give her milk: our milk supply was tins of evaporated milk mixed with water. Étienne, with his gift for nurturing, knew what to do at once. He found an empty plastic detergent bottle, soft to the touch and with a hole at the top. Together, they made up a batch of milk with warm water. She was resting in her box. Rodo held the bottle to her lips and squirted small amounts into her mouth at a time. She took it eagerly, licked her lips and reached for more.

'She must have been severely dehydrated when you found her,' I said. 'No wonder she's thirsty.' Rodo talked to her soothingly while she finished the whole bottle, as Étienne stood at the kitchen door and watched, his face lit with joy. Then Rodo fed her chunks of a banana that Étienne had cut up. She took each one carefully in her hand, put it in her mouth and chewed it slowly. I remembered what Jacques had said, that gorillas were unhurried and approached their food delicately. Like Rodo, I found it almost impossible to tear myself away from watching her. Each gesture and expression revealed a little more about her: I didn't want to miss a moment of it. I felt intoxicated by the privilege of having a great ape in our care.

Rodo asked me to check with Kruger at the morning radio session what the going price was for a baby gorilla. The people at Mayebut had wanted 15,000 CFAs (US$65) for her. Kruger's answer came back in his flat monotone, 'The purchase or sale of gorillas is absolutely prohibited under Gabonese law, Madame 'Enderson.' It was the ammunition Rodo needed. Next time he went to Mayebut, he would tell them.

Throughout the morning, we both stayed close to her to monitor her physical and mental state. Her enthusiasm for food was an encouraging sign. Better still, she could climb out of the box by herself and knuckle-walk around the room with no sign of a limp. However, her anxiety of the night before had resurfaced – she ground her teeth constantly. As long as she could see us, she remained in her bed, but when we moved to the next room, she climbed out and followed, screaming. When she caught up, she stopped and sat with her shoulders hunched and arms clasped tightly around her body, and rocked back and forth on her bottom. Her fear of abandonment seemed all-consuming.

In the wild, gorilla infants cling to their mothers' bodies for at least two years. If she were to survive and thrive, her care was going to be a full-time job.

'I'll just work in the office for the next few days,' Rodo said, 'until she settles in.' When Étienne had cleared away the breakfast things, Rodo spread out his geological maps on the dining room table to work until lunchtime, while she lay tucked up in her bed close by the legs of his chair.

Win hurried down from the workshop at lunchtime, eager to see her, and I watched the joy flood his face. 'She looks amazingly bright, considering what she's been through! How's she been this morning?'

Rodo looked down at her indulgently. 'She's had a bottle of milk and a whole banana.'

Win bent down and stroked her head. Any gentle touch seemed to soothe her. She closed her eyes and sighed deeply. 'I'd guess she's about four months old. How's the leg going?'

Rodo looked up with a wide grin: 'She's not even limping.'

Over coffee, we talked about possible names for her.

'She's gentle and delicate,' I said. 'It should be something feminine. What about Josephine?' We all liked that, so it was soon settled, and she would be called Josie for short.

Win felt that the wound should be bathed each day for a week to keep it clean, so in the late afternoon we set up a low wooden table outside with a bowl of warm water and disinfectant, some cotton wool and a clean towel. Rodo held her on her side while I did the bathing. The wound looked clean and healthy, with no discharge. All the stitches had held firmly, and Josie seemed unaware they were there. When I'd finished, she sat up, folded her arms, and met my eyes with a lingering look that seemed to say, 'I'm tired of all this fuss. Can't I just sleep?'

By then, the air had grown chilly. We knew she had to be kept warm or she could develop pneumonia. I thought for a while, then remembered an old woollen singlet I had tucked away in the flat. If I could adapt it to fit her, I calculated it just might work.

The singlet was twice as long as she was. I cut the lower half off so it came just to her bottom, tied a knot at the top of each armhole to make it smaller, then slipped the singlet over her head and slid her arms through the holes. It fitted perfectly, and to our relief, she accepted it with no fuss.

We sat with her in the guesthouse until dinnertime. Josie had been with us just twenty-four hours, yet already it seemed much longer. She made her need for bodily contact plain at every opportunity – leaving her bed, making her way across to Rodo and climbing unaided on to his lap, where she wrapped her arms tightly around his chest.

For a second night, Rodo barely slept. Josie spent most of the night climbing around the furniture and grinding her teeth, and only dropped off to sleep when she was allowed into his bed. In the morning, he discovered she couldn't be left alone in the bedroom while he showered and shaved. She screamed and shrieked, threw herself around in panic and knocked over furniture. In the end, he asked one of the surveyors to sit with her.

On the second day, the beginnings of a routine developed. Étienne had kept the leftovers from the dining room for her. She ate the boiled rice and cooked vegetables from a bowl on the floor, bent over it on all fours with her bottom in the air. She had a voracious appetite and finished every morsel. Then Rodo fed her a bottle of milk while he ate his own breakfast. Afterwards he took her outside to relieve herself.

That day, we gained another insight into her needs when Rodo handed her a whole raw carrot. She grasped it gently with both hands, focused all her concentration on it, then turned it over and over, exploring the smell and texture. But instead of biting into it, she started to play with it. For half an hour, she passed it from one hand to the other, dropped it and picked it up again. Then she tossed it on the floor without having taken a single bite.

'I think she needs some toys,' Rodo said. 'Have we got

anything?' He rummaged in the back of the sideboard and found an old ping-pong ball which he put in the box beside her. She picked it up with both hands, delicately rotated it and examined it closely before putting it down. During the morning, she picked it up and played with it again several times. It was clear she needed mental stimulation. Rodo searched the guesthouse, and by lunchtime had collected a small plastic bottle, some cotton reels, another ball and an old tape measure. That afternoon, she sat on the floor and picked each one up in turn, minutely exploring their shapes and textures. As we observed her intense concentration, single-mindedness and fine motor skills, it was impossible not to be awed by the sophistication of her brain.

By the third morning, Rodo had developed dark rings under his eyes. Josie's night behaviour had not settled, and he was becoming increasingly exhausted. But that morning we saw a marked change in her. She seemed more independent, content to stay in her box bed for longer periods or move about the room by herself, picking up whatever she found on the floor. Étienne and Bernard both gave her lots of attention and made sure she had food and drink. She had become used to the guesthouse environment, and seemed less anxious and fretful.

It was the moment to try an experiment to test her independence. We left her in the guesthouse with Étienne and Bernard and went about our normal tasks around camp for the first time in three days. It proved to be a milestone – she managed to tolerate our absence for a whole hour before becoming agitated.

We learned the boundaries of her tolerance by trial and error. Our next step was to see what would happen if Win,

Rodo and I all went outside, whether she would come with us. The three of us walked out the guesthouse door towards the clothes line. She followed on all fours, screeching in frustration. When she had almost caught up, we moved a few paces further and she repeated the routine. The third time, her frustration erupted into a full-scale tantrum. She threw herself on the ground, flailed her legs and arms in the air and screamed louder than ever. When we turned and moved back towards her, the transformation was instant. She sat up, looked at us, and grew perfectly calm again.

Each scrap of behaviour gave us a deeper understanding of her needs and psychological state. By the end of that day, her teeth-grinding had almost ceased.

On the fourth day, Rodo could neglect his work no longer. He needed to spend the entire day out of camp, leaving Josie and me to spend the day together. As I had a pile of paperwork to catch up on, I hoped she would let me get on with it.

I settled her in the blanket-lined box in the corner with all her toys, then sat down at my desk. In seconds she had climbed out and was knuckle-walking towards me. My eyes met hers, and she fixed me with her steady gaze. I knew it was going to be a battle of wills, and I doubted I could win. I walked over, picked her up and placed her back in the box, making soft crooning noises to soothe her. Meanwhile, Étienne and Bernard watched, amused, from the kitchen door.

'*Elle ne veut pas rester toute seule, madame!*' Étienne said. It was true – being by herself was the last thing she wanted.

On her next attempt, I ignored her until she reached the legs of my chair, where she sat quite still and looked up at me. I picked her up and we repeated the routine. Back at the box, I handed her the ping-pong ball, but she simply focused her gaze on me and held it. If she were going to be part of the Belinga family, I reasoned, she would have to learn some independence. Over the following hour, we repeated this sequence many times, and I didn't manage to do any work. In the end, I could no longer ignore her need.

She came over and paused beside my right leg, looking up. I looked into her eyes, made soft encouraging sounds, and patted my lap. She placed one hand on my thigh, gripped the leg of the chair with one foot, then the other, and climbed up. When she reached my lap, she placed her head and chest against my abdomen and wrapped her arms tightly around my waist. I felt her relax instantly. She breathed out a deep sigh, and I felt the rise and fall of her breathing against my stomach. All my nurturing impulses flooded to the surface. This was the first time I had held her. Was this how new mothers felt when they first held their child? I stroked her back softly with the tips of my fingers, then she nestled in and drifted off to sleep.

I forgot the paperwork and lifted my gaze to the windows above the desk and the view of forest-covered mountains. At that moment, meeting Josie's needs seemed the most important thing in the world. Her presence in our lives was a gift. How many people had held a great ape in their arms? I thought back to the sequence of events that had brought us here, to this wilderness, to this moment, caring for this orphaned creature whose brain and biology so closely matched our own. My thoughts were interrupted by a tiny movement as Josie adjusted her body against mine. I ran the fingers of my left hand up and down her back. With my right hand, I picked up a pen and wrote out an order for the following week's food.

That afternoon, to our dismay, Josie developed a runny nose and a cough. Étienne lit a fire in the guesthouse and we kept the doors and windows closed against the damp air. Josie moved over close to the fireplace and sat quite still, letting the heat seep into her bottom and back. Our drug cabinet, which held the bulk supplies of pharmaceuticals for the *infirmerie*, contained packets of children's aspirin and bottles of decongestant cough mixture. I marked out one bottle of cough mixture and a packet of aspirin to Josie in the drug register, and we began four-hourly doses.

Even this gave us fresh insights into her fine motor skills and lively intelligence. Each time we prepared to give her a teaspoonful of cough syrup, she reached out towards the spoon, gently grasped the handle and helped to guide it to her mouth. She must have loved the sweet syrupy taste, because she licked the spoon dry each time. That afternoon we started her on halves of aspirin tablets crushed up and mixed with jam.

As the days went by, Rodo lost more and more sleep. The dark rings around his eyes deepened, and he walked around in a daze. Although Josie had settled in well, she still couldn't be left with Étienne and Bernard for more than an hour. Beyond that, she would start screeching and running backwards and forwards trying to find us. The crisis came one day when she was left alone in the guesthouse for just ten minutes. Rodo returned to find his desk and all his papers smeared with her excrement. She had panicked, climbed on the desk, and tried to get out the window.

So we devised a roster system. Rodo would have her in the early mornings and nights, I would take her with me everywhere during workdays, and Win would look after her on Sundays.

We also agreed on a daily routine. Immediately after breakfast Rodo would bring her around to our flat, by which time I would be ready for work and take her into the office. She would have been fed and toileted already, so all I had to do was keep her near me. Her feeding had become much simpler. She had a permanent saucer of milk on the floor, which she lapped at whenever she wished. In the mornings and afternoons, she ate half a chopped banana and some vegetables, which she managed by herself, and at other times she had a bowl of boiled rice.

There was never any doubt about when and how often she needed the comfort of bodily contact. When Rodo was in the office, she would sit under his chair with both arms wrapped around one of his legs, and rest her head against him with her eyes closed. When I was in the office on my own, she would approach my chair obliquely or from behind, very slowly, without a sound. The first inkling I would have that she was there would be the feather-light touch of her hands closing around my leg, or one hand placed softly on my thigh as she paused in her climb halfway up the chair leg. Occasionally, she would climb in between my back and the back of the chair and curl up against me for as long as I sat there. But her favourite position was the lap embrace, where she sat facing me with her legs curled up and pressing into my stomach, her chest against mine, and her arms locked around my waist. That position gave her the maximum reassurance. She would remain there indefinitely without moving or taking any notice of what was happening in the room. She and I developed a regular routine: I would scratch her back lightly, she would relax her hold and drop off into a half-sleep. I could manage this quite easily while I sat at the desk operating the radio or writing.

She only became agitated when I moved about the room and didn't take her with me. If I left her on the chair, she would screech, climb down, and run after me. I learned that the best way to keep her calm was simply to let her cling to me all the time. When I stood up she simply clung tighter, as she would have in the wild. This allowed me to move about the room and still have both hands free.

I wasn't sure how she would cope when I took her in the Méhari for the first time on my routine deliveries to the *cas de passage* and the *économat*, and my trips up to the warehouse to work with M'Poko Lucien. But she took to it without a hiccup. When I drove, she sat perfectly still on my lap. When I walked around camp, she rode on my hip or sat with her bottom on my hand, clinging to my forearm. In that position she could see everything, and seemed to enjoy being swung. When I worked up in the warehouse, she sat quietly nearby and watched. With each day, my bond with her grew. Each morning I looked forward to the warm feeling of her body clinging to mine.

After a week, her wound had healed well. All the stitches were intact, there was no sign of infection, and her daytime behaviour was placid and relaxed. On the Sunday morning, a burst of bright sunlight broke through the thick cloud, bringing the first warm temperatures we had had all week.

Sundays were Win's day to look after Josie, to give Rodo

and me a break. They were also his only chance to relax and listen to classical music on the cassette player. Sundays had become even more precious for him since his work schedule had grown more demanding. He drove himself hard to meet all the project deadlines, and the fatigue showed on his face.

But this Sunday he announced, 'I'm going to give her a bath.' Josie had adjusted so well that she was content just to sit and watch while Win assembled everything on the wooden table out in the sun – a bowl of warm water, soap, a sponge and a towel. He rolled her on her back and she lay perfectly still while he sponged her all over. I sat nearby, taking in every small detail, full of wonder at her trust in us. He rubbed her down and applied a coat of antiseptic cream along the line of stitches, then they sat together in the sun while her coat dried.

When Josie was warm and dry, he picked her up and carried her into the flat. I watched as he chose a Tchaikovsky piano concerto and settled back to listen in a reclining chair with Josie face-down on his chest while he stroked her head and back.

The sunshine gave me a perfect opportunity to tackle a week's worth of dirty clothes. We still had no washing machine, so I lined up my usual row of plastic dishes and squeezed things by hand. The strains of Tchaikovsky reached me through the window of the flat, and because there was no work done on Sundays, the camp lay at peace, with just occasional bird calls echoing over the forest. I realised that the tumult of the first three months was now behind us, and I had begun to regain a sense of calm.

I returned to the flat to find Win and Josie both fast asleep in the chair, the sweeping phrases of the music washing over them. My eyes filled with tears as I thought back to what Josie had gone through. Now she was safe, and she knew she was in a caring environment. She'd made a remarkable recovery. Her capacity for learning had astounded us, and her human-like responses filled us constantly with wonder.

Meanwhile, Rodo grasped his first chance in a week to have some unbroken sleep. Before lunch, he joined us in the flat for drinks around the camping table. Josie, by then wide awake, sat on Win's lap. She was content just to sit still while we talked, calmly watching everything we did. But the sight of Win pouring beer into a glass caught her attention. She focused hard on him as he put the glass to his lips, then she stood on tiptoe, balancing herself on his legs, and reached out for the glass. Wrapping both hands firmly around it, she pulled it carefully towards her mouth. I had difficulty remembering she was a great ape and not a human child as Win guided the glass to her lips and she took a sip. When she had swallowed, she settled back on her haunches and looked around at each of us in turn.

Twice more in the hour that followed, she did the same thing. I thought back to what Eamon and Peter Telfair had told us – that Arthur the gorilla used to sit with them in the evenings and drink a glass of beer. When I had first heard it, I was convinced they were exaggerating.

After lunch, Win took her by the hand and walked her slowly from the flat down the grassy embankment, behind the clothes line, and up the slope to the edge of the tree line. He was concerned that her diet of human food might be deficient and that she might need more exercise. Thick secondary growth had sprung up in the clearing since Mario had had the helicopter pad made: plants with bright pink fruits at their base grew among a jumble of greenery. We knew they were a type of ginger that gorillas loved to eat.

Win let go of Josie's hand and she sat for some minutes looking around and smelling the forest for the first time in a week. The sight and smell of growing things must have stirred some of her earlier memories. Dappled sunlight played on her skin, moist rotting leaves were soft under her feet, and the buzz of insects droned in the afternoon stillness. Win stood perfectly still, careful not to distract her. She looked back at him, checking he was still there, then slowly began to crawl around, stopping here and there to pick tiny shoots, which she delicately placed on her tongue and chewed thoroughly before swallowing. At intervals she turned around to confirm that Win was nearby. Eventually, she found the bright pink fruits. She made for them unhesitatingly, picked one, and carefully prised out the flesh and placed it in her mouth.

She didn't range far, but seemed totally absorbed in the forest world. When she had eaten enough, she sat down, drew her knees up to her chin, crossed her arms and looked up at Win as if to indicate, 'Well, I'm finished. What now?'

I watched them at the forest's edge – Josie relaxed and calm, Win understanding her needs and giving her the chance to follow her instincts – and I marvelled at the miracle of their perfect communication. As the three of us walked hand in hand slowly back to the flat I felt like we were a family.

In the weeks that followed, I took Josie everywhere with me. Although her cold lingered, she seemed otherwise healthy. When I had washing to hang out, she came with me to the line and sat nearby on the grass. Each time I went out in the Méhari, she sat quietly in my lap. I had become so accustomed to her snuggling into me as I sat at the desk that sometimes I almost forgot she was there.

At first, I didn't stop to seriously consider how long Rodo could sustain his stoical tolerance of Josie's night behaviour. He rarely spoke about it. At midnight every night she would become playful and start cavorting around the bedroom; at dawn she would eventually tire. He lost more and more sleep, his bed linen and clothes were continually soaked with her urine, and he struggled to focus on work during the day. We all knew the situation could not continue indefinitely, but we pushed that thought to the back of our minds. There was no question of confining her to a cage: that would have killed her as surely as a hunter's bullet. In time, we came to the painful realisation that her long-term care required more resources than we had available.

Two unrelated events brought things to a head. First, Doug made one of his regular visits to review progress on the building program and the clearing of survey tracks. He told us that a party of senior technical specialists would soon visit the camp for several days, and that the smell of gorilla urine in the guesthouse could not be allowed to remain. We needed to find another home for Josie before they arrived. That same week, Jacques' family had finally arrived in Makokou and had moved into a large house. He knew the problems Rodo was having and offered a solution: his wife and three daughters had heard all about Josie and they wanted desperately to have her. She would find a loving home there with four people to share her care, he assured us.

It was a prospect we could barely contemplate. We loved her, we were responsible for her, and she had bonded with the three of us. Another change of circumstances might prove too great an adjustment for her. Every few days, Jacques reminded us of his offer. Then one Friday the decision could no longer be postponed. Josie would go down with Jacques to Makokou on the pirogue that afternoon.

I went about my work that morning weighed down with sadness. The wrench of having to part with her was almost too much to bear. She sat calmly on my hip while we moved about, unaware that her world would soon change completely. The three of us felt protective of her and afraid for her – letting her go felt like betrayal. We had no way of knowing whether she would adjust to the change, or be cared for as we had cared for her.

Rodo, Win and I made the trip to the *débarcadère* in the Méhari, with Josie occupying her usual place on my lap. When we arrived, the pirogue was waiting. Jacques supervised the loading of some empty fuel drums and iceboxes. Rodo stood silently on the riverbank. Josie, still in her woollen singlet, clung tightly to his leg with her eyes shut, almost as if she knew something was wrong. When all was ready, Rodo gave Jacques some food and drink for her for the journey, then handed her into his arms.

She clung tightly to him as he boarded the pirogue. The three of us stood together on the bank and watched as it moved slowly into the middle of the river. Then the outboard kicked in and the pirogue gathered speed. Her tiny form against Jacques' chest grew smaller and smaller until they rounded the bend and disappeared from view.

Each of us was too full of emotion to speak and we drove back to camp in silence. The parting had been inevitable, but that didn't ease the pain. Josie's time with us had been a journey of love, discovery and compassion, enriching us beyond anything we could have imagined. Now there was a void.

I was impatient to get to the radio the next morning to hear how Josie had fared on the trip downriver, and how she had responded to her new environment. The pain of separation lay heavily on me, compounded by a sense of guilt that somehow we had let her down. She had trusted us, and in the end we could not continue to give her the care she needed. My body felt like lead as I walked across to the guesthouse and switched on the radio. I missed her warm body clinging to me, her soft touch on my leg, and the routines we had shared.

'*Makokou de Belinga, Makokou de Belinga!* Jacques, do you receive me?'

'*Belinga de Makokou, Belinga de Makokou!* Receiving you, Nettie.'

'How is she, Jacques?'

'She handled the river trip well, Nettie, and she's doing fine.'

'That's great news, Jacques. Keep us posted, won't you?'

'Roger, Nettie, will do. Talk to you again at five.'

It was Saturday and I had a lot to do. Although I welcomed the distraction of work, I kept looking at my watch, waiting for the five o'clock radio link. Josie's first twenty-four hours in her new home would be crucial. At five I switched on the radio to find Jacques already calling me.

'*Belinga de Makokou*, Nettie, are you there?'

'*Makokou de Belinga*, receiving you loud and clear, Jacques. What's the news?'

'She still has a runny nose. I took her over to CNRS today so the vet could check her over. He said how well she had been cared for, and sends his congratulations to Win for the fine job he did on stitching her up. He said she's made a good recovery, but he's given her antibiotics for the respiratory infection.' (CNRS was the Centre National de la Recherche Scientifique, a distinguished French research body with a laboratory for tropical ecology located at Makokou.)

I felt myself relax: Josie was in good hands. 'Great to hear, Jacques. Well done. I'll pass on the message to Win – he'll be thrilled. Talk to you tomorrow. Over and out.'

For six days, all seemed to go well. Each morning, I asked after Josie at the radio. Jacques' wife came on air several times to say that their daughters loved having her and that she was faring well.

On the seventh day all that changed. Madame Poussain's voice came over the airwaves agitated and angry. 'She is behaving so badly, I'm thinking of sending her back to you!'

The words chilled me. If Josie was being disruptive, it could only mean that her needs were not being met. She was clearly stressed, and I feared she was heading for a crisis, but there was nothing we could do. I tried talking to Jacques' wife, but she was in no mood to listen.

The news came on Sunday morning. Eamon greeted Win and me at the guesthouse door, sadness etched into his face. 'I heard on the radio last night from Monsieur Poussain that the little gorilla died yesterday. I didn't want to tell you straightaway. I knew how upset you folks would be.' We stood there mute, absorbing the news like a physical blow.

'Does Rodo know?' I managed.

Eamon nodded.

'What happened – do you know?'

'She just turned blue and stopped breathing,' he said. I pictured her tiny body, fighting to the last against huge odds. Her life with us flashed before my mind, the image of her face, the touch of her hand. What had she suffered in those last days? Had they cared for her properly? I recalled the look on Eamon's face the night Josie had arrived, a look that seemed to say 'beware of caring too much'. He'd seen it all before, only much worse, but he hadn't had the heart to tell us.

Win and I walked back to the flat arm in arm and sat staring out over the forest until the tumult inside us had subsided. Our grief was too deep even for tears. Rodo buried his grief like the stoic he was. When we saw him later that day he was outwardly calm, but, like us, subdued and thoughtful. There was nothing to say. It was all over. In the morning, Madame Poussain came to the radio, her voice breaking as she told us, 'She died in my arms. We buried her in the river, with flowers.'

It was only months later that we heard something indirectly that made sense of her rapid decline. Apparently she had been kept outside at nights by herself, and had spent the hours of darkness fretful and agitated, trying to get in the door. We knew that warm body contact had been essential for her wellbeing, and that the stress and trauma of this deprivation would have hastened her death. But recriminations would have been futile. We kept our thoughts to ourselves, aware that few people could have matched Rodo's heroic self-sacrifice in letting her sleep in his bed. I remembered what Jacques had told us – that gorillas sometimes died of grief when separated from their long-term carers. It seemed the odds had been against Josie from the start.

Weeks went by before I could banish the endless cycle of these thoughts churning in my mind. Josie had become part of our lives – nothing could take that away. I was determined that somehow, sometime, I would do something to make her life and death count.

chapter twelve

Elephant tales and a village dance

I threw myself into work. The whole project was gathering such pace that all of us struggled to keep up with the daily demands. I shuttled between the guesthouse, the warehouse, the *cas de passage* and the *économat* delivering supplies and keeping track of stocks. In between, I dropped in wherever Win was working, in case he needed me to interpret or translate. But he rarely did: his French had progressed quickly. He knew no formal grammar, but his men had taught him the vocabulary he needed for building. One word at a time, he learned the names of tools, types of timber and building tasks. As construction was underway at several sites, he drove between them in the Kombi.

A special friendship had developed between Win and his head carpenter. Mehendje Bruno was quietly spoken, thoughtful and gifted. I often observed the instinctive rapport they had with each other – the language barrier barely mattered, as they seemed to know each other's thoughts.

The *combinée* had streamlined construction work dramatically. It could handle planing, spindle-moulding, and trimming rough timber to required thicknesses. The two smaller machines Win had ordered at the same time – a circular saw for breaking down the bulky 400 × 400 millimetre timber baulks from the sawmills, and a drop saw mounted on a bench for cutting sections of timber to required lengths – enabled the prefabrication of frames for all the new buildings.

Win thrived on the challenge of planning the entire building program, designing all the buildings, including the electrical, plumbing and septic systems, and supervising construction. Determined to avoid accidents, he trained the men in the safe use of the machines, and enjoyed the growing relationship with his team. It was the most demanding role of his life and called on all his skill and experience. And there was enough work to keep him going for a year, so when Doug offered us both a further six-month contract starting in the new year, we didn't think twice.

Our first issue of the *National Geographic* magazine arrived in November – the October 1975 issue. We had eagerly awaited its arrival, as we received no newspapers and had few books with us. I tore off the wrapping to find the image of Biruté Galdikas on the cover, walking in the forest of Borneo with a baby orangutan clinging to her left shoulder and an older juvenile on the ground, reaching up to take her hand. She was my age, and we even looked a bit alike, with long brown hair. She was dressed in jeans and a long-sleeved sweater, just like I wore on the coldest days.

I sat down and read the entire article on the spot. Some photographs showed baby orangutans playing, like Josie had. Others showed Biruté in dugout canoes on remote tropical rivers. Galdikas had become the third of Louis Leakey's 'ape ladies', dedicated to the study of great apes in the wild. Jane Goodall had been the first, and Dian Fossey had followed soon after. The *National Geographic* was helping to fund their research. I could barely tear myself away from the article. Biruté was forging a career working in an equatorial forest with great apes. If Josie had not come into our lives, the article would not have resonated with me so strongly. But as I stared long and hard at the photograph of this woman with the two young orangutans, I imagined the wonder and joy of working with great apes every day and earning a living at the same time. I saw it as a noble calling that required immense personal sacrifice, but that would be rewarding beyond anything else I could imagine.

I put the magazine aside and went about my daily tasks, but I couldn't put thoughts of it out of my mind. I had no academic background that would fit me for such a career and no idea of how I might go about pursuing it, but the seed had been planted. Could I aspire to working with gorillas, and combine my love and reverence for them with an academic career? It seemed like an impossible dream. I was a secretary and I was thirty years old. The chances seemed remote.

Eamon had an endless repertoire of stories. If he wrote them all down, I thought, he could publish a bestseller. Every chance I had, I encouraged him to tell them. They were always larger-than-life tales, and mostly revolved around animals and the way the Gabonese relied on them for food.

One night the conversation turned to elephants, and Eamon remembered one of his stories. 'I had a Pygmy come to my door one night. Pygmies are great elephant hunters, y'know. They don't even use a gun. They set a row of sharpened sticks on the track where they know the elephants go. Then when the elephant comes along and treads on the pointed sticks, it injures its foot and goes lame. After that, the Pygmies just come in underneath and stab it in the belly with their long-handled spears. Ever seen one? They're about six feet long, iron-headed, and boy oh boy, I wouldn't like to be in their way. Anyhow, this Pygmy came to my door one night. He knew we were having a little trouble feeding our workers, so he said, "*Patron*, I've just killed an elephant. Would you like to buy it?" So I said, "Well now, that depends. Do you have it with you?"' Eamon's eyes twinkled as he remembered. He always used humour when dealing with the local people. I'd seen it often, and they loved him for it. I tried to picture the scene – the tall laconic American and the tiny Pygmy – and how the Pygmy would have laughed till he almost cried.

'Come on,' I urged. 'Tell us another one about elephants.' I had always been drawn to elephants and I longed to see one in the forest, but they were elusive, and I doubted I would ever get my wish.

'Well, I think you'll enjoy this one. I was camped out in the forest working with a group of local men and their families. One day we got word that this elephant had been killed down by the river. We were running a bit short of food at the time, so I thought it'd be a good idea to let them have it, so I organised a truck to take them down there.

You've no idea how these people love to eat elephant – you've never seen anything like it. While we were driving down there, they were all singing and calling out, everybody was so excited. When we got there, I just stood back and let them go. I've never seen such a sight. As soon as we stopped, they all leapt out and ran at the thing like it was the last meal they were ever going to get. Men and women alike, it didn't matter. Well, they attacked that thing as if they were mad. Everybody had their own machete and there were arms and legs and knives flying everywhere. When they got through the skin, they just swarmed inside the carcass and started chopping and hacking. They seemed to be in some kind of frenzy and I was sure someone was going to get killed. Anyhow, it all ended peacefully, and everybody got back in the truck with their meat and went home for a big feast. If it happens again, you'll see.'

I didn't say so, but people hacking at an elephant carcass with machetes was a sight I never wanted to witness. 'Are there many about now?' I asked instead. I had often heard talk of the piles of elephant droppings out on the tracks.

'Oh, they're about. Not a lot of them, but they're certainly around. I saw one the other day when we were cutting an access road to one of the drill sites, and I've often seen its tracks in that area.'

Jacques had told me that the elephants in Gabon were pygmy elephants. They had evolved to be much smaller than the elephants of the savannas so they could travel more easily through the forest. Their tusks had a pinkish tinge. I knew that they also moved through low-lying areas close to the river, as people at Mayebut had told Rodo their plantations near Camp Six had been ripped up and trampled.

Eamon strode into the guesthouse one afternoon and presented me with four wiry black hairs about five centimetres long.

'There,' he said, 'if you ever get close to an elephant, you'll be able to get these too!' His whimsical smile played around his mouth. 'I didn't pluck them out myself, mind you. They were clinging to the bark of a tree where the elephant had been scratching itself.'

I ran my fingers along the fibrous strands and smelt them, trying to picture the elephant scratching. 'They're beautiful,' I said. 'I'll treasure them. Thank you.' I carried them carefully back to the flat and stuck them into my diary.

Though elephants remained elusive, we never knew from one moment to the next what wildlife we would see, what rare animal might be brought in, dead or alive. With the return of the wet season, game animals had moved back to the forest around camp, promising more fresh meat for the workers and their families. The men spent much of their spare time out hunting and trapping. They often shot duiker – the small antelopes that were plentiful – and the monkeys that provided easy pickings as they moved along open branches.

One day, Étienne pulled up at the guesthouse on his bicycle, with bloodstains all down his shirt and a smile that split his face. I'd never seen him look so proud. I raced outside to see what he'd taken.

He had a carcass trussed up on the carrier, and I watched as he untied it and laid it out on the ground. It had the head of a leopard and a sleek feline body, and was large enough to bring down a small antelope. I'd never seen an animal like this before. It was smaller than a leopard but bigger than a civet, and its coat was a dusky cream with muted spots.

'*Lui, il est trop méchant!*' he told me – it was vicious and dangerous.

'*C'est quoi, Étienne?*'

'*C'est un chat-tigre, madame!*' A tiger cat. He'd caught it in a wire snare – the wound showed clearly on its right front leg. I thought how beautiful it was, and how sad that it had become prey because, according to Étienne, tiger cats were quite rare. But I pretended to be enthusiastic so as not to spoil Étienne's moment of triumph. For him, it was a prestigious kill, and would provide abundant meat for his large family.

'I want to take your photo with it,' I said. He looked embarrassed, but called Bernard from the kitchen to help him hold it up.

'Thank you for showing me,' I said, as I snapped the picture. I realised he had brought it up to show us because he knew we would be interested. He strapped the carcass back on the bicycle and rode down to the village with his rifle slung across his back.

When I consulted our wildlife atlas, I found no mention of tiger cats in the equatorial forests of Africa. The atlas depicted a much smaller animal, the African golden cat, but its body shape and size were quite different from that of the animal we had seen. Positive identification of Étienne's tiger cat would remain a mystery that I hoped one day to solve (though I never have).

November also brought our first experience of a traditional Gabonese celebration.

'We've been invited to a coming-out-of-mourning party down at Mayebut tonight,' Rodo announced one day. 'Moagno Bernard's son is giving it. When someone dies, there's a mourning period of three to twelve months. After that, they hold a party.' Moagno Bernard was one of Rodo's workers.

'Terrific!' I said. 'That sounds like fun.'

Win, Rodo and I left after dinner, armed with folding chairs, pullovers, torches, cameras and insect repellent. It was the first time in months we had driven in the forest at night. Clumps of black cloud scudded across a bright moon, driven before a strong wind. A storm was gathering in the distance: rolls of thunder ricocheted over the forest, and the wind tossed the leaves by the roadside.

Win drove slowly, alert for any wildlife ahead. In the glare of the headlights, pairs of large red eyes stared at us from the undergrowth, but their bodies were invisible.

'They're probably bushbabies,' Win said. When we stopped level with them and shone the torch, they panicked and scrambled up the nearest tree trunk to the safety of the canopy. Bushbabies were small, brown, furry tree-climbers with huge forward-facing eyes. They were classified as archaic prosimians, an ancient life form which preceded the evolution of monkeys.

A few kilometres from Mayebut, another pair of eyes appeared in the tall grass by the road, hanging in the darkness like two amber orbs. As Win braked hard, a large sleek leopard moved into view and stopped just metres away. In all probability it had smelt us through the open window. It stood quite still, sniffing the air. Unlike the one that had visited our annexe, this leopard was in prime condition, its powerful, muscular body lithe and relaxed.

It remained still for less than a minute, then ambled across the road, paused to look back at us, moved into the thick vegetation and disappeared.

This was what I loved most about being in the forest – you never knew what you would see each time you went out. But I wondered about the implications of the leopard's presence for the people of Mayebut. In the forest, human settlements always attracted animals in search of food – elephants trampled vegetable gardens, gorillas raided banana plantations, leopards hunted for meat. Humans and animals competed for survival.

At Mayebut, the huts loomed as dark shapes in the clearing, faintly outlined in the moonlight. The giant triangular leaves of taro plants growing beside the huts shone like silver. A dog barked petulantly in the background, and the muffled sound of voices issued from one of the huts. Nearby, a group of old men sat huddled around a dingy hurricane lamp on the ground, their grave faces outlined in its glow.

There was no sign of a party. We climbed out and picked our way over ditches and around mud puddles until we found Moagno Bernard.

'What's happening, Moagno?' Rodo asked. 'Has the party been postponed?'

'*Non, patron*. We're waiting for the women to return with the tom-toms.'

Half an hour later, the first group of women emerged from the forest, carrying a metre-high wooden drum slung between them. It had been carved from a tree trunk into a tapered shape; antelope skin covered the top and trailed raggedly around the edge. A series of timber wedges, held in place with liana, allowed the drummer to adjust the tension.

The second and third drums arrived soon after – one a smaller version of the first, the other a slit drum made from a thick section of tree trunk and played with two sticks.

A crowd had just begun to assemble in the open when lightning cracked and flashed overhead and rain began to pound on the rusty tin roofs. Everyone rushed for the shelter of an open-sided pavilion in the middle of the clearing and huddled together inside it, with children laughing and squealing, dogs barking and babies crying as the rain grew heavier.

I breathed in the sweetness of the wet earth and watched the flashes of lightning illuminate the forest, feeling the people's excitement and anticipation all around me. In that moment I felt utterly at home, and I contemplated for the first time the magnitude of the change in me since we had come to Belinga. Some time in the past five months, the person I had previously been had disappeared and someone else had taken her place. Layers of my new identity were being added each day. I was being remade.

After the storm we moved outside again. People arranged themselves around three sides of a square facing inwards, and the musicians took up their position on the fourth side. Two other musicians joined the three drummers – a woman with rattles made from old gas canisters filled with pebbles, and a man with a length of iron pipe and a heavy wooden baton. A woman swept the dancing ground with a leaf broom and placed a lighted hurricane lamp in the centre.

I jumped, startled, as the band suddenly erupted into life. The two tom-toms throbbed in complex cross-rhythms, the stone rattles swished, and the iron pipe clanged. Underneath them, the slit drum boomed out deep visceral sounds that I could feel as well as hear – they reverberated through my abdomen.

A woman moved to the middle of the square and began shuffling slowly in a circle, throwing invocations to the crowd, who responded in a throaty chorus of guttural sounds. Then the other women rose to join her. They formed a circle, moving one behind the other, shuffling in a pattern of three steps and a pause. At the same time, they sang what sounded like a chant. Some had babies strapped to their backs. Abruptly – as if in mid-phrase – the music and dance ceased. As a singer myself, I couldn't work out how everyone knew the precise moment to stop.

The music began again with a more insistent rhythm. Several women emerged from a hut brandishing white monkey-tail fly-switches, and joined the others to form a new circle, facing inwards. They all bowed from the waist, then one at a time moved to the centre, twirling their fly-switches in the air and pivoting on the spot. Without warning, one of them singled me out, urging me to join in. I leapt up and joined the moving circle, shuffling sideways, waving my arms in the air and shouting. Then it was my turn to do a solo. Someone thrust a fly-switch into my hand and thirty female voices cried out, '*Allez, Madamo!*' (*Madamo* was a more familiar form of address indicating they felt comfortable with me.)

My love of dancing took over. I moved to the centre and whirled in a tight circle, brandishing the switch over my head in time to the clapping and singing. Win and Rodo looked on grinning. I had whirled back to the circle and handed on the switch, completely transported by the rhythms, when the music abruptly ceased on the offbeat, leaving me flailing my arms and legs while everyone else dissolved in laughter, cheering. I felt my cheeks burning with embarrassment, but the women were gracious. One by one they came over, shook my hand, and said '*Merci, madame!*'

The celebration continued long into the night. While the women danced, the men looked on. Rivulets of sweat streamed down the drummers' bodies. Their eyes were tightly closed, and I had the impression they would not have heard if anyone had spoken to them. Mary Kingsley would have heard sounds like this a century ago, I thought.

We took leave of our hosts around 2 am and drove back up the mountain with the vibrations of the slit drum still resonating in our ears. I wondered what my family would think if they could have seen me dancing by the light of the hurricane lamp in this tiny village, deep in the African wilderness. Could they understand anything of my life now? I doubted it.

chapter thirteen

Biologists and Bats

By Christmas, the appearance of the camp had changed radically. The place where the black and white colobus monkeys had played at the edge of the forest had become a bare, gravel-surfaced yard used for storing drums of fuel and parking bulldozers. Down where the old bamboo houses had stood, a series of new home sites had been cleared. Nearby, the first of the duplex mini-apartments was almost complete. Eamon's new stone house was already under construction, and six guestrooms had been created in the *cas de passage* for the team of Canadian drillers scheduled to arrive in several months.

A grid of test-drilling sites had been drawn up on the surveyors' newly made maps, each one requiring an access road. Eamon's dozer drivers had been hard at work on them: from the guesthouse windows, the raw scar of a new access road was visible along the side of Babiel, and on Bakota South new tracks and clearings had penetrated the forest. For me, these developments were the bitter corollary of the sweet. Every incursion into the forest meant more wildlife was at risk. From the outset, I had known this was inevitable; now it stared us in the face. But just a few months later my discomfort about it was to be eclipsed by a wildlife experience so remarkable that it would resonate with me for decades afterwards.

'There'll be some special visitors this weekend,' Eamon told me one morning. 'Annie Gautier-Hion and her husband will be coming up, along with Professor Brosset and a doctoral student.'

'You mean *the* Annie Hion, who worked here with the gorillas in the 1960s?'

'That's the one.'

'Is this just a social visit?'

'No, far from it. Annie and Jean-Pierre want to record the calls of *cercocèbe* monkeys, and Professor Brosset plans to revisit the bat cave where he carried out his research years ago. I believe the doctoral student, Louise, is hoping to collect some brush-tailed porcupines.'

I had never met a naturalist before, and the prospect of meeting Annie was heady. I felt I knew her already, because I had heard so much about her from Eamon and Jacques. She and her husband were in Gabon for a month's field work, staying at CNRS where Professor André Brosset was director.

'They'll drive up from Makokou on Friday afternoon and stay two nights,' Eamon said. The biologists had chosen an ideal time to come. It was February and the short dry season was still with us, which meant the new road via the Djadié River was open.

Their Land Rover, crammed with gossamer-fine mist nets, cages, cameras and sound-recording gear, pulled up outside the guesthouse late on Friday. A slim, vivacious woman stepped out, smiled warmly, and extended her hand. '*Bonjour! Annie Gautier-Hion, et voiçi mon mari, Jean-Pierre Gautier.*' They made a handsome couple, and their open friendliness attracted me straightaway. Rodo and I introduced ourselves and shook hands.

'*Bienvenue à Belinga!*' I said, and watched as Annie's gaze swept over the familiar sight of the guesthouse, looking much as it would have done a decade before.

André Brosset exactly fitted my image of a naturalist. He wore a long-sleeved shirt, a khaki camera jacket with rows of bulging pockets, jungle-green pants and sturdy boots. He could have been fifty, but his head of luxuriant black hair and carefully trimmed beard made him look younger. Louise Emmons, a slightly built American in her twenties, spoke quietly and looked scholarly. Her sandy hair, tied back in a ponytail, framed an elfin face.

'Eamon will be back soon,' Rodo said, 'but in the meantime, let me show you to your rooms.'

Next morning, I had my first chance to watch biologists at work. Eamon had spread the word that the scientists were interested in any small animals people could bring in, especially brush-tailed porcupines. Annie, Jean-Pierre and Louise had set themselves up at a long table beside the road, surrounded by equipment. By the time I arrived, they'd already recorded the calls of a band of *cercocèbe* monkeys moving through the trees several hundred metres away on the edge of camp. The monkeys were distinctive because of their huge voice boxes, which made the calls audible over long distances.

The carcasses of several small animals lay spread out on the table. They measured each one, weighed it on a set of portable scales, examined it closely, then recorded the information on field data sheets. I hovered in the background, fascinated, but anxious not to disturb them.

Annie looked over and smiled. 'Come and have a look.' As I watched and listened, I envied them a little – their passion was also their work. Their lives had direction and purpose, they were respected for their knowledge, and they were doing what they loved. Twelve years of officework had never once ignited my passion. If only I could do something similar to what they did, I thought.

Rodo, Win and I joined them for drinks before lunch, and I heard for the first time about the work being done at the research station in Makokou. CNRS was running a rehabilitation program for orphaned gorillas and chimpanzees, reintroducing them to the wild on an island in the river. Scientists from many disciplines also used the station as a base for their research. There were zoologists, botanists, entomologists and others who came for varying periods. André specialised in birds and bats. Louise's project involved radio-tracking the nocturnal movements of brush-tailed porcupines. She spent most nights alone on foot in the forest with a radio receiver, a grid map, a pen and a torch. I looked at her slight frame and wondered what she would do out there if something went wrong.

'Aren't you frightened in the forest?' I asked. Her reply gave me my first insight into her extraordinary courage and resilience.

'Not really,' she said nonchalantly. 'The only real risk would come from elephants. Sometimes it's so boring, I take a book.'

André had come to Belinga to revisit his old research

site, a cave called La Grotte du Faucon, which lay two hours' climb from the camp.

'It's the largest bat cave in Africa,' he explained. 'We calculated that up to a million bats of three different species live in it.' And he had another reason for revisiting the site. Some rare birds – bareheaded rockfowls, *Picathartes orea* – dwelt at the cave entrance. The birds had been officially classified as endangered and few people had ever seen them. He had studied them extensively in the 1960s and wanted to see how they were faring a decade later. As I listened, I was unaware of André's global standing in the scientific community. I saw a humble man, passionate about his work and fired with the energy of someone half his age.

Over dinner, he told us he'd engaged his former assistant, Mateba Louis, who was now on our workforce, as a guide for the next day. They would leave at nine in the morning for the two-hour climb to the cave. Annie, Jean-Pierre and Louise would remain behind doing their own work.

André cast his eyes quizzically around the table. 'I'd appreciate some company on the walk. Are there any takers?'

Rodo and I leapt at the chance. I looked across the table at Win. 'Would you like to visit the bat cave? André has just invited us.'

His eyes lit up and he beamed across at André. 'That would be wonderful! We'd love to.'

We woke early next morning to assemble our gear – bottles of drinking water, sweaters, spray jackets, cameras, torches and binoculars – and just before nine the five of us gathered in front of the guesthouse. Mateba Louis led the way up the dirt road towards the forest, where a track branched off behind the reservoir. André cautioned us to speak only when necessary and always in whispers, so as not to frighten any wildlife away.

The morning air was still cool, and moisture dripped from the leaves. The mountainside rose steeply, and we scrambled and slipped up the slope in single file, grabbing at exposed roots and struggling with the gear slung around our necks. At the top, the track levelled out. We padded through the dimly lit understorey, past spiders' webs heavy with droplets of water, around fallen forest giants and past thorny vines, the only sound the soft fall of our feet on the leaf litter. When we came to particular fungi or ferns, André paused to explain their special attributes and the uses the local people had for them. Several times we came upon elephant tracks in the mud.

'They often move over this ridge,' André explained. 'They follow well-worn paths.' The track wound around the mountainside like a snake, skirting giant tree trunks and massive boulders. We walked at a steady pace for almost two hours before André signalled that we were almost there.

A steep thirty-metre drop led down from the crest of a ridge to the cave. We clutched at tree trunks and roots on the way down, slipping on loose stones and sliding on our backsides to the bottom, where a pebbly creek bed wound through understorey vegetation. Banks of giant boulders stood between us and the creek, providing perfect cover.

André motioned us into absolute silence. The cave mouth lay only fifteen metres away, and if we were to see *Picathartes* at all, we had to remain hidden. At the first hint of our presence, they would fly off. We crept up one by one behind the line of boulders, then crawled on our hands and knees behind a thick clump of vegetation. Holding our breath, we slowly raised our heads just high enough to look through the gaps between the topmost leaves.

Less than ten metres away, on the bare expanse of smooth rock at the cave mouth, two *Picathartes* were performing a ritualised dance, a complicated hopping sequence, twisting and turning their bodies to right and left and cocking their heads from side to side. The two bald ovals on their heads stood out like the eyes of some creature from science fiction. They were the size of large pigeons, with sleek bodies and long thin legs.

As if on cue, a shaft of weak sunlight broke through the canopy and struck the rock platform, and for a few moments their brilliant colours were visible – rich wine red and mossy green on their heads, and dove grey on their wings and backs. Then something must have alerted them to our presence: in an instant, they had disappeared through the trees, leaving us gaping at the bare rock ledge.

André's joy at seeing them again shone from his face; Rodo, Win and I looked at one another, open-mouthed, stunned at the privilege of seeing them. Even when André signalled that we could stand up, we lingered, as if movement would break the spell.

We followed him down a dirt path towards the cave entrance. At the bottom, he crossed the creek bed and climbed up the left side of the cave mouth, pointing excitedly at something attached to the rock wall two metres from the ground.

'It's the nest!' he cried. The *Picathartes*' mud nest, threaded through with straggly bits of plant and twigs, was perfectly camouflaged. The structure exactly matched the colour of the rock and was partially concealed by overhanging grasses. We could easily have passed it by without noticing. *Picathartes* were poor breeders, and their numbers had dwindled steeply in the wild as a result of excessive collection. To see evidence that they were breeding must have been a dream fulfilled for André.

We stood poised at the cave entrance while he explained where we could safely walk once we were inside. For the uninitiated it could be treacherous, because the bats deposited several tonnes of guano on to the cave floor every day, and over millennia the droppings had built up to a depth of over a metre. During his research there, André had marked out a safe path to the back of the cave with vertical sticks. If we deviated from it, he warned, we would sink into the stinking sludge up to our chests.

With our torches on, we entered the gloom and moved slowly along the left side, where the guano was shallowest and we could balance against the rock wall. The surface was slimy and soft underfoot. The smell of the guano, a choking ammonia-like stench, filled our lungs and made breathing difficult.

At first, I saw nothing in the blackness. As we inched our way forward, a strange sound filled my ears, like a powerful wind rushing through a long tunnel but never reaching the end. Perhaps it was a trick of acoustics, I thought. But as my eyes adjusted, I realised the source of the sound – a frantic blur of moving bodies whirling above us. Hundreds of thousands of bats had simultaneously taken flight – countless fine-membraned wings all vibrating the air at once. Their furry black and brown shapes streaked in all directions, too fast for the eye to follow, the mass of moving bodies so dense it completely obscured the roof of the cave. Tiny high-pitched squeaks cut through the sound of rushing wings, like the piping of piccolos – the bats were all calling at once.

Until then, I'd had no experience of bats. I had grown up with all the myths and horror stories that surrounded them in western culture, yet now I felt no fear or repugnance. I was curious and excited.

The deeper we moved into the cave, the staler and more humid the air became. Our skin dripped sweat, trapping swarms of tiny black insects. Then I realised fine moisture was falling on us. Condensation from the cave roof I thought at first. But it was bat urine, falling like mist, wetting our hair and clothes.

We turned off our torches and stood still in the blackness, listening, smelling and feeling – immersed like deep-sea divers in total sensory bombardment. Then André switched on his torch and directed it to the cave wall. No rock was visible, because thousands more bats clung to it, crowded together, squealing, squirming and fighting, a seething mass of contorted upside-down faces protesting the disturbance.

The cave opened out into a vast high-ceilinged cavern. As we moved yet further in, the moving shapes of other life forms became visible. Pale insects that looked part-spider, part-scorpion crawled around the ceiling. A moving carpet of cockroaches and beetles swarmed endlessly over the guano, and the coiled form of a hooded cobra glinted on a rock ledge, waiting to strike at an unsuspecting bat. I felt we had entered another world, immensely far back in time, an entire ecosystem that had existed unchanged for numberless centuries.

At the far end, the combination of the heat and the acrid stench of the guano became overpowering and breathing grew even more difficult. It was time to turn back. I paused before we began our awkward progress back to daylight, and reflected on the miracle of this place – that it supported so much life, that it was so ancient, and that it also provided a home for one of the world's rarest birds.

Outside, we gulped in the clean, fresh air and squinted against the sudden brightness. Sunlight filtered through chinks in the canopy. The forest lay cool and quiet in the lull of midday. We sat down on some rocks beside the stream and washed the sweat, urine and insects from our skin, then swallowed mouthfuls of water from our bottles.

'The Pygmies come here sometimes to hunt the bats for food,' André said. I tried to picture the little people with their crossbows and poisoned arrows, or perhaps with their nets. André's mind had skipped back ten years, and he was reliving it. 'Each evening at dusk we would watch the bats exit the cave to feed, and at dawn watch them return to roost. I never tired of the spectacle; it took three hours for the stream of animals to pass over. By observing the speed and density of these movements, we calculated the size of the population.' He explained that the three species of bats were mainly insect-eaters; they exploited the food niche that birds occupied during daylight.

'Bats carry many parasites and diseases,' he said, 'including filariasis. Even the guano harbours a fungus which can be harmful to humans.'

I wished we could linger to witness the nightly exodus and the dawn return. I knew we would never come here again. My understanding of the cave had just begun, but our time had run out. We stood and stretched, drank some more water, then slowly began the steep climb out of the stream bed and the long trek home.

We reached camp mid-afternoon, just in time for farewell drinks before the scientists needed to leave. We gathered to sit in the old armchairs on the porch, overlooking the forest. Louise, Annie and Jean-Pierre wanted to hear all about the cave excursion, so, still on a wave of euphoria, I related in French everything we had seen. As I did, a group of giant casqued hornbills swished across the clearing, calling raucously. To me, they were the sound of Belinga. I never tired of seeing and hearing them.

While I had the chance, I asked Annie about the rehabilitation program that was underway for the orphaned great apes. I really wanted to see the gorillas and chimps, but hesitated to suggest we visit.

'How many apes do you have there, and how does the program work?'

Annie was quick to respond. 'Rather than tell you, why don't we show you? Come down for a weekend. There's so much to see – we'd love to have you.'

I looked across at Win and Rodo, who were nodding vigorously. 'Oh, we'd love to!' I breathed. 'Thank you!'

'You can have the two spare bedrooms in my house,' Louise offered. 'There's plenty of room. Just let me know over the radio when you can come, and I'll pick you up at the SOMIFER compound.'

Suddenly a new world had opened up to us. I hadn't dared to hope that we might see the apes. Now it was certain, I could hardly wait. The prospect of visiting the research station would keep me going for weeks as I battled the workaday frustrations of life in the camp. And it meant we would see these generous and dedicated scientists again. As we waved them off, I felt we had been uniquely privileged. André had shown us a natural wonder that only a handful of Europeans had ever seen. The sounds and smells of the cave, the prehistoric feel of the stinking darkness and the rush of those beating wings would stay with me forever. I hoped that *Picathartes* would continue to flourish, and that La Grotte du Faucon would always remain as we had seen it – timeless, hidden and filled with wonders. That night, I went to bed with my mind full of visions of an Africa before white people had ever come.

chapter fourteen

Gorillas in my soul

We had been at Belinga nine months. In all of that time, there had been no other white woman resident in camp, and my attempts to get to know some of the Gabonese women in the village had not succeeded. Many seemed shy and reticent, and I felt I would need to spend long periods around them before we could truly communicate with one another. I'd had to adapt to a masculine environment, where toughness and resilience were the personal qualities that counted most. My job had handed me more authority and autonomy than I had ever had in my working life, and my self-confidence had soared as I met the constant challenges and filled a crucial role in the management of the camp. My colleagues respected me, and I drew satisfaction from the knowledge that I had so far been equal to whatever life in the camp had demanded of me. The sense of empowerment was heady – for the first time in my life, I believed I could follow any career I chose.

Despite this strength and optimism, the daily frustrations of camp life continued to press in on me, and Win and Rodo felt them too. For the three of us, the antidote was always the forest. The noisier and more crowded the camp became, the more we felt the need to escape into the peace it offered. Six days a week, trucks and bulldozers rumbled past the guesthouse up to the maintenance bay. The constant stream of complaints from workers about rations or other grievances wore us down, and we found the only way to avoid being harassed was not to be there.

One Saturday morning, my tolerance ran out. Nothing had gone to plan, and I was fit to scream. When Rodo and Win came in for lunch, I saw that they were at boiling point too.

'Why don't we camp overnight at the Djadié tonight?' I suggested. 'The weather's fine. We could spend tomorrow swimming and exploring, and nobody could get to us. Come on! What do you think?' We had never done it before, but since Eamon had widened and graded the Djadié route, the drive to the river was an easy forty-minute run, and there was a wide sandy clearing at the riverbank where we could camp. 'We might even get to see an elephant,' I urged. Eamon had said that our best chance of seeing one would be to drive down to the Djadié at night.

The two of them needed little persuasion, so we spent the afternoon packing food, bedding and gear. Rodo would take the Toyota Land Cruiser; we'd go in the Kombi. At nine o'clock, we drove out into a clear, starry night. The forest lay bathed in silver from a bright moon: every leaf shone, and the soaring grey tree trunks stood out like columns in a cathedral. We led off in the Kombi, equipped with a game-spotting floodlight, and Rodo followed closely behind.

About twenty minutes out, we reached a fork in the track where the bulldozers had cut a bypass around a boggy area. The new section wound through dense forest, and piles of fallen trees littered the verges.

As we rounded a bend, the lumbering grey shape of an elephant appeared. It was side-on to us, slowly rocking from left to right and back again, blocking the road. My first wild elephant! I'd waited nine months for this moment. All I could think was how beautiful it was, how calm, how majestic.

We pulled up just ten metres away, with Rodo close behind, and climbed out. In the glare of the headlights it could not have seen us, but it would have smelled our scent and heard our whispered exclamations. It was so close we could see its tiny amber eyes glinting, and the pattern of wrinkles in its hide. Its tusks were tinged with pale pink just as Jacques had described. Moved beyond anything I could have expected, I swallowed hard to subdue the lump in my throat.

We must have stood watching it for ten minutes, although any sense of time had vanished. The elephant calmly stood its ground, the only acknowledgement of our presence a turn of its head in our direction. I wanted to fix this encounter forever in my mind, because I doubted it would ever happen again. I took in every detail – its sloping back, its round feet, the hypnotic swaying of its body. Its ancestors dated back to the woolly mammoths, and just as I had in the bat cave, I felt drawn back to an ancient world. I thought back to all the elephants I had seen in circuses and zoos, and the ones we had encountered on the roads in India with their mahouts on their backs, moving with grace and dignity through a dust-drenched landscape.

They had all spoken to my spirit. Now the great African forest had delivered me another gift.

We could go no further until the elephant chose to move away, and it had only two alternatives: continue down the road or move off into the forest. The latter choice was hazardous, as the road followed a ridge, and off to the sides, the land sloped steeply away. We watched it look around, assessing the options. In the end, it chose to re-enter the forest, moving slowly towards the mass of fallen trees, stopping to make sure the way was safe, then picking its way delicately over the logs and through the tangle of branches. On the muddy slope below it never once lost a foothold, placing its huge feet with total precision. We followed its progress with the spotlight until it had negotiated all the obstacles and disappeared among the trees.

Win sighed. 'That was really beautiful.'

'*Ja*, he wasn't scared of us, was he?' Rodo said.

'Eamon was spot on,' I said. 'He promised us one.' All the way to the Djadié, I thought about the elephant. I hoped it would never be hunted, and that the new road would not spell its death warrant.

At the river campsite, bright moonlight lit the expanse of white sandbank and shone off the surface of the water. Rodo had brought his small tent, so we helped him erect it on the sand close to the Toyota.

'Oh, this feels good already,' I sighed. 'What a glorious night.' I was cut dead by a throaty half-cough, half-bark that erupted from the swamp just metres away. Win reached for the spotlight and trained it on a line of branches overhead. I half expected to see a crouched leopard preparing to spring, but in the dappled moonlight there was nothing to see.

Then it came again – a roar, louder, more guttural, that sent the three of us running for the safety of the Kombi. We squeezed into the front seat, locked ourselves in, and shone the spotlight through the closed window. Again and again the sound shattered the silence of the river and set our imaginations galloping.

'Maybe coming here wasn't such a brilliant idea,' I muttered. We sat immobile for half an hour, scanning the darkness, alert for any movement. But none came, and eventually there was only silence.

'I'm going to sleep in the tent anyway,' Rodo announced.

'Rather you than me,' I said. 'You wouldn't get me out there.' Win and I climbed over the front seat of the Kombi onto the bed to avoid getting out, while Rodo made a dash for his tent.

'What do you reckon that was?' It was a rare occasion that Win couldn't answer a question about wildlife, but he had no idea about this one.

'I can't pick it. It's not one I've heard before.' We lay awake for what seemed a long time listening for a scream from Rodo, but it never came.

We woke to a bright, clear dawn. 'I've had a visitor in the night,' Rodo called out. 'Come and look.' A pattern of neat cloven hoof prints in the sand around his tent revealed that a small antelope, perhaps a duiker, had been nosing around.

I put the kettle on and made tea, and we sat on the sandbank and drank it in the cool of the morning. Flocks of egrets stirred on branches overhanging the river.

Hornbills and touracos called raucously from the canopy. As the sun climbed higher, it bathed the tree crowns in golden light. Before breakfast, we swam in the silky coolness of the river and floated on our backs, looking up at the sky. I could feel all the tension of the week ebbing away and the peace of the forest taking over.

All morning we swam, picnicked and explored, looking for tree orchids and ferns growing along the riverbank. Only one trial clouded the day for Rodo: tsetse flies attacked his legs and neck so badly that by midday his skin was covered in bright pink lumps the size of boils.

After lunch, we lay on the sandbank and let the warm sun dry us off. Already I felt myself bouncing back. When the time came to head back to camp, it seemed we had only just got away. I wasn't ready to go, but we wanted to return before dark. On the way we stopped at the place where we had seen the elephant, and I photographed its deep footprints in the soft mud.

All the benefit of our day away vanished the moment we pulled up at the guesthouse. We were just in time to hear one of the men asking Eamon for a vehicle to go out and collect the carcass of a huge male gorilla he had shot that afternoon. The hunter's face glowed with pride and elation.

Eamon told them they could take the Toyota utility. If I'd had a say they would have had to drag the carcass back on foot, if they could move it at all. The hunter had several others with him to help lift it. As they drove off, I caught Eamon's eye and shook my head.

He read my thoughts. 'You'll never stop 'em, you know. It's in their blood.'

At dusk, the Toyota pulled up in front of the guesthouse, and we came out to look, despite our revulsion. In the back, an old silverback lay slumped against the cabin, his massive face frozen in a mask of agony and shock. Half his hair had turned white, and his huge potbelly rolled over the tops of his legs. A gaping mouth revealed broken, dirty teeth. Win lifted up one of the silverback's hands and placed his own inside it – the small pink human one was dwarfed by the enormous leathery black gorilla palm.

Rodo, Win and I leaned in silence on the side of the ute tray and stared sadly into the animal's rigid face. Meanwhile, the hunter repeated over and over, '*Lui était très méchant!* He was very wicked. He attacked me.'

'Some attack!' Win grunted in disgust. 'The bullet's entered in the middle of his back!' In the background, the other men crowded around murmuring '*beaucoup de viande, beaucoup de viande*' – plenty of meat.

The tragedy was that the silverback had probably died trying to defend his family, but we guessed by his condition that he couldn't have moved very fast. He looked about fifty years old and we estimated he weighed over 200 kilos.

I realised then that Eamon was right: we were powerless to influence these hunting behaviours. They were part of a pattern that would be repeated over and over, irrespective of the ban the company had on paying for gorilla meat, and despite the fact that gorillas were protected by law. Trying to change these practices was like trying to stop the sun rising. Once again we could only look on, mute in the face of reality. Gorillas had no hope against guns combined with the hunger for bushmeat and a belief system that demonised them.

That night, we told Eamon about the roaring we'd heard at the Djadié.

'What do you think that would have been?' Win asked.

'Most likely a crocodile, I'd say. There are certainly some in those swamps. You're lucky it didn't come after you.'

Our weekend at CNRS was set for the middle of March. We would spend two days there and watch the field biologists at work. I thought about it constantly for weeks, and could hardly wait. The research station was not open to tourists, so for us to be invited there was a special privilege.

Win, Rodo and I left on the Friday afternoon for the drive to the Djadié. The day was crisp and fine. We crossed the river in a small pirogue, and were picked up in a company vehicle on the other side. At noon the next day, Louise called for us at the Roux house in a Land Rover. Already my heart raced at the prospect of what lay before us at the reserve. Again, I reflected on my transformation since we first arrived at Belinga. In the process of tackling my difficult job and learning about the forest and the animals, I had become a different person. My whole focus had shifted. The world of cities, traffic, consumerism and packaged entertainment meant little to me now – the life of the forest had pervaded my mind so deeply that I felt I belonged in this remote place. It was an identity I wore with pride.

As we bumped along in the Land Rover, I tried to picture the encounter with the great apes that awaited us. I believed it would be one of the most memorable days of my life, but even so I could not begin to imagine the wonder I would soon experience, and the profound effect it would have upon me. The half-hour drive took us along a red dirt road that ran parallel with the river and passed through small villages. At the gate of the reserve, a sign proclaimed 'Laboratoire de Primatologie et d'Écologie Equatoriale'.

'We have 100 square kilometres of forest here, abutting the river,' Louise explained. 'It provides us with a natural laboratory to study the entire ecology of the forest.'

'It's fenced?' Win asked.

'Yes. It has to be, otherwise people would come in to hunt.'

We approached a complex of low-rise buildings that nestled among flowering shrubs and gardens, and pulled up outside a low-set bungalow just in time to see André Brosset feeding fresh meat to a brown falcon perched on a tree stump in his garden. He strode over smiling and shook hands with each of us. '*Bonjour!* Welcome to the station! I'll see you soon at lunch.'

At Louise's bungalow we dropped our bags off and drove straight to the mess for lunch, where a dozen people, all wearing crumpled army surplus shirts and pants, sat around a long refectory table. Annie and Jean-Pierre greeted us warmly and introduced the others. Georges and Sylvie Michaloud, an outgoing young couple, managed the station. Hugo, a young French veterinarian, cared for all the primates. A French radio journalist, sitting at the far end of the table, was there to record field interviews. The others – all young men with tousled hair and intense expressions – barely stopped eating and talking to acknowledge our arrival.

I listened to the rapid-fire scientific conversation that ricocheted across the table. To my surprise, I could follow most of it. Everyone wanted to share their latest field news.

The botanist had finally located the fig tree he had been searching for. Hugo was nursing a scratched face from some aggressive chimpanzees, but had made some progress with a sick one. André had caught the falcon and Annie recounted her latest monkey sightings. Around the walls, poster-sized colour photographs of primates, bats, birds of prey, reptiles, fungi and insects gave the room the flavour of a natural history museum.

Louise explained that the reserve had been divided into a grid, with numbered areas marked on maps and a system of named tracks. Using these, the scientists could record precisely the location and movement of animals. The normal work of the station always had to go on, but we were welcome to watch whatever interested us.

We had just returned to Louise's bungalow when her Gabonese assistant ran in breathlessly from the forest, shouting, '*Madame! Il y en a! Le porc-épic! Venez voir!*' It was the breakthrough Louise had been waiting for – a porcupine had been caught in her trap. We followed her at a run out into the forest, and minutes later came to the wicker basket set on the ground. A small grey animal covered in spines, with a raffia-like brush at the end of its tail, crouched inside. To Louise's excitement, it was a female. She had been trying for six weeks to capture one so she could fit it with a radio collar. Now she would be able to track the nightly interaction between this female and the males she'd been tracking for some time.

Back at the house, we watched while she assembled the collar. They couldn't be made up in advance – once the battery was encased in its covering of epoxy resin, it started to use up power. I watched, fascinated, as she gathered everything in a canvas shoulder bag – some ampoules of anaesthetic, a syringe, thick gloves and the transmitter collar.

We all trooped back to the trap: the porcupine had to be anaesthetised before the collar could be fitted.

'This is going to be difficult,' Louise said. 'They're not easy to handle at the best of times, and she'll be panicky.' Her assistant had brought a soft, open-weave bag with him. They both pulled on gloves and, working together, transferred the animal from the trap into the bag. While the assistant held the bag tightly, Louise would inject the anaesthetic through the fine mesh.

We stood back and watched as the porcupine struggled and the first attempt failed.

'I must have hit a bone,' Louise muttered, withdrawing the bent needle. On the second try the needle went in, and within moments the porcupine was still. But when she lifted the limp body out of the bag, the porcupine's lips had turned blue. Louise felt for a heartbeat, but there was none. The porcupine had died of shock.

Louise said nothing, but the fatigue and disappointment showed in her face. It was a depressing outcome after six weeks of trying. We packed up the gear in silence and walked back, carrying the porcupine's body in the woven bag. Back at the house, she measured and weighed it and noted its general condition. I thought as I watched what a lonely and unforgiving life she had chosen for herself, and how tough she needed to be to survive it.

Louise squared her shoulders and looked us in the eyes. She was not about to allow this crisis to ruin the plans she had for us: 'Tonight we're going to visit some singing bats,' she announced.

***

At nightfall we assembled on the riverbank, where a *pinnassier* had a small pirogue waiting. The bat colony was accessible only by river. Louise issued each of us with a miner's headlamp, so that when we had to scramble up the muddy bank we would have both hands free. We sat quite still, one behind the other in the pirogue with our knees drawn up to our chests, and it moved out into midstream. To me, the river felt altogether different by night – small noises were magnified, the insect chorus sounded clearer, the call of a night bird echoed hauntingly through the darkness. In the prow, the *pinnassier* shone a light on the surface ahead.

We travelled for perhaps four kilometres before pulling in to a thickly overhung bank, then switched on the headlamps and climbed out onto a slippery mud track. On all fours, we mounted the steep bank and came out on a narrow trail that ran parallel with it.

Louise led us silently in single file for perhaps half an hour, then suddenly motioned us to stop. A sound like a miniature hammer striking a tiny anvil came from directly over our heads: 'Tuc! Tuc! Tuc!'

'There they are!' Louise whispered. I recognised the call immediately. It was the same one we had heard many nights and early mornings at Belinga – clear, regular and metallic. I nudged Win and whispered, 'That's it! That's what that sound was!' We stood quite still and listened to the metallic taps cutting through the night air. As more bats began calling, the 'tuc, tuc, tucs' crosscut each other in complex syncopated rhythms.

The owners of these extraordinary voices were *Hypsignathus monstrosus*, hammer-headed fruit bats, the largest bats in

Africa, with wingspans of ninety centimetres. We couldn't see them, but I had seen pictures of them. The males' huge, elongated heads resembled miniature horse's heads, and their nasal area, a mass of convoluted fleshy membranes, gave them a grotesque aspect. Their enormous voice boxes extended for half the length of their bodies, and were what produced the powerful call, which was critical to their reproductive strategy.

During the dry season, the males congregated in vast numbers at well-established locations on riverbanks, and sang in chorus at dusk and dawn. These all-male aggregations were part of an extraordinary pattern of mating behaviour. Females were drawn to the colony from far off in response to the chorus. Then, from all the potential mates, they chose the one whose call attracted them the most. The scientists at CNRS knew this colony well, because the bats returned there every year.

We had left too late to hear the chorus at its peak, Louise explained. Only a handful of bats were still singing, and soon they would fall silent for the night. I tried to imagine the hypnotic effect of these syncopated metallic sounds when the whole colony was calling at once, and wished I could have been there to hear it.

We waited until the 'tuc, tuc, tucs' had ceased altogether, then began our trek back to the pirogue. On the way, Louise narrowly missed stepping on a hooded cobra that lay across the path.

At the station we turned in early, because in the morning we would travel out to meet the great apes on the island. I lay in bed and thought about the lives of these dedicated biologists. When we finally left Africa, I didn't want to return to the empty world of officework I had left behind. I believed I was destined for something better, a profession that would be intellectually satisfying. My thoughts turned to the three 'ape ladies', and the idea that had been haunting me for months – that I might one day follow in their footsteps.

It was another fine clear day. We met Hugo at the riverbank, where a pirogue loaded with bunches of ripe bananas was beached on the mud. Hugo was about thirty, with clear olive skin and fair wavy hair. He had a ready smile, and a gentleness that fitted him perfectly for working with great apes.

'Before we go, I'll just tell you a bit about our great ape rehabilitation program,' he said. 'We began eight years ago. We raise the orphaned gorillas and chimpanzees for three years, then, if we think they're ready, we release them on to one of the forested islands in the river, and supplement their natural diet with food drops every couple of days. It's an experiment in rehabituating them to the wild.

'At the moment, we have all the animals on one large island. They've formed themselves into two separate groups, one entirely of chimpanzees and the other a mixed group of two chimpanzees and two gorillas. We won't get out of the pirogue at the first group, because they're a bit aggressive at the moment. I had to anaesthetise and move them a few weeks ago, and they're very wary of me now. That's how I got these scratches on my face.'

I could feel my excitement mounting as we boarded the pirogue. I had anticipated this day for so long. My new Pentax camera with its 300 millimetre zoom lens was slung around my neck, and Win had brought his movie camera.

A deep silence blanketed the river as we approached the island ten minutes later. The *pinnassier* cut the outboard, and we drifted slowly into the muddy bank. Thick forest cloaked the island – a mosaic of green shapes, clear in the morning light. Huge rope-like loops of mottled grey liana crisscrossed the understorey and hung from the high canopy.

The chimpanzees grew highly excited at our arrival, screaming, hooting and swinging from vine to vine. We watched their performance from the pirogue. It could have been a scene from millions of years ago. I sat speechless and had another of my 'pinch me' moments – could it really be me, here, seeing this?

Hugo explained that the group comprised one male, two senior females – Dodo and Albertine – another female, and two juveniles. When the initial excitement had abated, Dodo climbed down from a tall tree and headed straight for the pirogue, where she reached into the prow, grabbed the nearest bunch of bananas and hauled it up the muddy path. We watched as she climbed back up the same tree, trailing the heavy bunch behind her, settled herself on a sturdy branch, and began to eat, skilfully balancing the bunch in front of her.

Meanwhile, the *pinnassier* unloaded two more bunches. Albertine came down to the pirogue next with her two-year-old infant Josephine, and dragged a bunch up to the clearing. We watched them for perhaps twenty minutes, filming and listening to Hugo's commentary.

'Some of these animals have been on the island for five years,' he explained. 'Dodo is eight now. She's the dominant female.' I had guessed that by her confident behaviour. There were many questions I wanted to ask, but it was time to move on to the opposite end of the island.

As we approached the shore, there was no sign of the animals.

'You must be very quiet here, and make no sudden movements,' Hugo warned, 'and you need to put your camera out of sight. It might frighten them.' The *pinnassier* ran the pirogue up on the bank, and we stepped out.

A narrow earth track led from the water's edge to the line of trees. Suddenly two chimpanzees emerged from the underbrush and bounded down towards us. First one then the other leapt up into Hugo's arms, hugging him tightly and rubbing their faces against his cheek. He cradled each one to his chest, rubbed their backs and talked to them – a ritual of mutual ecstasy. In their excitement, the chimps threw themselves about and greeted Rodo, Win and me in turn. One launched itself at me with its arms outstretched. I scooped it into my arms, hugged it to my chest and stroked its back and head. Lost in the joy of the moment, I looked into its face.

Hugo looked on amused. 'That's Bouéni,' he said.

Bouéni looked back at me exuberantly and pouted his lips for a kiss. I buried my face in his, nuzzled up to his cheeks, and planted a kiss on each one. He had his legs locked around my waist and seemed set to continue our love affair indefinitely, but I gently eased him to the ground, where he took up a position with his back against my legs while I rubbed his shoulders and head. I tried to picture the years of dedicated nurturing he must have had in captivity to give him such trust in a stranger.

We turned to move up the narrow path towards the vegetation. At that moment, one of the gorillas appeared at the top of the track. He was an impressive sight –

thickset, with a prominent brow ridge framing deep-set eyes. He stood quite still, regarding us with an intense expression, then moved tentatively down the path in a shuffling gait, his knees bent and his arms straight, occasionally touching the ground with his fists.

I was at the front of the group. I was excited, fit to burst, but knew I must maintain an outward appearance of calm. I hoped this magnificent animal might passively accept our presence, but I didn't expect more. I had no idea what the protocol was for greeting a gorilla. I shot an inquiring glance back at Hugo, who watched from behind.

He quickly reassured me. '*Celui-là, il est très, très gentil. Il s'appelle Ikata.*' His name was Ikata, and he was extremely docile. Ikata was now just metres away from me. Every hair of his lustrous coat shone in the sun. His eyes, lit with a mild curiosity, fixed on mine. No-one spoke: everyone watched the two of us. Then he reached out both arms towards me, and moved in closer. This was my cue: I stretched mine towards him, palms facing upwards. Would he trust me enough to let me touch him?

There was no precedent in my life for this moment. I was approaching an eight-year-old male gorilla who had never seen me before. He already had the strength of several men. All I had to rely on was Hugo's assurance that he was gentle. In seconds, I'd taken in everything about him: his round-topped head, not yet mature enough to have the sagittal crest that would mark him as an adult male; the leathery texture of his fingers and face; the pushed-in shape of his nostrils; the cleanness of his thick black hair; and the intensity of his gaze. His body language conveyed a deep calmness; his movements were relaxed and deliberate. He was not afraid – so, taking my cue from him, nor was I.

Slowly we approached each other until less than a metre separated us. I held my breath. Then, with exquisite gentleness, Ikata moved forward and enfolded me in an embrace of greeting. In my wildest imaginings, I had never anticipated this. Time seemed to stop. I was both inside the moment and outside of it – abandoned to the ecstasy, yet somehow aware of myself.

We were the same height, his face level with mine, just inches away. As he took my measure, I moved one hand up and rubbed the domed top of his head, made small noises of reassurance, and stroked the sides of his face as I looked into his eyes. He moved closer, nestled his face against my cheek, and extended one arm around my shoulders. His delicate touch belied the enormous power in his hands. As he honoured me with this extended greeting, I continued stroking his back and head. All this time, he made no sound. My mind raced. This gentle animal trusted me completely – how could it be?

As I looked into Ikata's serene face, a fine intelligence looked back, and in those few moments, the boundary between our species dissolved. We communicated, across millions of years of evolution, what was common to us both. Beyond speech, I stood motionless, transfixed. I'd had to live thirty years and come to this African wilderness to discover my vocation.

Eventually, Ikata transferred his attention to the others, and we all moved up the track to a clearing which served as the feeding station. There, the second gorilla, a female named Pascaline, sat quietly on her own. The *pinnassier* had brought a bunch of bananas up and placed it on the ground near her. She took no notice, and focused instead on the sight of Win's and Rodo's bare arms and legs.

Ikata calmly sat on the ground, his belly collapsing into rolls, his legs loosely crossed and his arms folded across his chest. I sat opposite him, cross-legged on the ground with the bunch of bananas between us. Glints of sunlight filtered through the canopy and patterned the leaf litter on the forest floor with patches of gold. I was immersed in his world, conscious of no-one but Ikata and myself. At eight years old, he was sub-adolescent. For the moment, Hugo had said, he was still playful. He loved nothing better than being jostled in a bout of mock wrestling. He would not be sexually mature for another three years.

He reached out and picked a single banana from the bunch, peeled it and took each mouthful fastidiously, smearing no fruit on his face or chest. He ate just two before turning his attention back to me, reaching out and lightly touching my arms and legs. When he noticed the gap between my socks and trousers, he reached out, lifted up the edge of one trouser leg with his thumb and forefinger, and bent over to look inside. I sat quite still as he explored the texture of my skin with his leathery fingers.

Then I moved in and faced him at close range. This must have been the signal that I had presented myself for social grooming: he reached across and pulled gently at the strands of my long hair tied back in a ponytail. Bit by bit, he teased it out of the elastic band until all the hair fell loosely over my face, then ran the strands gently through his fingers, focusing intently on the texture of the hair, and fossicking on my scalp. I could scarcely believe my feeling of connectedness with him, but I was conscious that one inadvertent move on Ikata's part and he could scalp me.

I slowly eased the clumps of hair out of his grasp, careful not to alarm him, and tied them back out of reach. The grooming session was over. He sat back, resumed his Buddha position, and stared impassively into space.

Hugo's voice reached me as if from far off. 'It's time to go.' I stood slowly and took a last look at Ikata sitting placidly in the sunlight. I wasn't ready to leave. For me, this had been a day like no other. I wanted to laugh, cry and shout out that I had finally decided what I wanted to do with my life. Like Biruté Galdikas, I would study to be an anthropologist and, if things worked out, I would work with great apes, as she, Jane Goodall and Dian Fossey were doing. I kept the decision to myself, but 13 March 1976 would resonate through my life for all time – the day I looked into Ikata's eyes and glimpsed eternity.

We made our way slowly back to the river, Bouéni and the other chimp following us down to the pirogue, still seeking attention. I stroked them and talked to them. It was too soon to leave – I wanted to spend hours with them – but Hugo was waiting. As we pulled away from the bank, I hoped that Ikata, Bouéni and the others would survive to breed. They were being given every chance, but there were no guarantees.

That night, back at Louise's bungalow, I lay awake a long time with a jumble of images jostling in my mind – the island in the river, the dead porcupine, the hammer-headed fruit bats – and the feeling of Ikata grooming my hair. Overriding it all was the vision I had now embraced for my future.

On our last morning at the reserve, Hugo invited us to his house for drinks. We arrived to find him bottle-feeding twin two-month-old chimpanzees. He cradled one in the crook of his arm and held a bottle of warm milk to its mouth, while the other managed its bottle by itself. They were fed every few hours, day and night. As I watched him nurture them, I saw the depth of his commitment to all the animals in his care. For him, it was not just a job – the animals' needs took precedence over everything. Like everyone on the station, his work was his passion.

When the twins had finished their bottles, Hugo carried them outside onto the lawn. Their soft pink faces and huge expressive eyes were never still as they took in their surroundings, romped together, cuddled each other and played with small toys. It was impossible not to feel kinship with these great apes. We are so like them; they are so like us. The longer I watched them, the more entranced I became. Sitting with these fragile and delicate infants, I thought about Josie and how dependent she had been on us. I had no doubts now about the course I had set for myself. Above all else, this was what I wanted to do.

Just before lunch we farewelled everyone, tried to convey our gratitude for their generosity, and left for the trip back. On the way into town, we told Louise about our campsite at the Djadié. We were determined to persuade her to take a break away from her punishing routine.

'Drive up and meet us at the Djadié next weekend!' Rodo urged. 'We can camp there overnight and swim in the river in the morning.' Louise looked across at us wearily and brushed a strand of hair from her eyes. A smile played around her mouth, and she took a deep breath. 'I'd like that,' she said quietly.

'Wonderful!' Rodo beamed. 'It's all settled then.' It was agreed that Rodo would drive down in the Toyota, we would follow in the Kombi, and Louise would meet us there in a CNRS vehicle on the following Saturday afternoon.

The day of our rendezvous with Louise dawned wet and muddy – the first storm of the 'long wet' had struck the day before. Camping at the Djadié in those conditions was not an appealing prospect, so we made an alternative plan. Rodo would drive down there, pick up Louise, and bring her back to camp for the weekend. They arrived back just on dusk and pulled up outside our door. She was in buoyant spirits and greeted us both with a hug.

The rain had held off all afternoon, but a storm was building as I showed her to her room.

'Drinks in our flat in fifteen minutes!' Win called out. 'And you'll be eating with us, Louise.' Rodo left to shower and change, and returned carrying ice-cold bottles of Regab beer and a packet of nuts.

'I've just learned there's a dance on in the village tonight,' he said, 'and we four are invited!'

'What's the occasion?' I asked.

'I think it's some kind of ceremony to cleanse Madame Elizabeth and Augustine's new house of bad spirits, and make it safe for them to live in.'

I turned to Louise to explain: 'Augustine is the village head, and Madame Elizabeth is the most senior woman. According to Eamon, she's actually a witch.'

'We'll need to take some beer with us,' Rodo said. 'They'll want us to have a good time, and if they see drinks in our hands, they won't be concerned about their hospitality. They'd probably hesitate to offer us palm wine, and if we don't bring beer, they'll feel compelled to buy some. I don't think we should put them in that position.' Rodo was close to the men and understood their customs.

We walked down to the village by torchlight just after nine o'clock. Louise had her portable tape recorder, as she wanted to capture some music and singing. The importance of the occasion became immediately evident. A palm-leaf pavilion had been erected beside the new house, with fires lit at the entrance, and people sat around the sides facing inwards with the drummers seated at the far end.

Chief Augustine and Madame Elizabeth were sitting at the entrance. They stood and greeted us, and Madame Elizabeth ushered us to a row of plastic chairs that had been arranged for us. She was an imposing figure, tall, solidly built, with a commanding presence. Her broad, high cheekbones framed alert eyes. Her skin was smooth, the colour of milk chocolate, and her mouth often widened into a broad smile, revealing more gaps than teeth. She wore a brightly patterned length of *pagne* wound around her, with an overblouse and a headscarf.

About forty people were gathered in the pavilion. While Madame Elizabeth circulated among the guests, chatting, Chief Augustine, a small thin figure, looked on passively. I thought – not for the first time – that his wife's powerful presence seemed to have eclipsed him long ago.

I took my seat beside a young woman with a baby on her back. 'What's going to happen tonight?' I asked her.

'Madame Elizabeth is going to dance!' she said proudly.

'Just by herself, no-one else?'

'*Oui.*'

'Why isn't everyone going to dance?' I asked.

'Because Madame Elizabeth dances the best,' she

replied. It didn't sound as though I would have a chance to repeat my attempt at Gabonese dancing that night.

While two men stoked the fires, the other musicians arrived – women with rattles and men with lengths of iron pipe and wooden sticks. They began warming up, and Madame Elizabeth broke into a slow shuffle in front of them, throwing out comments to the crowd.

Just then, rumbles of thunder sounded directly overhead, and flashes of lightning arced over the forest like strobe lights. In minutes, the storm had hit, and everyone fled the palm-leaf pavilion, scrambling for the shelter of the new hut. It was of the same construction as all the village houses – puddled mud over a sapling frame – with two rooms and a bare earth floor.

We all sat cross-legged on the ground, pressed closely together around the walls, facing inwards, where hurricane lamps had been set up and a fire lit. The acrid smell of sweat mingled with the fragrance of burning sap, and the fire threw dancing images onto the ochre-coloured walls. At one end of the room, the musicians set themselves up afresh, and Madame Elizabeth retired unobtrusively to the adjacent room.

Time stretched and warped as we waited for something to happen. Around us, a hubbub of voices rose above the crackle of the fire. Some people smoked the rank-smelling Gabonese cigarettes. Children sat and stared impassively and babies slept as the rain drummed on the corrugated-aluminium roof. The air inside the hut soon turned hot and fetid: Rodo opened his bag and handed each of us a bottle of cold Regab.

Our eyelids had begun to close when the door to the adjoining room opened to reveal a terrifying figure framed in the doorway. A collective gasp escaped from everyone seated around the floor. The figure stepped into the room, acknowledging no-one. Its skin was covered in thick white paint, its features picked out in black, red and blue. On its head was a grotesque wig of animal skins, with spiralling wisps of straw projecting in all directions, giving its face a Medusa-like appearance. It was a woman wrapped from the chest down in a stark white sheet; at her waist, a girdle of leopard-skin strips supported a rustling overskirt of straw. Two men accompanied her, one on either side, dressed in flowing white robes and white skullcaps. When I recovered from the initial impact, I realised the woman was Madame Elizabeth.

The drummers began beating out a slow, ominous rhythm, and the three figures processed forward and started circling the fire. Madame Elizabeth's demeanour had changed utterly from earlier in the evening. I peered hard at her face as she passed by. It was as fixed as a mask, with no flicker of recognition of anyone, and her eyes seemed focused on some distant point.

At a shout from the crowd, the two men in white dropped into the background and the whole band crashed into life. Madame Elizabeth's body became instantly charged with a raw energy. She circled the fire, her gaze fixed on the flames, and her voice rose in a guttural chant. The music grew louder and faster, and with it her movements grew more frenzied until her whole frame shook. Rivulets of sweat poured from her forehead, streaking her make-up into bizarre patterns.

Then the music ceased abruptly and she collapsed onto a low wooden stool, withdrawn, still acknowledging no-one. Once recovered, she began again: her chants intensified and she directed invocations at the crowd, who made long, complicated responses. The ritual seemed to be building to some kind of climax. I had no idea what to expect, but she had created an atmosphere of terror in the room, and I started to feel uneasy.

Her performance continued for perhaps an hour and a half until, towards midnight, the band fell silent and Madame Elizabeth abandoned her dancing and moved with a small group of men and women – including the drummers – to sit in a circle around the fire. We watched them pass a flask of powder from hand to hand. Each person tipped some on to their palm, placed it on their tongue and swallowed it with a mouthful of water. I had heard about *iboga*, a hallucinogenic drug made from the roots and bark of a tree that was used in rituals of the secret Bwiti cult, and I wondered whether this was it. Then palm wine was poured into a glass and each person in the circle drank a sip from it. At the same time, lumps of resin from the atanga tree were thrown on the fire, sending a sharp, spicy perfume into the air. The obvious parallels with the Christian communion rite struck me, and I wondered whether this part of the ritual reflected the influence of missions.

After that, torpor settled over the room. People spoke in whispers. Outside, the storm had abated, and the sound of rivulets cascading down the hillside filled our ears. The four of us sat respectfully and waited. The heat had made us thirsty, so Rodo passed out the remaining bottles of beer. Louise had managed to record some of the music.

Another hour passed before one man in the circle stood up and shouted to the crowd to clear him a space, prompting the mass of seated figures to retreat toward the walls. He started circling the fire and taunting the crowd with wild gestures. The drummers took up their positions again and played in a frenzy of abandonment, gyrating their bodies and rolling their eyes – the drug appeared to have taken effect. The dancer's body trembled convulsively. At intervals he lunged at people in the crowd with a bare dagger and transfixed them with grotesquely bulging eyes.

I sensed the climax was approaching. The man threw himself on the ground and moved around on his bottom, with his bare feet just touching the burning wood and his eyes rolling like a madman's. Jumping upright again, he careered around the fire, lurching precariously. Then in an instant he had lost his balance and fallen headlong into the live coals, sending a spray of them towards the front row of spectators. The crowd drew back in horror, then several men leapt to their feet and dragged the dancer clear of danger. Dazed and physically spent, he appeared to feel no pain, and allowed himself to be carried off to recover.

The proceedings had come to a temporary lull. It was after one o'clock, and our numb legs and backsides cried for reprieve, so we stood and stretched, then picked our way through the crowd to where Chief Augustine sat quietly in a corner. One by one, we gravely shook his hand and thanked him.

Outside, the air had chilled after the storm. The forest dripped, and frogs sang in a chorus of clicks, squeaks and chirrups. A jumble of questions rattled around in my head. What beliefs underlay the rituals? What did they mean? How ancient were they? I doubted I would ever know the answers – our time at Belinga would be much too short.

We all slept late next morning. Over breakfast, Win and Louise talked food and cooking, and she asked if she might bake a cake for lunch. There were lemons from an old tree near the *cas de passage*, and we had flour, baking powder and spices in the cupboard. I left Win to show her where things were and drove down to invite Rodo up for coffee and cake in an hour.

I didn't realise it at the time, but that Sunday was to be the last before the influx of new staff and contractors arrived. The camp lay at peace, with insects buzzing and birds feeding outside our windows on the heads of grass seed. By the time Rodo arrived, the homely smell of baking filled the flat.

Louise's lemon teacake came out of the oven golden brown and fragrant. We sat around the table talking, eating and drinking coffee, and looked out over the forest. As we chatted, I reflected on the long chain of circumstances that had brought the four of us together from opposite parts of the world. The chances of our meeting would have seemed nonexistent just a year earlier.

Before she left, Louise thrust her home address into my hand. 'I hope I'll see you again before you leave. If not, you can always contact me in the States.' As we saw her off, we could not have guessed that this intrepid, slightly built woman would go on to have a distinguished research career in tropical mammalian biology. She would discover new species in South America and elsewhere, and thirty years after our time in Gabon would be described as one of the greatest tropical biologists to have ever lived.

chapter fifteen

RAIN, RAIN, RAIN AND NEW PEOPLE

The onset of the big wet coincided with the long-awaited arrival of expatriate staff and the drilling contractors from Canada. The expatriate population in camp ballooned from nine to seventeen, propelling my battles over fresh food supplies to a new level of frenzy. The *vivres frais* normally arrived twice weekly, when flights operated between Libreville and Makokou. I had doubled the size of the orders, and waited anxiously for each consignment that came up on the pirogues. But I hadn't bargained for how much the wet season could disrupt transport throughout the country.

The problems began one day in April. I had waited all day for a consignment, but when the truck arrived from the *débarcadère* all the driver had on board was hardware and drums of fuel. I felt my anger rising, and at the five o'clock radio session I gave Doug a blast. 'What the hell's happened to our *vivres frais*? We got absolutely nothing today! How are we expected to manage?'

Doug's voice came over the air through a burst of crackle. 'Nettie, I know for certain the *glacières* were loaded on the plane. Godart specifically told me he supervised it himself.' Godart was SOMIFER's accountant and manager in the Libreville office. 'I'll look into it and let you know first thing tomorrow.' My imagination went into overdrive – if they'd been loaded, then what had happened to them in transit? After I finished at the radio, I put Étienne and Mambo Bernard in the picture, as they had been expecting ingredients for that evening's meal, then drove down to the *cas de passage* to tell Samba Bernard and Léon the same story. We had plenty of tinned vegetables to fall back on, but I knew that everyone's tolerance for them would wane quickly.

At nine o'clock the following morning, I switched on the radio and called up Libreville. Doug's voice came on, sounding harassed. 'Nettie, you're not going to believe this. The *glacières* were loaded all right and the plane left, but on the approach to Makokou the pilot couldn't land because the weather was so foul and the beacons at the airport were out of order, so the son-of-a-bitch was forced to turn around and come back to Libreville.'

'Oh great!' I groaned. 'What do we do now?' It was a reprise of the supply problems we had experienced in the lead up to the *fête* eight months before, except that now I had less patience with the chaos that constantly dogged our endeavours and we had twice as many people depending on the food supplies.

'Nettie, I'll charter a special plane if we have to. Give me a couple of hours to work on it, and let's talk again at eleven.' By the time we spoke again, Doug had arranged a charter. It would leave Libreville that day. With any luck the food would reach us within a day and a half.

The three *glacières* arrived late the following afternoon. I expected the worst, since they had been in transit for so long, and wasn't disappointed. I opened them to find squashed tomatoes and wilted celery covering what lay underneath, and a jumble of ruptured tubs of yoghurt that had leaked all over the bags of eggplants and capsicums. The cheeses, meat and salamis had fared better, though, and some of the cabbages and cucumbers looked salvageable.

Étienne looked on in dismay as I sorted through it. He shook his head. '*Les légumes sont fatigués, madame,*' he said. Tired vegetables – yes, that captured it perfectly, I thought. Étienne's highly individual way of expressing himself always brought a smile to my face – like the night he had encouraged me to eat up some remaining salad at dinner because '*Ça ne dort pas, madame,*' – it doesn't sleep. From that night on, I could never think of a lettuce salad without recalling that it wouldn't sleep.

At the afternoon radio link, I told Doug the food had made it, but that it seemed an expensive way to move perished vegetables around the countryside – the air charter had cost US$1000. It was to be the first of five charters in the three weeks that followed, however, as the depredations of the weather and the unreliability of the navigation beacon at Makokou combined to disrupt aircraft movements. Our radio links became more frequent – two in the morning and two in the afternoon – to coordinate the movement of extra pirogues and keep us informed. As the radio sessions gobbled up more and more of my time, I cursed the wet season and the chaos of Africa and began to look forward to the time, just months away, when I wouldn't be doing the job any more.

I often started work before 7 am and finished after dark – much depended upon the arrival and departure times of pirogues. All the empty containers – 200-litre fuel drums, gas bottles, *glacières* and *cantines* – had to be returned promptly to Makokou. If we didn't keep them moving, Kruger would become testy because it messed up his system. So I established a routine of assembling the empty gas bottles, *glacières* and *cantines* at the door of the guesthouse the night before, ready for the truck driver to load. The non-return of empty fuel drums emerged as a sore point from time to time, but I couldn't help that, as I had no control over them and no idea of their whereabouts. Whenever Kruger got cranky about them, I referred him to Eamon.

Each month the cash and stock at the *économat* had to be reconciled to ensure the company recouped its outlays on the huge volume of merchandise purchased for resale in the village. The *économat* now stocked over 150 different lines, from bicycles to double foam mattresses, and everything had to be accounted for. And because I felt sorry for Rodo at the end of each month when he had to prepare the 100 pay packets for the men, I also worked with him adding up the hours and deducting any advances people had received.

My tiny salary was laughable given the job to be done, but I rarely thought about it. Like everyone else, I did whatever was necessary to keep things running. When I did stop to ponder it, I weighed up the frustrations of the job against everything our life in the camp had brought: our time with Josie, the visit to the bat cave, and my hour with Ikata. Those were the things that would remain with me forever, whereas I knew the chaos would pass.

* * *

For me, the arrival of the two new expatriate couples brought fresh faces and the promise of a fuller social life at last. My nine months as the only white woman in camp had ended. Both men were geologists, both the wives were nurses, and all had worked elsewhere in Africa. The recently married French couple, Michel and Marie-Claire, had come to Gabon from Mauritania. Michel looked to be about forty, tall, with thinning hair and an ebullient personality. Marie-Claire was younger, tall and slim with olive skin, quietly spoken and serious. She'd spent a year delivering babies in Mauritania, and as I grew to know her I formed the impression she could handle almost any situation with equanimity. It had been agreed that she would run the *infirmerie* once they settled in. Like most of the French people we had met in Gabon, neither of them spoke any English.

By contrast, the American couple, Jim and Carol, had come straight from a year's work in Sierra Leone, where the national language was English, and they only spoke a smattering of French. Jim was short and stocky. He reminded me of the sort of Australian men who had gone to Papua New Guinea as *kiaps* or patrol officers in the 1950s: he wore khaki shirts and pants and a broad-brimmed hat, and used words sparingly. Carol had enough zest and personality for both of them. She was in her twenties, with an engaging smile, long brown hair and a zany outlook. I warmed instantly to her and knew we were going to get on.

The two couples moved into the brand-new mini-apartments that Win and the carpenters had recently finished. Rodo and Jacques had moved into similar ones several weeks earlier. Each dwelling was equipped with power, bottled gas for cooking, showers and a septic system with flushing toilets.

I had little contact with the team of Canadian drillers once they began work. They came from the French-speaking part of Canada, but I soon discovered that I could understand very little of what they said. I was puzzled until Jacques explained that the French they spoke derived from a much older form of the language, and had changed little since the time of the early French settlers. I wasn't the only one having trouble – the Gabonese workers couldn't understand them either. All four of them were short and muscular and they smoked a lot. Although they were courteous whenever I met them, they were used to a rough life in frontier environments, and seemed uncomfortable talking to a woman. They kept to themselves, so I had no opportunity to get to know them. They moved into the suite of upgraded rooms in the *cas de passage* and took their meals there alongside the surveyors.

The chance to get to know Carol, Jim, Michel and Marie-Claire better came at Easter. We invited them and Rodo to our flat for cheesecake and sangria on the Saturday night. It was the first gathering we'd had in the flat, and it made me realise how much I had missed a normal social life. Win spent the afternoon baking a lemon cheesecake, using dozens of the miniature tubs of Petits Suisses – a soft white cheese intended as infant food – that Libreville had been sending us. He sprinkled the top with grated lemon rind and spice, so that when it came out of the oven it looked like an illustration from a gourmet cookbook.

Rodo arrived carrying a small box, but wouldn't tell us what it contained. Only when we had finished the sangria, demolished most of the cheesecake, told stories and laughed a lot, did he reveal what was inside – six hens' eggs, one for each of us, finely painted all over in brilliant colours and intricate patterns. No two were the same.

I thought at first they were ceramic. 'Where did you get these? Did your mother send them from Germany?'

'No, no. I had Étienne hard-boil them for me, and I painted them myself this afternoon with felt pens. That's what we do in Bavaria at Easter.' He presented each of us with one and wished us happiness.

I had never seen their like. The delicate patterns could have been Persian miniatures. 'Rodo, they're exquisite!' I said, and hugged him hard. All the trials of the past months had not toughened Rodo or lessened his sensitivity. With this gesture, he'd made us all feel like a family, even though we came from four different countries. Everyone was in such high spirits by the end of the evening that we decided to have a barbecue at the Djadié the next day, weather permitting.

Wind-swirled fog swept through the forest as we drove out in convoy after breakfast. Win had packed steaks and Carol had brought potatoes and onions to bake in the fire. On the way we stopped to watch bands of monkeys leaping from tree to tree, hornbills in flight, and a family of partridges feeding at the edge of the road.

The fog had cleared by the time we reached the river. Jim and Michel gathered wood and built the fire while Win coated the steaks with powdered garlic, and Marie-Claire, Carol and I wrapped the potatoes and onions in foil. With glasses of red wine in our hands, we sat in a long line on an old upturned pirogue to watch the fire burn down to coals. I felt myself relaxing into a warm and mellow state. The fragrance of the burning wood, the peace of the river and the camaraderie all conspired to consign the worries of the camp to somewhere beyond the borders of my mind.

We lingered over the juicy steaks and jacket potatoes, not talking much, just listening to the cries of birds echoing through the forest. After lunch, everyone swam in the river and lay on the sandbank to dry off. Only a change in the weather forced us to pack up and leave. Light rain soon developed into a downpour that lasted all the way home. When we arrived back, the camp was quiet: there had been no crises, and Eamon had done the radio link for me.

Now that the apartments were finished and occupied, Win and his men were able to concentrate their efforts on finishing Eamon's house in time for the arrival of his wife from America in May. Doug had christened the house 'Eamon's Palace' because of its size and luxurious design. Win had designed it as a showpiece, using the finest local timbers for the internal finishes. The floors were varnished wood, exposed beams supported the roof, and a huge stone fireplace dominated the living room. Like the guesthouse, it was built in natural stone – rough lumps of red ironstone that blended in with the red earth. It occupied an elevated site just below the forest line, and the front windows afforded views out over the camp towards the village. As each week passed, I watched it take shape, and with it saw Win's creative satisfaction blossoming.

Just when it seemed that things were starting to settle down around the camp, a bombshell dropped: Jacques, our experienced and tireless mechanic who could fix anything anytime, had had enough. He submitted his resignation and would be gone in a month. We found it difficult to imagine how the camp could function without him, and braced ourselves for an increase in the chaos.

Ever since our weekend at CNRS and my encounter with Ikata, I thought constantly about my dream of becoming an anthropologist. Apart from the excitement I felt at the prospect, there were many practical things to sort out. It wasn't just my future at stake: I had Win to consider. How would he feel about my embarking on a degree in my thirties? What would it mean for us financially if I had to give up work to do it? How would his life change if I spent four years burying myself in books and assignments?

I chose my moment to broach the subject. It was a Sunday when we had a morning to ourselves, with no distractions.

'Sweetheart, what would you say if I said I wanted to go back to university?' I began.

Win's eyebrows shot up and he fixed a searching gaze on me. Then he swallowed hard and readjusted his weight in the chair. 'I'd be delighted for you. I think you're capable of doing anything you set your mind to – you've proven that time and time again. What do you have in mind?'

'Well, I've been thinking about Josie and Ikata, and rereading that article about Biruté Galdikas working with the orangutans in Kalimantan. I can't get it out of my mind. And Jane Goodall and Dian Fossey, too. They've all forged good careers working with great apes. It's not something I would ever have contemplated before we came here, but I want to try. I'd like to do something for gorillas, and I really want to be with them. If I could make my living working with them, I couldn't imagine anything more wonderful. But I'd need a formal qualification first and I believe that, with my humanities background, that should be anthropology.'

Win's mind immediately turned to the practicalities. 'What would be involved if you did? Where would you start? How would you get into it?'

I had few answers. 'I'm not sure. I'm not even certain that anthropology would be the best pathway, but Biruté has an undergraduate degree in anthropology, so that's what I'd investigate first.'

'So how do you find out?'

'Well, I'd have to contact some universities once we finish here. Assuming we go back to Brisbane, the University of Queensland would be the obvious first port of call, but I don't know what they offer or even whether I'd get in without a science background.'

'And would you do it part-time or full-time?'

'I'd probably have to do it part-time and work during the day, to pay for the fees. The only problem with that is I'd be forty before I finished. If I did it full-time, you'd have to support me. Either way, it wouldn't be easy.'

We sat in silence for a few moments, looking out the louvre windows onto the forest. I could see Win was weighing up all the likely ramifications. We both loved the forest and the gorillas, and after our time at Belinga we were unlikely ever to settle into a conventional suburban life. And he knew that once I had set my heart seriously on something, I pursued it relentlessly. I always finished what I started and didn't do things by halves.

He looked hard at me. 'Well, if that's what you want to do, I'll support you every step of the way. You know that, don't you? I want you to be happy, and I want to see you fulfil your potential, because you haven't been able to do that so far. I've had my chances – now it's your turn.'

'Thank you, sweetheart.' My eyes misted over and I hugged him hard. I could have hoped for no greater expression of devotion and commitment than that. Our love and partnership were stronger than ever, and together we would plan and work steadily towards a new future.

Win and me at the Adventurers' Club in Brisbane, soon after we first met in 1970. It was a party night, and Win had cooked dinner for about 100 people. (Photograph © Bill Atkinson)

On the riverbank, waiting for the *pinnassier* to fix the outboard motor. Belinga camp could only be reached by travelling upriver for a whole day on a pirogue. We wore heavy clothing against the dry season cold.

A village we passed on our first trip up the Ivindo, on our way to Belinga. The people lived by fishing and hunting, and grew crops of maize, cassava, taro and bananas.

My first view of the cloud forest around Belinga in daylight left me speechless. From that moment I realised we were entering a world few were privileged to know.

Belinga camp from Belvédère, a vantage point from which we could look down into the Republic of the Congo. Surrounded by endless forested mountains, we sometimes forgot that another world existed outside.

The guesthouse at Belinga, built from the local ironstone. Office, dining room, kitchen, living quarters and radio shack, it was the hub of the camp.

Interior of the guesthouse at Belinga. The hard hats and rain jackets hanging on the fireplace were in constant use. Workspace and relaxation area, the guesthouse was where I spent much of my time.

The Gabonese workers' village at Belinga. Constructed from puddled mud over sapling frames, the huts consisted of two rooms with cooking fires outside. Specialist workers occupied prestige spots at the top of the hill.

A block of mini-apartments under construction at Belinga. Win introduced modern building methods to the area. The Kombi played a crucial role in transporting materials and men.

Rodo, Win and I loved to drive out on the old forest tracks wildlife spotting. Fallen trees often blocked the way, but Rodo was prepared for this one.

We made weekly trips to buy manioc from women in the local villages. Here at M'Vadhi, the SOMIFER pirogue is beached alongside the women's small pirogues. Their trips often involved hours of paddling each way.

Women and children at M'Vadhi village, Upper Ivindo, on our manioc-buying day. Bundles of manioc lie on the riverbank, ready to be loaded. This commerce, organised and managed by the women, provided vital cash.

A traditional Pygmy shelter at M'Vadhi, contrasting with the mud hut most widely built throughout the country. We were shocked and dismayed to see Pygmy families in poor and degraded conditions.

I make friends with children and a puppy at M'Vadhi. I wondered what future these children might have in this remote location, with limited educational opportunities and the ever-present threat of disease.

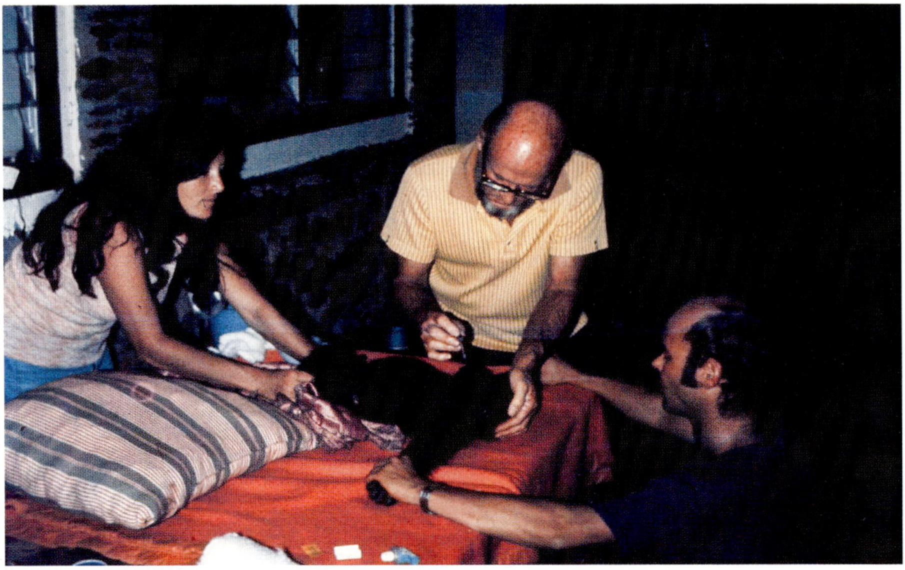

Win sedates Josie with red wine prior to surgery, while Rodo and I steady her arms and legs. This was the beginning of our journey of love with her that was to change my life.

Josie on the Citroën Méhari. She became part of our Belinga family. Her intelligence and vulnerability kept us on an emotional seesaw between joy and sadness as we shared each day.

Left: Josie with Win in our flat, drinking from his glass of beer. Once she realised she was in a loving environment, she relaxed. On Sundays, Win would take her to the edge of the forest to forage.

Below: Josie clinging to me at the radio on the day she left us. I was weighed down by the sadness of her imminent departure, and fearful for her future.

Boisterous Bouéni, a young male chimpanzee, leapt into my arms on an island near the CNRS research station in Makokou. Reared in captivity, he was a relentless attention-seeker.

On the island, where Hugo brought food drops of bananas every few days. Bouéni's gobbling style of eating contrasted with Ikata's fastidious feeding habits. In the wild, gorillas and chimpanzees would never live together.

Ikata has peeled a banana and explores its texture delicately. Sharing this moment in the forest with two of our closest relatives filled me with wonder, and I felt the force of a different destiny tugging at me.

Bouéni soon abandoned his food in favour of another cuddle. Honoured by his trust, I savoured this precious encounter, wishing it would last forever.

Bananas forgotten, Ikata embarks on a grooming session, teasing my long hair out of its rubber band and fossicking gently on my scalp. Incredulous, I felt I had entered, at least in part, into his world.

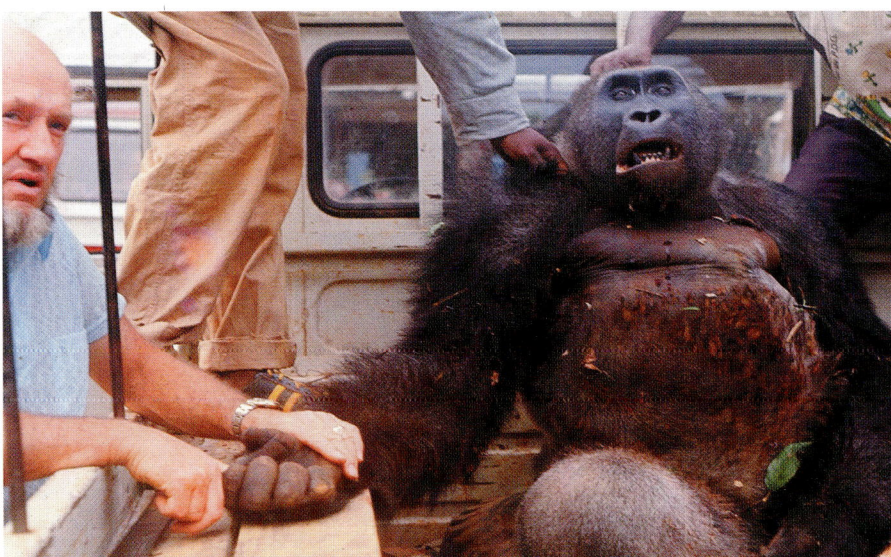

The horror of a slain silverback gorilla at Belinga, shot through the back by local hunters. Gorillas were demonised in the local culture, and killing one brought prestige as well as meat.

A gorilla's skull picked clean by ants – another distressing sight that would haunt me forever. Our efforts to stop gorilla killings proved fruitless. Their protected status under the law meant nothing in this remote forest.

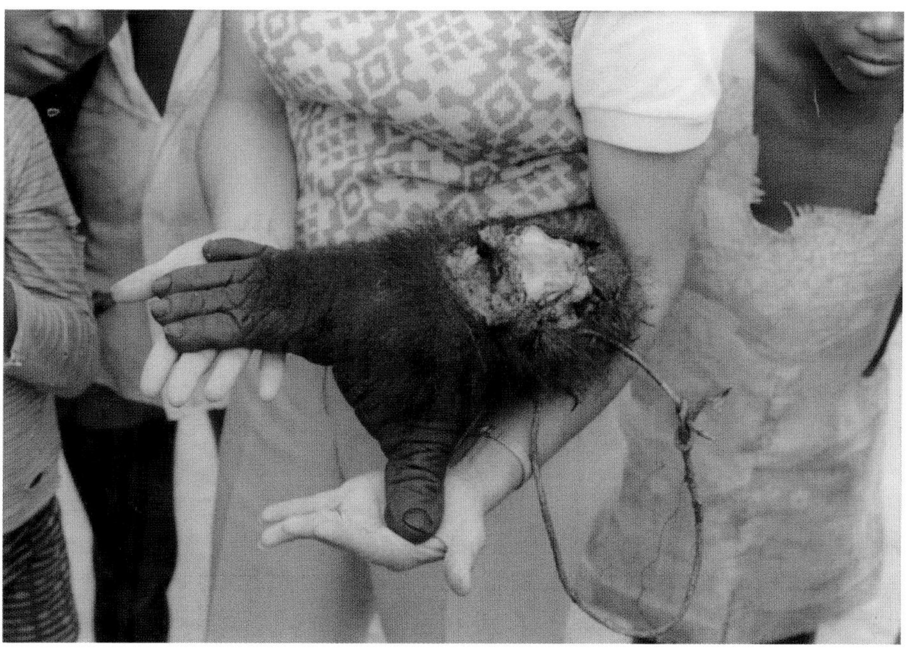

A hunter's grim trophy – a gorilla's severed foot on a rope – twirled triumphantly in the air by a young boy at Mayebut.

Bwiti dancers at Belinga, performing for visitors. The Bwiti cult is widely practised in Gabon, and involves the use of the hallucinogenic drug *iboga*. Many symbols of Christianity were incorporated into the performance.

Test drilling for iron ore on Babiel. A team of Canadian drillers brought twenty tonnes of equipment with them and extracted core samples from sites all around Belinga. The associated destruction of forest distressed us.

Win and Rodo inspect Eamon's house under construction. The walls were built from local ironstone, readily available all around the camp. Gabonese stone masons were well versed in using this material.

Win in front of Eamon's completed house – the detached kitchen behind and the great forest just metres away. The luxurious house drew universal praise. Eamon's wife wanted Win's name engraved on a plaque outside.

Win and me with the Kombi back in Brisbane in 1992. The sign-writing was what had led to our year at Belinga. A vehicle with a unique history and appearance, it became well known around Brisbane.

A privilege I never expected to have: meeting Jane Goodall in Brisbane in October, 2008. She has inspired me for over thirty years. (Photograph © Julia Hoy)

chapter sixteen

THE BITTER AND THE SWEET

The beginning of May heralded our last three months in the camp: at the end of July our contracts would end, and we would return to the world we had left behind eighteen months before. Soon we would have to decide whether that world would be Australia or England.

We knew that leaving would not be easy. Our life in the forest had taken hold of us so deeply that it had become part of who we were. Living in the mountain wilderness had changed how we saw ourselves, and created a world in which cities and highways, technology and possessions were only incidental to our lives. It had opened our minds to another way of being, where we found joy in the presence of native animals, in the cycle of the seasons and the exquisite colours and shapes of fungi, fruit and insects. Each time I thought about leaving I felt the bite of sadness. But beneath that, there were forces driving us to go.

When we had first arrived, we had little concept of the impact the project would have on the forest and wildlife. That realisation took time. It wasn't that vast areas of forest were being cleared: that would come later, if the iron ore were ultimately mined. Rather, it was the steady encroachment of local access roads for surveying and drilling that disturbed the animals and made them more vulnerable to hunting. It was the noise from dozers and graders that shattered the silence. We had never stopped to consider at the outset that creating a settlement of over 500 people, where before there had been none, would generate an insatiable demand for bushmeat.

Now we had seen for ourselves the slaughter of gorillas and chimpanzees. We had witnessed hunters parading their kills of a silverback and other endangered wildlife. We had watched the *sous-préfêt* shoot the fish-eating eagle from a pirogue, and seen the rare bongo antelope cornered and gunned down. Indirectly, we were complicit in this simply by being there. That was the dark side of being in the forest, the bitter, inescapable reality, and it created a dilemma of conscience that we couldn't ignore. Even if Doug offered to extend our contracts, we could no longer countenance being a part of the problem. We knew hunting would always be a way of life for the people who lived in the vast interior of Gabon – they had lived that way for thousands of years – and for outsiders to criticise how they obtained their food would be presumptuous. But it didn't alter our distress at the slaughter of rare animals.

Overlying all of this was the weariness we both felt, the battle fatigue from pitting ourselves against forces we couldn't control. Life at the frontier seesawed between the excitement and unpredictability of wildlife encounters on the one hand, and the frustration and chaos that dogged our endeavours on the other. Our day-to-day life engendered ambivalence – a love/hate mixture increasingly veering towards the hate end of the spectrum. I now understood the pressures that had driven Mario to leave, and I guessed that they also underlay Jacques' decision to go.

For weeks, Win and I weighed up the pros and cons of returning to Australia versus going back to England. Australia was on the other side of the world. If we went back, the chance to travel abroad again might never come, we reasoned – whereas if we resumed our life in London for a while, we could work and save for the future and take some holidays in Europe at the same time. Besides, England had the added attraction of being an ideal place to explore my study options. I could visit the libraries, zoos and museums, and begin reading everything I could find about anthropology. London Zoo even had gorillas.

The more we considered it, the more we favoured England. We weren't ready to be absorbed back into the life we had left behind in Brisbane three and a half years before. In fact, the mere thought of it felt like a negation of the people we had become. So, in the end, the decision was easy. We would fly back to Europe in the summer and take up where we left off.

'The first thing we'll do is have a holiday in Greece!' Win said. 'We've earned it.' It sounded a brilliant idea to me. I thought back to our time in Greece three years before – the clear Mediterranean light, the stony hillsides, the white churches against a turquoise sea and the ruined temples set in cypress groves. Yes, I thought, I could stand a dose of Greece.

Eamon's wife, Noni, arrived early in May. She was a veteran of the early days of Belinga, having lived there during Eamon's first tour of duty in the 1960s. When we met, her guarded expression told me nothing of how she felt to be back. I tried to picture how she would have looked when she'd last lived at Belinga. Now she was in her late fifties, small and motherly, with steel-grey hair, a subdued manner and, I thought, a long-suffering air. I had sewn curtains for her new house the week before, partly because I wanted her to feel welcome and partly because without them, she and Eamon would be living in a fishbowl.

One morning we sat down together over tea in the guesthouse and I asked her about her life in Gabon in the old days. I never tired of hearing the history that the old hands could tell me. She brightened, and seemed to welcome the chance to talk about it. She spoke slowly and carefully in her Midwestern accent.

'When we first came to Gabon, we stayed in the deserted mission house at Ndjolé while we waited for a trailer home to be provided. The only water supply was from the river. One day I had to entertain the American ambassador and his wife. There were no chairs, so all I could offer them to sit on were dirty mattresses. They sat on those filthy things with such aplomb, as if they were tapestry-covered sofas!' She smiled gently at the recollection.

As I listened, I warmed to this quiet woman, whose demeanour suggested she had endured much during her life. She reminded me of the pioneering women of early America I had seen in films. Even in the luxury home she would soon occupy, I knew she would need all her resilience to cope with life in the new Belinga.

I wish I had asked her more about which deserted mission house she meant, because there had been more than one in the Ndjolé area. Mary Kingsley had been there, and gone on to nearby Talagouga, where an American missionary, Dr Nassau, had established the earliest mission in the region in 1882. Others had followed. I discovered decades later that Caroline Alexander, an American scholar who became fascinated by Mary Kingsley, had travelled to Gabon in the 1980s to retrace Kingsley's journeys and written about it in a book called *One Dry Season: In the Footsteps of Mary Kingsley*. When I read her account of a visit to the ruined Catholic cathedral at Asange, near Ndjolé, shivers rippled across my skin, and I thought of Noni and the old mission house:

> I approached the cathedral, whose heavy double doors surmounted with great bosses stood closed with an air of finality, as if they had been sealed shut irrevocably and forever; yet they swung easily open when I pushed them. I stepped into the cavernous cathedral nave, which, stripped bare as it was of all pews and of every scrap of decoration, resembled a medieval dining hall more than it did a church . . . All along the high side walls, the jungle had come peering in each window, groping with its sinuous tendrils into this private darkness, and leaf by leaf consigning it to a forgotten secrecy . . . Impossible to describe the feeling of desolation harbored in this grandiose and gutted structure . . .

Even as I listened to Noni over tea in the guesthouse, long before I had read Caroline Alexander's book, I thought how transitory human endeavours were in these African tropics. White people came, built structures, pursued dreams and ultimately left. Then mildew and decay took over, turning everything back into a ghost of itself. That would be the fate of the Belinga camp too, I knew. Ultimately the forest reclaimed everything.

Win and I told Doug that we would definitely finish up at the end of July.

'You know we could find things for you to do if you wanted to stay a bit longer,' Doug cajoled.

'Oh, I don't doubt that,' Win replied, 'but actually we're ready to go. We've reached an end point and we need to move on.' We didn't elaborate, but Doug could see we'd made up our minds and he didn't press the offer.

'Well, Nettie, we'll need someone to take over all the things you've been doing. How do you think Carol would go?'

'She'd be a natural,' I said. 'She's bright and energetic and she rolls with the punches. She'll pick up the French pretty quickly once she's in the job.'

'Okay. I'll have a talk to her and see if she's interested.' When Doug approached her about it, Carol didn't hesitate. She needed something to do and saw the job as a challenge. We agreed that I would start teaching her the ropes as soon as possible.

There would be little time to focus on our future in the weeks ahead, as the pace of change was about to escalate even further. After more than ten months, the surveyors had completed their work. For them, the job had been a nightmare. The punishing terrain, tight deadlines and the delay in arrival of their equipment – combined with vehicle problems and the hardships of the wet season – had pushed them to their absolute limits. At the farewell party Eamon put on for them, they made no secret of their delight to be going home. I hadn't come to know them much, except for big Andy, the Yorkshireman, whose hair I had cut whenever he couldn't stand its unruliness a moment longer. I would always remember his good nature and ready smile, even when there was little to smile about.

Doug broke the news one day that we needed to plan for the visit of a high-level delegation in mid-June. The Comité Technique – a twelve-member body of experts representing all the partners in the consortium – would hold a meeting at Belinga to coincide with the end of stage one of the project, a chance to showcase everything that had been achieved in the first eighteen months. The vice-president of Gabon, Monsieur Mébiame, would be among the party, so the guests would need to be housed and fed in as close to VIP manner as we could manage for three days and nights. We had just four weeks to prepare. I hoped there would be some respite from the chaos that usually surrounded us to allow me to get on with the complex task of organising it, but that was not to be: two unusual events provided unwelcome distractions.

The first of these involved one of our domestic staff. One day, Mambo Bernard turned up for work drunk. Normally immaculate, his clothes were dishevelled and his speech slurred, and he lurched when he walked. Étienne, who rarely drank, was clearly upset. He took me aside and whispered that he couldn't work with someone in that state.

I had never had to discipline any of the domestic staff, and I felt more disappointed in Bernard than angry with him because I liked and respected him, but I couldn't let it go. For some minutes, I racked my brain as to the best way to handle it. Then I remembered a sanction that Mario had occasionally invoked – suspension from duty for three days. It was known as *mise à pieds*. As a result, the worker lost pay, and it usually proved effective. I checked first with Eamon to be sure of my ground. When he concurred, I took a deep breath and strode into the kitchen to find Bernard swaying between the stove and the bench. I looked him in the eye and assumed my sternest expression.

'Bernard, go home now – and don't come back for three days. You're drunk!' I was sure he would want to argue. Instead, he looked back at me blearily, struggled to take in what I had said, then hung his head and lurched out through the dining room and down the road towards the village.

That left Étienne the only one on duty in the guesthouse. He turned to me looking desperate – there was dinner for five to be prepared, but he didn't cook. 'Madame, what am I going to do?'

'*Ça va, Étienne,*' I soothed. 'We'll get you some help.'

I drove down to the *cas de passage* to look for Patrice, a new cook who had joined us the month before, and told him we needed him up in the guesthouse for a few days while Bernard was away. We drove back together in the Méhari, and I saw relief flood Étienne's face when we arrived. I left them to sort out dinner and prepared to do the five o'clock radio link.

I doubted we would see Bernard until the end of the week, but the next morning he came to the door, nursing a severely swollen black eye and looking sheepish.

'Madame, why did you send me away?'

'Because you came to work drunk, Bernard,' I said. 'That is not acceptable, and we cannot tolerate it.'

'But madame,' he pleaded, 'I've done nothing wrong.'

As calmly as I could, I explained what we expected of him and that I didn't want this situation to happen again.

He looked at the ground, shifted from one foot to the other and murmured, '*Oui, madame.*' His eye looked extremely painful. The lid had completely closed over and the whole socket was suffused with a pattern of bright purple and black. It looked so bad I thought his sight might be permanently affected. As he turned to walk away, I called after him, 'What happened to your eye?' I assumed he'd been in a fight, but the truth was even worse.

'It's my wife, madame, she hit me with a rock!'

My shock must have shown. I would never get used to the domestic violence that erupted in the village far too often. 'Well then, you must go down to the *infirmerie* straightaway and let Madame look at it,' I insisted. 'You have a very nasty injury.'

'*Oui, madame.*'

I thought Marie-Claire should look at it, in case he needed to go to Makokou to see the doctor: we had a responsibility to attend to the health of the workforce. He left then, dejectedly nursing the eye, and slowly walked down the hill towards the clinic.

The eye must have been all right, because when he returned to work at the end of the week, the swelling had gone down and his sight appeared unaffected. I said no more about the incident, and we behaved as though nothing had happened. After that, the tensions between the domestic staff seemed to subside.

I didn't have long to wait before the second distraction convinced me that things in the camp were spiralling out of control. Late one Friday afternoon, two gendarmes from Makokou turned up unannounced, ostensibly to report on law and order in the camp. They'd travelled upriver in a company pirogue. Eamon, Rodo and I met them at the guesthouse door, where they were swaggering and strutting in uniform, each with a shotgun slung over his shoulder.

'We'll be staying for the weekend, and we'll need rooms,' the surlier of the two informed us. Rodo, Eamon and I looked at each other, took in the sight of the weapons and read each other's thoughts. We were likely to be in for a rough weekend, but they had us over a barrel.

'Well, I think we can manage that,' Eamon said in his calm Midwestern voice. I had already decided to keep well out of it; I didn't want anything to do with them. The problem was, we could hardly refuse them accommodation, as the rooms vacated by the surveyors were still empty.

'Dr Krol here will show you to your rooms,' Eamon intoned with exaggerated courtesy, nodding towards Rodo. When they had left for the *cas de passage*, Eamon turned and gave me an outsized wink.

I didn't see them for the rest of the weekend, but I soon discovered how they had spent their time. On the Sunday afternoon, I decided to check the state of the fridge in the guesthouse. Étienne and Bernard sometimes forgot to clean out rotting vegetables, and unless I reminded them about it, the bottom of the fridge would fill up with a soup of fetid brown liquid and slimy red and green solids.

When I opened the freezer compartment, six pairs of eyes, fixed in their death stares, and six open mouths full of stained teeth greeted me just inches away from my face. One had a small red fruit still stuck to its tongue. I was face to face with six powder puff monkeys, each tied up into a ball with its own long tail, unskinned, ungutted and just as they had been when the gendarmes' cartridges had brought them down. Trickles of dried blood spattered their black hair. The white patches on their noses that gave them their name stood out pathetically against their startled faces.

I felt my blood pressure skyrocket. 'What the hell is this?' I shrieked – uselessly, as it turned out, because there was no-one around to hear me. I slammed the freezer door shut and strode out of the guesthouse back to our flat. Win was sitting by the window reading.

'Come and look at this!' I shrilled. I didn't stop to explain. Win trailed in my wake as I marched back to the guesthouse and flung the freezer door open.

'Look what they've done! How dare they?' While I fumed, Win's sense of the ridiculous took over, and he dissolved into uncontrollable laughter.

'It's not bloody funny!' I bellowed. 'Monkeys carry all sorts of diseases, and they're shoved up against the food that people here are going to have to eat!' Win was doubled up, his face flushed bright red: it was the biggest laugh he'd had in months. I couldn't decide whether to be more outraged at the gendarmes' arrogance in stashing their spoils in our fridge, or at the prospect of the diseases that might be passed on from the carcasses stowed alongside our frozen meat.

Maddeningly, I was powerless to act because of who the perpetrators were. I wanted to hurl the carcasses out into the forest, but I didn't dare – just as when the *sous-préfêt* had shot the fish-eating eagle, I had to bite my tongue. If I ran foul of officialdom, both of us could be kicked out of the country at a moment's notice. There was nothing to be done but go back to the flat and have a stiff whisky.

The gendarmes left early the following morning and took the frozen monkeys with them. I didn't see them go, but if I had, I would have noticed what else they were carrying off. It was only later that one of our welders told Jacques they had pulled rank and obliged him to fabricate a metal coffee table from company materials for them to take back as a souvenir. The coup de grâce was revealed later still: we found they had wrecked one of the toilets in the *cas de passage* during drunken revelry on the Saturday night. If this was how the constabulary behaved, I thought, there wasn't much hope for the rest of the population.

'Two months to go,' I lectured myself. 'Keep cool. Two months and we'll be out of here.' The gendarmes must have enjoyed their stay so much that they spread the word in town, because once the dry season had begun and the Djadié route was open, the sight of uniformed men with rifles driving into camp on a Friday afternoon ceased to be unusual.

I had a suspicion that all this stemmed in part from Eamon's laissez-faire approach. I had seen it in action often enough. Whatever the men asked for, Eamon would almost always agree to. He seemed incapable of refusing them. If I turned down a worker's request I regarded as unreasonable, he would go straight to Eamon, who would override me. Many of the families had relatives in Makokou, and word of Eamon's benevolence spread quickly. By then, I had worked out that Eamon saw himself as some kind of father figure to the Gabonese, an attitude that must have carried over from the early days when the country had been newly independent.

In mid-May, Carol began working beside me. She had only a smattering of French, so the prospect of having to conduct the radio links by herself once I had gone terrified her. But she was smart and eager to learn.

'Don't worry,' I assured her. 'I felt just the same when I started out. You'll get the hang of it after a while.' She shadowed me each day and I briefed her on transport logistics, routine procedures and the problems she could expect to face. Gradually I introduced her to all the men who would report to her.

'How did you learn all this?' she asked.

'Blood, sweat and tears,' I replied with a grin. 'No pain, no gain.' She nudged me playfully and we both dissolved into giggles. It was the most adaptive response to the madness that surrounded us. I knew Carol would be all right.

A fortnight before Jacques left, he brought the new mechanic up from Makokou for a familiarisation visit. Monsieur Bertin would take his place at the end of the month. When Jacques' last day came, I looked around at the faces in the room as we gathered to say goodbye and saw only sadness. Monsieur Bertin stood quietly on the fringes, saying little. I had given Jacques our contact address back in London, and I had his home address in France written in my diary.

'We'll see you in September,' I promised, 'on our way through to Greece. *Au revoir, Jacques, et bonne chance!*'

'*Au revoir, Nettie,*' he said, and kissed me on both cheeks in the French fashion. He shook hands with everyone, then we watched as he climbed into the blue Land Rover for the last time and turned the key. The last we saw was his arm waving out the window before he turned the bend in the road and headed for the *débarcadère*.

Rodo, Win and I exchanged looks, remembering Mario's anguished departure nine months before. The project had been plagued by staffing problems from the outset. I couldn't work out whether it was intrinsically unmanageable, or whether this was normal in remote Africa when white people tried to achieve things. In two months we would be gone too, and all the daily frustrations would become fading memories. I wanted to leave on a high note, to carry part of the spirit of Belinga with me, and to cherish the gifts that my year in the forest had given me. I knew I would leave with a mixture of joy and sorrow – but it would be mainly joy.

The high point of Win's achievement at Belinga came early in June, when Eamon and Noni's house was at last finished. The last coat of varnish on the floors had dried, the ceiling beams glowed reddish brown against the white panels, and the solid timber of the bar top gleamed. Win had drawn on his lifetime's experience of architectural design to create the house in the best tradition of African wilderness lodges. The huge stone fireplace dominated the living room and would provide essential warmth in the cold dry-season nights. When he showed Noni through for the first time, she gasped with astonishment.

'You should record your name on a plaque on the front wall so people will know in the future who created it,' she urged. I knew Win would never agree to a suggestion like that. It wasn't his style. He derived satisfaction from projects perfectly executed and designing buildings that gave enduring joy to those who lived in them.

He grinned dismissively. 'But who'd be there to see it?' Eamon, in his understated way, congratulated Win and thanked him for what he acknowledged was an extraordinary effort.

It was such a monumental achievement that I wanted a memento of it, just for us. I persuaded Win to put on a clean set of clothes and we drove up together that afternoon so I could take his picture standing in front of the house. After that, I photographed all the fine architectural detail inside.

Word of the house quickly spread around the camp, and soon all the staff wanted a guided tour. It was a triumph too for Win's chief carpenters – Bruno, Jean-Jacques, Nestor and Joseph. They had never worked on such a building before, and their pride in it shone in their faces.

The first half of June passed in a frenzy of preparation leading up to the arrival of the Comité Technique. Carol and I spent whole days planning menus, checking the bedrooms were ready and trying to anticipate the visitors' every need. Win put aside all other work to complete the refurbishment of the guesthouse and make eight new dining tables. By the time the party arrived on the night of 14 June, the guesthouse had been transformed. The walls gleamed with fresh white paint, and Carol had sewn floral curtains for all the windows and re-covered the lampshades with matching cloth. Potted ferns decorated the corners, and the new dining tables were covered with bright cloths I had cut out from lengths of *pagne*. As Doug ushered the party through the door, the look of amazement on his face told me all our efforts had been worthwhile.

While the guests were served welcome drinks, Carol put the final touches to the batch of pizzas she had made for their evening meal; on a nearby bench, the three lemon cheesecakes Win had baked sat ready on platters. The dining room hummed with conversation, some in English, some in French, and I caught snippets of it as I moved about serving food and removing empty plates. Everyone thought the guesthouse charming, and they found it hard to imagine how such hospitality could be offered in a remote camp 600 kilometres from the coast and 700 metres up in the mountains.

In the morning, the flags of all the consortium partners were raised on the hillside above the guesthouse – Gabon, the USA, Germany, France and Romania – a reminder that Belinga was a flagship development for Gabon, and due protocol had to be observed. The delegates' program would include a tour of inspection of the entire camp, a visit to the drill sites, and a formal meeting to review progress and discuss future plans. Rodo had also organised a special dance performance by a group from Makokou for Saturday night, and Eamon and Noni would host a cocktail party at their house on Sunday evening.

Carol spent Saturday cooking a huge pot of curried lamb for their evening meal. Noni baked apple pies and Win had carved a miniature ebony souvenir for each guest from an ancient log that Eamon had brought in from the forest on a dozer. I hovered in the background, washing dishes, setting tables and emptying bins.

The guests arrived for their pre-dinner drinks in a buoyant mood, full of enthusiasm for what they had seen and eager to see the dance performance that would soon follow.

Down in the village, where we gathered after dinner, three large bonfires burned fiercely in a clearing below the bottom row of huts. Plastic chairs had been set out for the thirty of us, facing a palm-leaf pavilion where the musicians had set themselves up at the back.

A troupe of male and female Bwiti dancers had travelled up from Makokou two days beforehand – Rodo had organised their accommodation in the village and provided them with rations. They had been using the empty schoolhouse in the village for rehearsals.

Clusters of workers and their families had gathered on the sidelines. The night was cool and clear, with bright stars. I had brought the camera – this would be my only chance to capture such an event before we left.

The clanging, thumping music began, as always, without warning. When the dancers appeared in a long line from behind the pavilion, they looked like apparitions from some voodoo ritual in Haiti. Every face was painted white, obliterating the dancer's identity, and their features were outlined garishly in blue, red, orange and black. Some had blood-red crosses painted on their foreheads. The shuffling line of figures circled the fires, trance-like, their eyes glazed.

Some wore long white robes, like priests, with crimson sashes. Several women wore white veils like nuns. To one side, a colour photograph of Pope Paul VI had been pinned to a post. Strips of leopard skin dangled from some dancers' waists. They carried an eclectic mix of objects – fly-switches, bells, lamps, flags on sticks, torches and rattles – which they twirled in front of them or over their heads. I peered at their faces as they swirled past. Many seemed drugged, their faces expressionless, their eyes fixed in a vacant stare.

As the intensity built, some dancers prostrated themselves before the fires. Some leapt over the flames to the accompaniment of a dirge-like chant from the others. In the forest setting, the dance had a mesmerising effect.

My eyes began to close and my breathing slowed.

I was startled awake by the gasps of the audience at the sight of six male dancers, wearing only loincloths and bunches of fresh leaves, cavorting in a frenzied dance. One member of each pair carried the other on his back and they whirled in tight circles; their eyes rolled, their mouths gaped in an attitude of menace, and their nostrils flared. The other dancers were nowhere to be seen. Was this the African embodiment of Caliban, I wondered – the wild man of the forest, closer to animals than to humans?

My head spun with the tumult of images – swirling red and white figures, drugged men leaping fires, wild naked men glistening with sweat. Then, suddenly, it was all over. The thudding drums fell silent, the rattles no longer swished, and the dancers vanished. In their place, an eerie quiet hung over the clearing.

We held our applause until one of the men nearby confirmed that the performance had ended. Then there was clapping and cheering, handshaking and a hubbub of voices, as everyone speculated on the meaning of what they'd seen. My eyes swept the faces of the guests – chatting, gesticulating, laughing – and I knew the performance had given them what they wanted, a glimpse of the raw Africa they wouldn't find anywhere else.

On the final night, we all gathered in Eamon and Noni's house for the farewell cocktail party. I watched the reactions of the visitors as they entered the living room, the looks of admiration as they took in every detail. Noni stood behind the panelled bar, setting out plates of food. Doug circulated, working the crowd of dignitaries like a diplomat. I could tell the entire visit had impressed the Comité beyond anything they could have expected. And as I stood, having another of my 'pinch me' moments, I saw a colossal black-and-white image of a gorilla mounted on the wall beside the fireplace. It was Arthur, the much-adored lowland gorilla who had loved to wrestle. My eyes misted over and I thought of Josie and Ikata. I knew why Eamon had put it there.

Towards the close of the evening, Vice-President Mébiame took me aside and asked me in French about the forest and why I liked living at Belinga. I told him it was the most wonderful thing that had ever happened to me, that the world of the gorillas, the colobus monkeys, the leopards and the elephants had set my spirit on fire.

He smiled wistfully and said, 'I would like to have had that privilege myself. I have never seen most of those animals.'

chapter seventeen

Partings

As the time of our departure approached, I wanted to fix forever in my mind all the changing images of wildlife that accompanied the seasons, especially the visits of migratory birds. The rainbow bee-eaters of North Africa – the ones we had seen in Saharan oases – spent six months of the year with us. I loved their exquisite colours – green, yellow and blue – and their high piping calls as they dipped and whirled in the air catching insects. Swallows also came south to escape the northern winter. They perched in hundreds on our powerlines like a parade of soldiers in black and navy uniform. Large black and white storks sought refuge in the clearing, ahead of fierce storms and gales. I had watched them trying to circle for a landing as the wind buffeted their huge wings. They looked ungainly with their long thin legs dangling down, but they were graceful and elegant fliers on a calm day. Cattle egrets also visited, their snowy white feathers and bright yellow beaks conspicuous against the green of the forest and the red of the ground. Belinga provided a natural resting place for the birds on their long journeys, because they could pinpoint the clearing from far off. For me, the sight of these large flocks resting from their epic migrations was one of Africa's great spectacles.

From late June, I had more time to focus on the wildlife and forest, because Carol had been steadily taking over the various parts of my job. On 29 June, she did her first radio link in French without any assistance. I sat beside her, ready to help, but she didn't need me. A week later, she took over all of my tasks.

Suddenly I had nothing particular to do. For several days I felt myself in limbo, alternating between relief at the shedding of the burden, and emptiness because I was no longer needed. When that phase passed, the realisation dawned that at last I was free to go out on the tracks photographing whenever I wanted. I took the Méhari out often in the afternoons to capture images of the forest backlit by gentle sun. I stopped frequently, examining the minutiae of spiders' webs, the patterns on butterflies' wings as they sucked up salt from animal dung, the blossoms on the flowering vines that grew by the roadside. Each time I went out, the tinge of loss tugged at me. Soon I would leave it all behind.

Win had one last endurance test to face – driving the Kombi back to Libreville on the first stage of its journey back to Europe. Despite all it had done in Africa, it was still in good condition and we weren't ready to part with it. Kruger had sent the company barge up the day before to transport it downriver, and Win would be gone about five days. We would keep in touch by radio. I watched as the barge, laden with empty fuel drums and *cantines*, women, children, and the Kombi, pulled slowly away from the bank. The sight took me back a year to the night we had landed at Mayebut and driven up the mountainside in the van for the first time.

That evening, I spoke with Win on radio. The river trip had taken ten hours, because the water level was dangerously low. He would leave Makokou at first light in the morning and hoped to reach Libreville by seven o'clock that night. Optimistic, I thought, but didn't say it.

I heard nothing until two days later, when he came to the radio in the Libreville office, his voice husky and flat with exhaustion.

'It was a nightmare trip. The route was worse than ever. The mud bogs were thirty metres long. When I got stuck and tried to winch out, the handle sheared off, so I had to wait for someone to tow me out. At the first river crossing the ferry had broken down and was relying on a truck arriving at either bank to tow it across with cables. The second one was even worse. Lines of trucks were queued up either side because the ferry could only take two at a time. But I had a bit of luck there. There was a gendarme who asked me for a lift to Libreville and he managed to get us to the head of the queue. We got across just on dark, and were making good time when the engine started to splutter and stall – the old problem of water and dirt in the petrol – so I had to keep stopping to clean the fuel filter.'

'And did it get better after that?'

'Nope. I made dinner for the two of us about nine o'clock and we slept in the van – the gendarme in the front and me in the back – and the *fourreaux* feasted on us all night. We left early next morning with just 300 kilometres to go. The route was drier, but littered with rocks. We'd just started when we had the first blow-out. I fitted the spare, but you won't believe it, within half an hour we'd had another one. By then, the gendarme had had enough, he flagged down the next vehicle and left me to it. It took me till mid-afternoon to limp into town on three good tyres and a flat. I'm staying at a *cas de passage* here in the African quarter. I haven't slept. The place is full of mosquitoes and surrounded by barking dogs.'

'A month to go, sweetheart,' I soothed. 'The worst's over now.'

'On the bright side, I'm having dinner with Roger tonight. I'll talk to you again tomorrow.' I knew that a night of Roger's cooking and conversation would soon restore his spirits.

When we spoke on the radio the next time, Win was full of good news. He had spent the morning at the port and booked the Kombi on a container bound for Bordeaux. Better still, since all containers from Libreville normally returned to Europe empty, only a nominal charge had been payable.

'And I'm bringing Roger back to camp with me for a visit,' he said. 'He's going to be in Makokou anyway to install a new aviation beacon. We'll be up on either Monday or Wednesday.' It was wonderful news. We could return some of his lavish hospitality, and he would see Belinga at last.

They arrived on the Wednesday night, Roger in high spirits after the river trip by pirogue. He could hardly wait to see the countryside. He'd never lived in the interior, and now we – who had been new to Gabon just a year before – would be his guides. We chatted late into the night: he wanted to hear all about the project and what our life had been like.

The following day was one of those rare sparkling ones where every leaf shone, the sky was clear, and it hadn't rained for a week. After breakfast, I took Roger out in the Méhari to Babiel, where we could look out over the mountains and forest to the north. After lunch, Win took him on a tour of the camp to see all the new buildings, especially Eamon and Noni's house. Then in the late afternoon we drove down to Mayebut and walked to the abandoned gold settlement at Camp Six. We knew the area was a favourite haunt for elephants, because the old houses were surrounded by banana trees. The elephants hadn't long gone: we arrived to find the ground strewn with freshly flattened vegetation and the red mud scored with their footprints. We stood and listened for any hint that they were still around, but there was none – we had missed them. Just before dusk, we drove up to Belvédère, the highest point on the mountain behind camp, and watched the sun set over the camp.

That night I cooked *lapin moutardé* for the three of us – rabbit in mustard and wine sauce. We lingered long over the meal, reminiscing and telling our African stories. So much had happened since our first meeting at the beach campsite in Libreville a year before.

Roger left early next morning to return to Makokou. We would see him in Libreville in the days before we left, and better still, he had invited us to visit him in France during the summer while he was home on leave.

By early July, I thought all the most confronting events were behind us, and we would coast gently up to our departure date. Yet, unwittingly, we were about to put ourselves in the way of critical danger.

It was a fine balmy afternoon with no wind, and we were not needed in camp. As we had many times before, we decided to go out game-spotting in the Méhari. We planned to be gone only an hour, and as usual we didn't bother to tell anyone where we were going. Win was dressed in lightweight shorts and rubber thongs, and I had on my standard work clothes – jeans, a T-shirt and sneakers. We took the road to the Djadié along Bakota South, with the vinyl top of the Méhari folded down so we could see all around.

Bands of monkeys shrieked their alarm calls ahead of us and giant casqued hornbills called raucously overhead. Dense secondary growth two metres high flanked the route. We skirted piles of fresh elephant dung in the middle of the road.

We drove far out, scanning ahead for any sign of gorillas or a leopard. Soon it was dusk, when the bats left their roosts to feed, and flashes of reddish brown darted across in front of us. Their numbers quickly swelled to a continuous stream. Thick cloud had blanketed the sky, and visibility was low as we began the return journey, listening to the first stirrings of the insect chorus.

That was when the Méhari's engine faltered and cut out.

'What the hell?' Win pumped the accelerator, turned the ignition off and on, and pushed his foot to the floor again. In the gathering darkness, the only sound was the insects. We waited ten minutes and tried again, but nothing happened. The fuel gauge showed half full, and the instrument panel gave no hint of the problem.

By then, all light had gone. With no torch, no weapon, no communications equipment and no protective clothing, we were totally vulnerable. We knew no-one else would use the road that night. We had no food or water, and in the unlikely event that anyone missed us, they wouldn't know where to start looking. The choices were stark: huddle in the Méhari until daylight, or walk back to camp in the dark. The risks were enormous either way. The Méhari's soft vinyl top and plastic windows would be no barrier to a hungry leopard, and the mosquitoes would guarantee us a sleepless night. In the end, we chose the path of action: we would take a gamble and set out on foot.

It must have been after six o'clock, but we couldn't be sure because it was too dark to read our watches. Heavy cloud obscured the moon so that only a faint glimmer came from the wheel tracks on the laterite. I was conscious of fear, but I knew I couldn't afford to let it take hold – I needed to stay focused on the task and have faith that everything would be all right.

'We're going to have to feel our way by following the wheel tracks,' Win said. 'We'll go in single file. You set the pace and I'll stick close behind you.' I peered at the ground and placed my right foot in the shallow depression of a wheel track, then my left foot in front of it, heel to toe. Either side of the route, beyond the wall of secondary growth, the mountainside dropped away steeply. If we encountered a female elephant with young, we would have nowhere to run. We'd heard that a leopard usually wouldn't attack when there were two or more people. I held on to that thought.

'We need to avoid brushing the leaves at the sides and disturbing anything venomous,' Win said. 'Just keep to the middle.' We were climbing a steep rise. Win's rubber thongs slipped and slid and he struggled to keep them on.

'You know, if we could make enough noise, we might scare off any animals ahead,' I said after we had been going perhaps fifteen minutes.

'It's worth a try,' Win's voice sounded behind me. I began to bellow out a nursery rhyme at the top of my voice, 'Three blind mice, three blind mice, see how they run . . .' over and over, pumping up my confidence. In time, my footsteps fell in with the rhythm. When I got tired of that tune, I switched to another, then another. The longer I kept them up, the stronger I felt.

We'd been going about an hour when Win shrieked, 'Aaagghh! Something's just bitten my toe. I think I've trodden on a line of safari ants!' He ripped one thong off and flailed blindly at his foot and leg with it. If the ants attacked us, we would be in desperate trouble. They moved in columns of millions, and nothing could stop their advance. They marched straight through people's houses, and if an injured or trapped animal lay in their path in the forest, they devoured it alive.

'Don't stand still here!' Win shouted. 'Keep going as fast you can.' I stamped my feet hard and strode out as fast as I dared. All around us, the insects clicked and whirred.

Just then, something moved in the vegetation beside us. We both froze. Goosebumps formed on my skin and my heart thumped. I held my breath. All I could hear was the drumming of my pulse in my ears. There was still no moon and blackness enveloped us. I had no idea what we would do if something came at us at this range. We had no way of knowing what had made the noise, and my imagination leapt into overdrive: was it a leopard, a wild pig, an elephant? Perhaps it was just a small antelope, timid and harmless. I knew that panic would be disastrous. I had to remain calm and have faith that we would make it. We waited for a minute, perhaps two, but the sound didn't come again, so we moved off, warier than before.

'How long do you think we've been going?' I said after a while. It was as though we were moving through an endless black tunnel, and time was meaningless.

'Oh, maybe an hour, maybe more – it's hard to say.' I thought back to our time in the Sahara when we had broken down. It was the only other time I had felt my life could be in danger.

We must have been walking for an hour and a half when Win called out, 'Stop! Listen!' It was the faint low-pitched throb of a motor way off in the distance.

'That's the generator!' Win shouted. 'We're probably only half an hour away!' We quickened our pace as much as we dared. The danger had not passed, but I felt a surge of confidence – we'd covered most of the distance.

The rhythmic hum of the generator gradually grew louder, until finally we rounded a bend and saw lights glinting through the trees.

'We did it!' I whooped, and punched the air. Soon we could make out the shapes of trees around us in the faint glow. Then we were at the edge of the clearing, where the brightly lit guesthouse beckoned with warmth, safety and familiarity. I stopped to hug Win, and we strode towards the pool of light.

It was after eight o'clock: we had walked for two hours. If someone had suggested we would ever do that in the African forest at night, I would have laughed in their face. Back at the flat, Win examined the stinging red lump on his toe and discovered a safari ant had embedded itself in his thong. We decided not to disturb Eamon with the news about the Méhari that night, as there was nothing anyone could do until morning.

After breakfast, he received the news with characteristic calm, drove out in the Toyota and towed the Méhari back to the workshop. Eamon was not given to exaggeration, so when we saw him later in the day, his solemn expression and few words left us in no doubt about how close he felt we had come to disaster. 'You were twelve kilometres out,' he said. 'You are two very lucky people!'

Twelve kilometres through the forest at night, unarmed and utterly defenceless: it was a feat only for the brave, the foolhardy or the desperate.

Monsieur Bertin pored over the Méhari that afternoon, and by the time we called in, late in the day, he'd found the problem. He leaned on the bonnet and wiped his hands on a greasy rag. 'Water in the petrol!' It was the handiwork of the *pinnassiers*. Yet again they'd been selling off petrol to villages along the river and topping up the 200-litre drums with muddy river water, and somebody had forgotten to filter the fuel when the Méhari had been filled up. Win and I exchanged glances and quietly groaned. '*C'est l'Afrique*,' I muttered, and we drove down to the flat to celebrate our survival.

Rodo was on leave in Germany for the whole of July, but we would see him briefly in Libreville on our way out. Doug had taken holidays for a month, too. In their absence, Sam Sims, a senior American geologist, moved into camp as acting director. We took to him immediately. Beneath his ready humour, Sam seemed sensible; he would run a tight ship, and that was what the place needed.

Win's work in the camp was almost over. Every construction project had been completed, and he had more free time than he'd had in a year. One afternoon we drove down to Mayebut just for the pleasure of being out, and so I could take photos of the people.

It was another fine, clear afternoon, with gentle sunlight playing over the thatched mud huts. When we arrived, a group of children were playing at the river's edge, the little ones naked, the older ones splashing about in their clothes. I listened to their laughter as I stood on the riverbank photographing. Then a voice behind me, calling out '*Madame! Madame!*', caused me to whirl around. It was one of the teenage boys. He had something to show me that he was excited about. I thought it might be a large beetle on a string, or perhaps a frog or a lizard. Instead, he produced from behind his back a severed gorilla's foot on the end of a piece of rope, and twirled it triumphantly over his head.

I felt the familiar horror, and a knot formed in my stomach. The foot had not begun to putrefy, so I knew the kill was very recent. I took it in both my hands and looked at it closely. The four smaller toes were separated from the big toe by a wide gap – that was how gorillas gripped tree trunks and branches. The foot looked as if it had been hacked off with a machete. It was large enough to have belonged to an adult. Win and I stared at it in silence and sadness. These hunting patterns were never likely to change, laws or no laws. There was nothing to say, and all the joy had gone from the afternoon. I handed the foot back and we drove away.

We were back at Mayebut later that week to meet an incoming pirogue when we discovered the grizzly sequel to the episode. A massive gorilla's skull, picked clean by ants, lay propped up on the ground against the wall of a hut. Its heavy sagittal crest, like the ridge on a centurion's helmet, projected across the top from front to back. The large eye sockets gaped as empty black holes. The bare nasal bone gave no hint of the unique nose print that had once covered it.

The skull looked too big to have belonged to the same animal whose foot I had held, which suggested that at least two animals had been slain. This was a memory of Mayebut I would rather not have taken away with me, but to these hunters, a gorilla was of no more intrinsic worth than an antelope or a pig. It was all edible meat, and besides, a dead gorilla couldn't raid banana plantations. Even if I lived my life out here, I would never get used to the slaughter.

Eamon gave us a farewell party in the guesthouse two nights before we were due to leave. Étienne had picked flowers in our honour and arranged them in a vase at the centre of the table. Carol made pizzas and spaghetti; Michel showed slides of his latest exquisite wildlife photographs; Eamon told jokes; and one of the Canadian drillers played his mouth organ and sang ancient folk songs in the strange nasal patois that we found so hard to follow. I thought, as I moved around the room chatting, that we couldn't have been a more diverse group, plucked from the corners of the earth and thrown together on a mountain in the wilds of Africa. But there was a sense of community that transcended all our differences.

Next morning, I walked up to the warehouse to say goodbye to M'Poko Lucien. We had worked closely together for a whole year. He had seen me at my most harassed, yet his calm gentleness and honesty had made my days bearable when all around us was in chaos.

He stood at the door of the warehouse in his white hard hat, his eyes sad and his mouth drooping at the corners.

'When will we see each other again, madame?'

'I don't know, M'Poko. We are going back to Europe. Perhaps we will not come to Africa again.'

'Where can I write to you, madame?'

'As soon as we know where we will live, I will write to you,' I promised. 'It will be somewhere in London.'

'It won't be the same without you, madame.'

'*Merci, M'Poko,*' I said. 'Thank you for everything. You have been kind and gentle and we have worked well together. And now I would like to take your photo.' He stood up straight with his clipboard in hand, looking serious while I took the picture. Then we shook hands and I promised again to write.

'*Au revoir, madame.*' As I turned to walk back down the hill he had tears in his eyes, and so did I.

When the day came to leave – 2 August – we had little luggage. Most of our things had gone with the Kombi.

My other important farewell was to Étienne. Of all the domestic staff, he was the gentlest, the most sober, the most caring. He had been there since the beginning, always quietly working in the background, a calm presence when everything around was in tumult. I shook his hand, thanked him for all his kindness and wished him and his family good luck. He looked distracted during this interchange. As I turned to go, he called after me, 'Madame, madame, I have something I want to ask you.' By this time, we were outside the guesthouse. He took me aside behind the privacy of the hedge, and drew something from his trouser pocket.

'Madame, I think I am very sick.' He handed me a small glass jar full of blood and what looked like body tissue. He was embarrassed, I could see, but his alarm overrode it.

'I have been passing this, madame, for some time,' and he indicated his bowels. 'Can you get someone to look at it?' I was stunned. I thought I knew what it meant.

'Of course I can,' I said. I took the jar from him. 'Please no,' I prayed silently. 'Not Étienne, not with seven children.' It hit me like a physical blow. Étienne was only in his late thirties, perhaps forty. I thought back to our first week at Belinga, when I used to quiz him about witchcraft, sorcery and spirit beliefs as he served our evening meals. He would earnestly recount to me examples of sorcerers' powers, and assure me that there were people in Makokou who could perform magical acts like restoring felled trees to life overnight. My affection and respect for Étienne had begun in those very early days, and deepened with time. He could neither read nor write, and to me he seemed as innocent as a child, guileless and without malice, yet he had the gift of caring for others. It seemed to me the most brutal turn of fate. Why couldn't it have happened to one of the wife-beaters in the village? Why this good man?

I looked hard at his anxious face, the furrowed brows, the troubled eyes, and I found no words to comfort him. What could one say to a man who had realised he was dying? I wanted to take his fear away. At that moment, he seemed small and vulnerable. I took a deep breath to still my sadness.

'Take care of yourself, Étienne,' I said.

'*Oui, madame,*' he replied solemnly. I stowed the jar safely in my shoulder bag. Sam Sims waited nearby in the Toyota, ready to drive us down to the Djadié crossing, and I turned to take my last look at Belinga, heavy with thoughts of the tragedy that awaited Étienne and his family. This was the day I had both longed for and dreaded for months: on the one hand it brought escape from the madness in the camp; on the other, it meant the end of our time in the forest – the most exhilarating period of my life. Soon we would return to one of the biggest cities in the world.

I tried not to dwell too long on everything we were losing – that would be too painful. But even as I tried to steel myself, I felt something infinitely precious slipping away. I would never be able to look out over that vast forest again, or watch black and white colobus monkeys cavorting on vines at the edge of the clearing. I would never hear again the giant casqued hornbills calling, or watch the touracos feeding on the fruit of the *parasolier* tree. And when we were back in England or Australia, would anyone understand what it was I had left behind? An ache settled in my chest, a longing I knew would always haunt me. The last lesson Belinga taught me was that one could never have the sweet without the bitter. The more one loved, the more one had to lose.

Win climbed in beside Sam and I got into the back seat and wound down the window so I could wave. My last sight of Étienne was of him standing, framed in the doorway of the guesthouse, waving back, still wearing his floral apron.

***

Kruger had a driver waiting on the other side of the Djadié crossing to take us to Makokou, and the staff at CNRS had invited us for a farewell lunch at the research station. We sat around the long refectory table in the mess with Louise, André, the Michalouds, Hugo and Irene, whom we had met only recently, but who had given us the keys to her Left Bank apartment in Paris to use on our stopover. I had a lump in my throat most of the time. If not for these people, we would never have glimpsed the world of the western lowland gorillas, the bats, the orphaned chimpanzees and the brush-tailed porcupine. I was bursting with the intensity of it, but I didn't know how to tell them.

Our plane was due to leave in the late afternoon. At the airport, Kruger had checked our bags in with Monsieur Loupin, our old friend the storekeeper, in his other role as the Air Gabon agent. For all his hard-headedness, Kruger and I had reached an accommodation. Underneath his tough exterior he had a kindly heart, and I felt sorry for him stuck there in Makokou, every day a battle against the odds.

The dusty terminal was crowded with women, children, baskets of live chickens and rolls of bedding. We stood in the midst of them, waiting for the boarding call. Then out of the crowd appeared the figure of Mehendje Bruno, Win's chief carpenter. He had come down to see us off. Win's face lit up, and I watched the two of them shake hands. Theirs had been a remarkable partnership; together they had done work as fine as any in the world. Bruno had tears in his eyes as he said goodbye. '*Au revoir, patron.*'

'*Au revoir, Bruno. Bonne chance!*'

Just as the call to board sounded, a car pulled up beside the terminal and a group of CNRS staff jumped out, there to see us off. There was just time to shake hands before we joined the rush for the boarding ladder. We paused on the top step to look back and wave: our last sight was of Kruger, Bruno and the CNRS people standing behind the chain-wire fence, with the red dust of Makokou blowing in their faces.

Doug and Gina met us at Libreville airport and drove us to our lodgings in the African quarter to check in, before we went on to their new home at Tahiti for dinner. We talked long into the night, and brought Doug up to date with everything that had happened while they were on leave. Just before we left, I took Doug aside and gave him the glass jar with Étienne's blood in it.

'I think he has bowel cancer,' I said. 'Can you make sure this is tested? I promised him I would look after it.'

'Sure, Nettie. No problem.'

The next day we spent time with Rodo, who was in transit back to Belinga from leave. The three of us felt like a family. Wherever our lives took us in the future, that bond would not change, because it had been forged in hardship and isolation and through love of Josie. We planned a rendezvous in Europe in a year's time, once he'd finished at Belinga.

'Promise you will write,' I insisted. 'I want to hear everything that happens.'

He looked sad. 'It won't be the same without you two up there.' I hoped that Carol and Jim would become his family in the months ahead. He needed people around him who cared.

'Nothing will be the same for us either,' I answered.

Then we left him and set out for the SOMIFER office, where some final paperwork awaited.

The day before we left, Roger drove us to Libreville airport to watch the ceremonial welcome for President Valéry Giscard d'Estaing of France who had arrived at the start of a state visit. Gabon's ties with France remained strong sixteen years after independence: over 30,000 French nationals still worked in the country, throughout all sectors of the economy and industry.

Hundreds of Gabonese women had assembled in lines in the open air, representing the forty language groups in the country. Each group was dressed in distinctive costume, a spectacle of red, yellow, green and blue patterns in the strong sunlight. When the president appeared, they burst into vigorous dancing and song and became a moving sea of colours, upturned faces and waving arms. I climbed a small tree nearby and perched on a branch to take a photo. I would be unlikely to witness such a sight again.

Our Swissair jet lifted slowly out over Cap Estérias, bound for Geneva, then Paris. The Atlantic was grey-green and calm, just as it had been when we first arrived in Libreville the year before. From my seat at the window I couldn't see the forest: we had left it far behind. The Kombi was already well on its way to Bordeaux, where we would collect it in three weeks' time.

I thought back to my youth in Brisbane, to myself as a shy primary-school girl. I remembered when my language teacher at secondary school had chosen me to take part in a French-speaking competition because I was the best speaker in the class. I had been fifteen. Paralysed with stage fright, I had declined, never suspecting that fifteen years later my French would open doors to a world I had never heard of. I recalled the night Win and I had met at the Adventurers' Club in Brisbane six years earlier, and how my life had changed irrevocably from that moment on – how he had inspired me to embrace a life of risk and adventure.

A part of me never wanted to leave Africa. As I sat in the plane with the whine of the engines in my ears and the Atlantic far below me, I knew a part of me would always remain at Belinga. In my role at the camp, I had given of myself as never before. I had battled isolation, culture shock and the privations of a frontier posting, but ultimately I had thrived. I was stronger and wiser, and I had finally grown up. Life at Belinga had shown me a world beyond my imagining. I had held great apes in my arms, and in those moments I had glimpsed eternity. Whatever happened in the future, I would be bound to Josie and Ikata forever. The feeling of Josie clinging to my body would never leave me.

Even then, I suspected that my encounters with the great apes would become the defining events of my life. They would mark me out as uniquely privileged, and form the nucleus of my new identity. Powerful images of Jane Goodall, Dian Fossey and Biruté Galdikas flooded into my mind. These women had followed their dreams – surely I could too? It would mean a long academic journey – years of study, a significant drop in income, and little leisure time. But the idea of sacrifice seemed integral to it. I would give it my all because that was the only way I knew how to be.

I had no idea whether there would be barriers to my entry into a degree program in anthropology, such as my lack of a science background, but I was committed. I felt responsible to Josie, Ikata and all gorillas orphaned, injured or killed through human ignorance or cruelty. The vision of myself returning to Africa and working with gorillas would sustain me through the long years ahead.

Everything seemed possible as I stared out the aircraft window at the ocean far below. I reflected how important it was for people to take chances in life – to grasp the moment and make a leap of faith. That was what Win and I had done when we went to Belinga. Now I was speeding towards a new future.

I looked around at the other passengers. Many of them looked like French nationals going home on leave. Two Gabonese religious sisters sat together several rows in front of us, and there were businessmen in suits who probably worked for oil or mining companies. I wore my new identity with pride: as someone who had engaged with remotest Africa, I had earned my place in this company.

'*Vous voulez un apéritif, madame?*' The flight attendant's voice broke my reverie.

'*Je veux bien, merci,*' I replied, almost without thinking. Then I settled back and allowed the western world to draw me back in.

Epilogue

Our life at Belinga transformed and inspired us. On our return to Australia we realised we could never settle in suburbia again, so we bought a thickly forested bush property outside Brisbane, where Win built our first home, largely from recycled materials. We have lived here since 1980. It is home to an abundance of wildlife, including a breeding pair of powerful owls, and the forest has grown and flourished. We have watched it withstand fire, frost, drought and flood – each time, it recovers when conditions improve. The gums produce blossoms, the parrots and flying foxes descend on them to feed, and the wallabies graze on our front lawn. Whenever I look out the window, I think of Belinga.

I began my degree studies in anthropology in 1978, and graduated with first-class honours from the University of Queensland in 1983, when I was thirty-seven. Anthropology was just one of several pathways into primatology, but the only one open to me. Afterward I worked as an anthropologist for several years, teaching in universities and doing some consulting.

Although in my heart I still wanted to work with gorillas,

I had to face some harsh realities. Dian Fossey had been murdered in her bed at the Karisoke Research Center in 1985; Win and I needed to establish a solid financial future for ourselves; my salary as a junior academic paid me less than I had earned as a secretary; and we needed to spend some time with our families after so many years abroad. The prospect of spending years in Africa isolated in a forest seemed to run counter to all the personal priorities that pressed in on us.

So I set aside my idealistic dream, and took a job as an administrator in a university. Win was approaching sixty and I had become the primary breadwinner. For sixteen years, photographs of Josie and Ikata adorned the walls of my office, and everyone who came in asked about them. When I told the story, many choked back tears. They all said I should write it down. So when I stopped being a university administrator, I dusted off my diaries and began writing.

My time with Josie and Ikata remains at the core of my identity even today – I have been where few others have trodden. I still want to give something back, partly to honour the gifts these great apes gave me, so I provide financial support in various ways. I am a zoo parent of the western lowland gorillas at Taronga Zoo, I have adopted an orphaned juvenile orangutan in Borneo through the Australian Orangutan Project, I belong to the Australasian Primate Society, and I support gorilla conservation and research through membership of the Berggorilla & Regenwald Direkthilfe in Mülheim, Germany. And whenever I can, I talk to people about gorillas, how gentle and sensitive they are, how desperately they need our protection, and how close we humans are to them in so many ways.

In 1996, twenty years after we left Gabon, an outbreak of Ebola virus killed twenty-one people in the village of Mayebut II. They had eaten the flesh of a dead chimpanzee they'd found in the forest. In the cruellest twist of fate, the killing process had reversed – instead of people killing the apes, the ape's flesh killed the people. The virus is believed to have been responsible for the dramatic fall of up to fifty per cent in the population of western lowland gorillas and chimpanzees in the upper Ivindo region and adjacent areas of the Republic of the Congo. But fresh hope for the long-term survival of western lowland gorillas emerged in August 2008 when wildlife researchers announced that an estimated population of 125,000 of these endangered animals had been discovered living in an area of remote forest 18,000 square miles in extent in the Republic of the Congo. Subject to independent verification, this discovery would double previous population estimates.

As for Belinga, the iron-ore deposit was never mined at the conclusion of SOMIFER's exploration program in the 1970s, partly because the world steel price plummeted. However, all that is changing now. The Gabonese government has signed an agreement with Chinese mining interests to re-explore the Belinga deposit, mine the ore, and build a railway to transport it to the coast. Work has already commenced on road construction and the establishment of worker camps. Despite the world economic downturn, the Belinga project appears set to proceed.

Win and I continued to receive news of the camp and its people long after our departure. As promised, I wrote to M'Poko Lucien from London and still have two letters written in his clear hand in perfect French, asking when I planned to return. We were deeply saddened to learn that Nganga Étienne had died of bowel cancer in the late 1970s.

Travelling in France, we visited Jacques Poussain and his family at their home, and were treated to a lavish traditional French lunch prepared by his wife. Jacques had found work elsewhere, and they were looking to the future. We also stayed with Roger Bonnet and his wife at their home in Toulon, on the way back from our holiday in Greece. As always, Roger cooked for us, and in return Win did some carpentry on their house. Roger subsequently took up a posting in troubled Chad. I corresponded with him for many years afterwards.

Carol wrote to us in London, her letters full of the chaos that faced her daily, but she never lost her sense of humour. We had no further contact with Eamon after we left Belinga, but we heard he'd returned to live in the United States earlier than planned.

When the exploration program at Belinga concluded, Doug and his family left Gabon. Doug wrote regularly, visited us in London and later sought us out in our forest home in Australia. A diligent correspondent, he wrote to us from all over the world for decades.

Our bond with Rodo has remained unbreakable for over thirty years. He wrote to us regularly from Belinga with news of events great and small, and I have kept all his letters. When his tour of duty there ended, we drove from London to Germany to spend time with him. Now retired, he phones, emails and writes from his home in the German countryside. The photograph on the cover of this book shows Josie clinging to his legs on the day she left us.

Shared experience would link me to all of these people; nothing could alter that. Time, the great deceiver, still tricks me even now when I think of our life at Belinga: surely it was only yesterday . . .

GREAT APE CONSERVATION ORGANISATIONS

In the three decades since we left Africa, great ape conservation has become a global issue. All great apes – gorillas, chimpanzees, orangutans and bonobos – are endangered in the wild and need human support if they are to survive. Jane Goodall, Biruté Galdikas and countless others have devoted their lives to this cause. Dian Fossey paid the ultimate price.

There are many organisations dedicated to this conservation task. They rescue orphaned and injured apes, care for them in sanctuaries, teach them the skills they need to survive in the wild, and, where possible, release them into protected areas. At the same time, they conduct education programs, lobby governments to preserve native forest habitats, raise funds to support their work and engage in many other vital tasks including field research. They also encourage members of the public to adopt or sponsor a great ape by making an annual donation which is used to provide for their needs.

The following list is by no means exhaustive, but for those wishing to know more about the work being done to support the survival of great apes, or to become involved in some way, these websites will provide an excellent starting point:

- The Jane Goodall Institute (JGI): www.janegoodall.org
- The Dian Fossey Gorilla Fund International: www.gorillafund.org
- United Nations Environment Programme Great Apes Survival Partnership (GRASP): www.unep.org/GRASP
- The Australian Orangutan Project (AOP): www.orangutan.org.au
- Orangutan Foundation International (OFI): www.orangutan.org

Glossary

atelier du bois	woodworking shop
bâton	stick of manioc
cantines	lockable tin trunks
cas de passage	visitors' lodge
combinée	multi-function wood machine
débarcadère	landing stage
économat	village shop
fourreaux	midges
ghiques	jiggers (parasitic insects)
glacières	iceboxes
infirmerie	infirmary
magazinier	shopkeeper or warehouseman
méchant	wicked
mouche rouge	red fly
pagne	printed cotton cloth
pinnassier	boatman
sous-préfêt	deputy district governor
vivres frais	fresh food

Acknowledgements

I am deeply grateful to many people for their advice and encouragement in the writing of this book. First and foremost I thank my husband, Winston Henderson, for his unswerving love, support and belief since I wrote the very first draft in 1977. I thank my dear friend Rodo Krol, who shared our life at Belinga and was eager to read everything I wrote. My special thanks go to Amanda Lohrey who inspired me to pick up the manuscript I had set aside decades earlier and embark on the long process of turning it into a book. The University of Queensland, through the grant of an Australian Postgraduate Award, provided financial support allowing me to work on the book full-time for two years. I am grateful to my agent, Lyn Tranter, for her enthusiasm about the manuscript and her energy in finding a publisher for it. Stuart Glover read many drafts, and brought expert editorial advice to bear on my text. Bronwyn Lea helped me to grow as a writer through her sensitive readings of my work. Kim Wilkins and Jay Verney generously afforded writerly advice before I began.

mbers of the 2006–07 M.Phil (Creative Writing) class the University of Queensland provided insightful feedback on my drafts. My special thanks go to Alison Urquhart and Elizabeth Cowell, my wonderful publisher and editor at Random House, for their wholehearted commitment to the book and for being such congenial colleagues. I thank Emma Collier-Baker for the time we spent discussing our mutual love, gorillas. Many others – family, colleagues and friends too numerous to name – have helped through their constant interest and enthusiasm to keep my faith alive along the way. They know who they are.

I am deeply indebted to André Brosset, Annie Gautier-Hion, Louise Emmons and Hugo who welcomed us so warmly to CNRS at Makokou, and were our scientific guides in the Gabonese forest.

For their camaraderie, humour, generosity of spirit and for all they taught me, I thank our many Belinga colleagues and friends, especially DJY, PG, GP, MM, Nganga Étienne and M'Poko Lucien. And I am grateful to Roger Bonnet for taking us under his wing in Libreville and opening his home and heart to two grimy Australians.

My lifelong gratitude goes to Josie and Ikata, who opened up the world of western lowland gorillas to me and changed me forever.